THE COMPLETE AIR FRYER COOKBOOK

800

Amazingly Easy and Affordable Air Fryer Recipes to Fry, Roast and Bake for You and Your Family

Stephanie Robins

Copyright © 2020 By Stephanie Robins

All Rights Reserved.

No portion of this book may be reproduced or duplicated using any form whether mechanical, electronic, or otherwise. No portion of this book may be transmitted, stored in a retrieval database, or otherwise made available in any manner whether public or private unless specific permission is g anted by the publisher.

This book does not offer advice, but merely provides information. The author offers no advice whether medical, financial, legal, or otherwise, nor does the author encou age any person to pursue any specific course of action discussed in this book. This book is not a substitute for professional advice. The reader accepts complete and sole responsibility for the manner in which this book and its contents are used. The publisher and the author will not be held liable for any damages caused.

TABLE OF CONTENT

Introduction   1

Chapter 1 The Basics Guide of Air Fryer   2

The Mechanics of an Air Fryer 2
Why I Love Air Fryer Cooking 3
A Guide to Picking the Perfect Air Fryer 5
Kitchen Accessories and Techniques for Air Frying 7
Kitchen Staples and Spices From the Pantry 9
Achieving the Perfect Time and Temperature 10
Air Frying Cooking Timetable 11
Cleaning and Caring for an Air Fryer... 12
6 Beginner-Friendly Tips for Cooking Air-Fried Food 13
Prioritizing Health With Every Mouthful 15
FAQs About Air Fryers 17

Chapter 2 Staples Recipes   19

Juicy Caesar Salad Dressing 19
Vinegary Enchilada Sauce 19
Simple Flavor Packed Teriyaki Sauce 19
Milky air fryer Grits 19
Easy Shawarma Spice Mix 20
Milky Air Fryer Baked Rice 20
Sauce Flavored Asian Dipping Sauce 20
Classic Marinara Sauce 20

Chapter 3 Healthy Breakfasts   22

Grilled Breakfast Tater Tot Casserole. 22
Milky Chocolate Banana Bread 22
Air Fried Eggs in Pepper Rings........... 23
Meaty Canadian Bacon Muffin Sandwiches 23
Eggy Sausage and Cheese Quiche..... 23
Glazed Strawberry Toast...................... 23
Syrupy Breakfast Blueberry Cobbler.. 24
Eggy Spinach, Leek and Cheese Frittata 24
Milky Buttermilk Biscuits...................... 24

Air Fried Peppered Maple Bacon Knots 25
Eggy Veggie Frittata 25
Sumptuous Breakfast Cheese Sandwiches... 25
Syrupy Vanilla Granola 26
Tasty Turkey Breakfast Sausage Patties 26
Cheesy Spinach and Bacon Roll-ups . 26
Baked Egg in a Hole.............................. 27
Sweet Milky Monkey Bread.................. 27
Baked Asparagus and Cheese Strata. 27
Milky Spinach and Bacon English Muffins... 28
Oily Cinnamon Sweet Potato Chips.... 28
Air Fried Ham and Cheese Toast 28
Syrupy Banana and Oat Bread Pudding 29
Baked Bourbon Vanilla French Toast. 29
Milky Hash Brown Casserole 29
Eggy Hash Brown Cups 30
Eggy Crustless Broccoli Quiche......... 30
Milky Western Omelet 30
Creamy Bacon and Egg Bread Cups.. 31
Cheesy Fried Cheese Grits.................. 31
Cheesy Egg Florentine with Spinach . 31
Juicy Chicken Breakfast Sausages 32
Meaty Breakfast Casserole.................. 32
Fried Potatoes with Peppers and Onions 32
Cheesy Artichoke-Mushroom Frittata 33
Baked Mini Cinnamon Rolls 33
Baked Whole-Wheat Muffins with Blueberries.. 34
Coconut Brown Rice Porridge with Dates 34
Milky Maple Walnut Pancake............... 34
Sweet Cornmeal Pancake..................... 35
Milky Mixed Berry Dutch Baby Pancake 35
Aromatic French Toast Sticks 35
Oily Corned Beef Hash with Eggs....... 36
Tomato-Corn Frittata with Avocado Dressing 36
Cheesy Rice, Shrimp, and Spinach Frittata 37
Cheesy Mini Brown Rice Quiches....... 37
Olives, Kale, and Pecorino Baked Eggs. 37

Baked Quesadillas with Blueberries... 38
Air Fried Egg and Avocado Burrito..... 38
Cheesy Avocado with Eggs 38

Chapter 4 Fish and Seafood 40

Oily Cauliflower Fritters 40
Cheesy Tuna Patties............................. 40
Golden Breaded Fish Fillets 41
Roasted Parmesan-Crusted Halibut Fillets 41
Lemon-Honey Snapper with Fruit 41
Juicy Swordfish Steaks 42
Cheesy Salmon with Asparagus 42
Easy Fried Salmon Patties................... 42
Air Fried Crispy Fish Sticks 43
Oily Basil Salmon with Tomatoes 43
Cheesy Parmesan-Crusted Salmon Patties... 43
Vinegary Hoisin Tuna 44
Mustard-Crusted Sole Fillets............... 44
Yummy Oily Teriyaki Salmon............... 44
Herbed Salmon with Roasted Asparagus 45
Oily Fish Tacos 45
Air Fried Milky Cod Fillets 45
Ginger Flavored Tuna Lettuce Wraps. 46
Honeyed Halibut Steaks with Parsley 46
Baked Golden Beer-Battered Cod....... 46
Milky Cajun and Lemon Pepper Cod .. 47
Juicy Salmon Bowl............................... 47
Baked Tilapia with Garlic Aioli 47
Aromatic Baked Cod Fillet................... 48
Butter-Juicy Salmon Steak.................. 48
Scallops with Broccoli and Bean 48
Lemony Red Snapper Fillet 49
Roasted Scallops with Snow Peas 49
Crispy Breadcrumb Scallops 49
Garlic-Butter Shrimp with Sausage ... 50
Savory Tilapia Fillet............................. 50
Breadcrumb-Crusted Fish Sticks........ 50
Air Fried Paprika Shrimp 51
Buttery Catfish Cakes with Cheese 51
Aromatic Coconut-Crusted Prawns.... 51
Air-Fried Pecan-Crusted Catfish 52
Aromatic Parmesan Fish Fillets 52
Savory Roasted Shrimp 52
Cheesy Shrimp Salad with Caesar 53

Parmesan-Crusted Hake with Garlic Sauce 53
Aromatic Air-Fried Scallop 54
Roasted Crab with Onion and Tomato 54
Baked Flounder Fillets......................... 54
Coconut Milky Fish Curry with Tomato 55
Breadcrumb-Crusted Catfish Nuggets 55
Aromatic Shrimp with Parsley............. 55
Air Fried Bacon-Wrapped Scallops 56
Buttery Shrimp with Cherry Tomato ... 56
Breaded Calamari Ring with Lemon... 56
Rice Shrimp Patties.............................. 57
Aromatic Air Fried Shrimp 57
Panko Crab Sticks with Mayo Sauce .. 57
Tangy Shrimp.. 58
Shrimp Paella with Artichoke Heart ... 58
Buttery Scampi..................................... 58
Savory King Prawn............................... 59
Fired Shrimp with Mayonnaise Sauce 59
Crispy Crab Cakes with Bell Peppers 59

Chapter 5 Red Meats 61

Meat and Rice Stuffed Bell Peppers ... 61
Baked Apple-Glazed Pork 61
Cheesy Beef Rolls 62
Savory Lamb Loin Chops 62
Beef Meatballs with Marinara Sauce... 63
Bacon-Wrapped Filets Mignons........... 63
Air Fried Beef Satay 63
Air Fried Carne Asada.......................... 64
Buttery New York Strip........................ 64
Air Fried Venison 64
Homemade Salsa Beef Meatballs........ 65
Panko Crusted Calf's Liver Strips........ 65
Air Fried Lamb Kofta 65
Easy Thai Curry Beef Meatballs 66
Baked Beef and Tomato Sauce Meatloaf 66
Air Fried Lahmacun (Turkish Pizza).... 66
Baked Beef Steak 67
Rump Steak with Broccoli 67
Air Fried Veal Loin............................... 67
Air Fried Steak and Spinach Rolls...... 68
Savory Steak with Mushroom Gravy .. 68
Aromatic Steaks with Cucumber and Snap Pea Salad..................................... 69
Cheesy Stuffed Beef Tenderloin 69

Crusted Beef Steaks.................................. 70
Air Fried London Broil 70
Air Fried Beef Kofta................................ 70
Baked Zucchini Ground Beef 71
Crispy Golden Schnitzel 71
Breaded Golden Wasabi Spam 71
Easy Lamb Chops with Asparagus..... 72
Golden Lamb Chops 72
Crispy Bacon-Wrapped Sausage 72
Cheesy Beef and Pork Sausage Meatloaf 73
Bacon-Wrapped Hot Dogs 73
Crispy Pork Tenderloin 73
Golden Lemony Pork Chop 74
Chuck and Sausage Sandwiches........ 74
Teriyaki Pork Skewers........................... 75
Bangers and Cauliflower Mash 75
Air Fried Pork Rib................................... 75
Nuts Crusted Pork Rack 76
Roasted Lamb Chops with Potatoes .. 76
Savory Pork Butt with Chilled Sauce.. 77
Pork Steak and Squash......................... 77
Cheesy Sausage and Mushroom Calzones... 78
Crunchy Tonkatsu 78
Teriyaki Country Pork Ribs.................. 79
BBQ Sausage, Pineapple and Peppers .79
Crispy Lechon Kawali 79
Baked Pork Chops and Apple 80
Air Fried Pork Tenderloin..................... 80
Roasted Ribeye Steaks 80
Bo Luc Lac 81
Chessy Asparagus and Prosciutto Tart 81
Roasted Pork Chop 82
Balsamic Sausages and Red Grapes . 82
Baked Beef and Spinach Meatloaves . 82
Spicy Pork with Lettuce 83
Authentic Char Siu 83
Paprika Pork Chops 84
Dijon Pork with Squash and Apple 84
Tangy Sriracha Beef and Broccoli 85
Pork Cutlets with Aloha Salsa............. 85

Chapter 6 Poultry 87

Chicken Tacos with Peanut Sauce...... 87
Maple-Rosemary Turkey Breast.......... 87
Homemade Air-Fried Chicken Wings . 88
Stuffed Chicken with Bruschetta 88
Panko-Ctusted Chicken Fingers 88
BBQ-Honey Basted Drumsticks.......... 89
Apricot-Glazed Drumsticks 89
Baked Garlicky Whole Chicken........... 89
Classic Hawaiian Chicken Bites.......... 90
Bacon-Wrapped Cheesy Chicken 90
Cheesy Chicken and Pepperoni Pizza 90
Broiled Goulash...................................... 91
Buffalo Chicken Drumettes 91
Breaded Chicken Nuggets.................... 91
Chicken, Bell Pepper and Onion Rolls 92
Barbecue Chicken Tostadas with Coleslaw... 92
Cajun Chicken Drumsticks 92
Balsamic Marmalade Duck Breasts.... 93
Strawberry-Glazed Turkey Breast 93
Fried Chicken and Roma Tomato........ 93
Chicken Thighs on Waffles with Honey 94
Golden Chicken Schnitzel 94
Air-Fried Korean Chicken Wings 95
Cherry-Glazed Whole Duck 95
Panko-Crusted Chicken Livers 96
Honey-Glazed Chicken Breasts 96
Air-Fried Duck Leg Quarters 96
Air-Fried Crispy Chicken Skin............. 97
Paprika Chicken Skewers 97
Baked Turkey and Carrot Meatloaves. 97
Panko-Crusted Chicken Cutlets.......... 98
Golden Sweet-Sour Chicken Nuggets 98
Tangy Cilantro Chicken Breast 98
Peach-Glazed Chicken with Cherry 99
Cheesy Dijon Turkey Burgers 99
Baked Cheesy Marinara Chicken........ 100
Herbed Dijon Turkey Breast 100
Spicy Chicken, Sausage and Pepper.. 101
Chicken with Mashed Potato and Corn. 101
Parmesan Chicken Skewers with Corn. 102
Chicken Thighs with Veggies.............. 102

Chapter 7 Vegan and Vegetarian 104

Smoked Paprika Cauliflower 104
Air-Fried Cheesy Broccoli Tots 104
Air-Fried Winter Veggies...................... 104
Kung Pao Tofu 105
Homemade Maple Pecan Granola....... 105

Spicy Honey Broccoli	105
Balck Bean Cheese Tacos	106
Baked Veggies with Basil	106
Lemony Tahini Kale	106
Tortellini and Vegetable	107
Roasted Veggies Balls	107
Caramelized Eggplant with Yogurt	108
Caramelized Wax Beans	108
Bell Peppers with Garlic	108
Thai Spicy Veggies with Nuts	109
Roasted Cinnamon Celery Roots	109
Balsamic Asparagus Spears	109
Roasted Honey-Glazed Carrot	110
Asian Spicy Broccoli	110
Garlicky Stuffed WhiteMushroom	110
Baked Turnip, Zucchini, Onion	110
Teriyaki Cauliflower Florets	111
Cornflakes-Crusted Tofu Sticks	111
Breaded Eggplant Slices	111
Roasted Ratatouille	112
Potato and Asparagus with Cheese Sauce	112
Air-Fried Cheesy Cabbage Wedges	113
Ratatouille	113
Cheesy Vegan Quesadilla	113
Rosemary Butternut Squash	114
Panko-Crusted Green Beans	114
Herbed Broccoli with Yellow Cheese	114
Crispy Veggies with Mixed Herbs	115
Roasted Veggies and Rice	115
Garlicky Carrots with Sesame	115
Italian Spiced Tofu	116
Crispy Chili Okra	116
Panko Parmesan Zucchini Chips	116

Chapter 8 Vegetable Sides 118

Air-Fried Broccoli with Hot Sauce	118
Maple Brussels Sprouts	118
Baked Scalloped Potatoes	119
Roasted Spicy Cabbage	119
Parmesan Buttered Broccoli	119
Balsamic Asparagus	119
Tangy Sweet Potatoes	120
Cheesy Corn on the Cob	120
Panko-Crusted Cheesy Broccoli	120
Cheesy Corn Casserole	121
Air-Fried Acorn Squash	121
Breaded Brussels Sprouts with Sage	121
Crispy Parmesan Asparagus	122
Arrowroot-Crusted Zucchini	122
Tangy Balsamic-Glazed Carrots	122
Russet Potatoes with Yogurt and Chives	123
Rosemary Red Potatoes	123
Golden Butternut Squash Croquettes	123

Chapter 9 Appetizers and Snacks 125

Roasted Tuna Melts	125
Roasted Sausage and Onion Rolls	125
Deviled Eggs with Paprika	126
Homemade Baked Almonds	126
Stuffed Mushrooms with Cheese	126
Sardines with Tomato Sauce	127
Stuffed Jalapeño Poppers with Cheese	127
Air-Fried Cheesy Zucchini Tots	127
Lemon-Pepper Chicken Wings	128
Cheesy Green Chiles Nachos	128
Mozzarella Pepperoni Rolls	128
Cheesy Sausage Balls	129
Parmesan Cauliflower Florets	129
Air-Fried Edamame	129
Garlicky Button Mushrooms	130
Roasted Honey Grapes	130
Golden Hush Puppies	130
Browned Ricotta Capers	131
Homemade Paprika Potato Chips	131
Smoked Sausage and Mushroom Empanadas	131
Parma Prosciutto-Wrapped Pear	132
Air-Fried Polenta Fries with Mayo	132
Air-Fried Pickle Spears	132
Honey Snack Mix	133
Sweet Roasted Mixed Nuts	133
Shrimp Toasts with Thai Chili Sauce	133
Crispy Cinnamon Apple Chips	134
Apple Wedges with Yogurt	134
Fast Carrot Chips	134
Crispy Spiced Apple Chips	134
Stuffed Mushroom with Ham	135
Caramelized Cinnamon Peach	135
Air-Fried Crunchy Chickpeas	135
Spicy-Sweet Walnut	136
Panko-Crusted Avocado Chips	136

Muffuletta Sliders with Olives 136
Spicy Kale Chips 137
Green Tomato with Horseradish 137
Easy Spicy Tortilla Chips 137
Air-Fried Old Bay Chicken Wings 138
Roasted Parmesan Snack Mix............ 138
Golden Italian Rice Balls..................... 138
Fast Cripsy Artichoke Bites................. 139
Barbecue Herby Sausage Pizza 139
Air-Fried Breaded Chicken Wings 139
Bacon-Wrapped Stuffed Dates 140
Super Cheesy Sandwiches................... 140
Golden Mushroom and Spinach Calzones.140
Cheesy Crab Meat Toasts 141
Cod Fingers Gratin 141
Bruschetta with Tomato Sauce 141
Cheesy Corn and Black Bean Salsa ... 142
Cuban Turkey Sandwiches 142
Caramelized Peach Wedge 142

Chapter 10 Desserts   144

Tangy Cake.. 144
Blueberry Cupcakes 144
Buttery Shortbread.............................. 145
Rhubarb Oatmeal Crumble 145
Baked Coconut Cake............................ 145
Baked Apple Fritters 146
Buttery Chocolate Cookies................... 146
Walnut Butter Baklava 147
Blueberry and Peach Galette............... 147
Berry Crisp with Coconut Chip 148
Pecans Nuts Cookies 148
Creamy Raspberry Muffin 148
Baked Apple-Peach Crisp.................... 149
Buttery Chocolate Cheesecake............ 149
Buttermilk Cake 149
Pumpkin Pudding with Vanilla Wafers 150
Coffee Coconut Cake 150
Baked Walnuts Tart 150
Peach-Blueberry Tart 151
Chocolate Cake..................................... 151
Baked Sweet Apple 151
Apple Wedges with Apricots 152
Caramelized Fruit Kebabs 152
Tangy Cake... 152
Breaded Banana with Chocolate Sauce 153

Lemony Cheese Cake 153
Baked Chocolate Pie............................ 153
Fudge Pie 154
Blackberry Butter Cake....................... 154
Air Fried Pineapple Rings................... 154

Chapter 11 Casseroles, Frittata, and Quiche   156

Cauliflower and Chicken Casserole.... 156
Cheesy Chicken Crouton..................... 156
Spinach and Chickpea Casserole........ 157
Beef and Mushroom Casserole........... 157
Baked Corn Casserole 157
Cheesy Green Bean Casserole 158
Chessy Sausage and Broccoli Casserole 158
Ritzy Chicken and Vegetable Casserole...158
Smoked Trout and Crème Fraiche Frittata.159
Pastrami Cheese Casserole 159
Cheesy Vegetable Frittata................... 159
Riced Cauliflower Okra Casserole...... 160
Cheesy Chicken Ham Casserole......... 160
Ritzy Turkey Breast Casserole 160
Tilapia and Rockfish Casserole 161
Goat Cheese and Asparagus Frittata . 161
Broccoli Cheese Casserole 161
Cheesy Spinach and Mushroon Frittata.162
Grits and Asparagus Casserole 162
Beef and Chile Cheese Casserole....... 162

Chapter 12 Wraps and Sandwiches   164

Prawn and Cabbage Egg Rolls Wraps 164
Golden Cod Tacos with Salsa 164
Air Fried Avocado Tacos...................... 165
Beer Cod Tacos 165
Cheesy Bacon and Egg Wraps............ 166
Spinach and Cheese Pockets.............. 166
Pork and Carrot Momos..................... 166
Cheesy Potato and Black Bean Burritos 167
Air Fried Cheesy Steak 167
Sumptuous Spring Roll....................... 168
Aromatic Beef and Onion Tacos 168
Golden Chicken Burgers 169
Golden Chicken Empanadas 169
Air Fried Crispy Spring Rolls 170

Beef Burgers with Korean Mayo 170
Golden Tilapia Tacos 171
Shrimp and Zucchini Potstickers 171
Turkey Sliders with Chive Mayo 172
Air Fried Cream Cheese Wonton 172
Eggplant Hoagies 172
Cabbage and Pork Gyoza 173
Baked Turkey Hamburger 173
Cheesy Chicken Taquitos 173
Cheesy Potato Tortilla 174
Cheesy Chicken Wraps 174
Avocado and Tomato Egg Rolls 174
Crispy Chicken Egg Rolls 175
Beef Burgers with Mayo 175

Appendix 1: Measurement Conversion Chart 176

Appendix 2: Recipe Index 177

INTRODUCTION

Growing up, I was never a big fan of diets. I thought that they were a sadistic form of punishment, ruling what you can and cannot eat. I was raised in a big Italian family where food was treated as a way to socialize, express love, and connect with others. This meant that my typical Sunday roast meal was full of meats, pastas, and deep-fried treats that my mom prepared for the whole family. It wasn't until I moved to another state for work—and had to prepare meals on my own—that I realized just how unhealthy my diet had been for so many years. Don't get me wrong, I absolutely enjoy all types of foods and dishes. My only concern was the impact of the kinds of foods I was eating on my health.

My first docto's visit for a general check-up didn't go so well. In fact, my blood pressure was so high that I needed to be hospitalized. At that moment, all I could think about was how I was going to explain missing a day of work to my manager; however, I should have been thinking about how critical my health condition was. It's safe to say that this was the wake-up call I needed to adjust my eating habits and improve my slowly deteriorating health. However, I had a few "terms and conditions" of my own. First, I wasn't going to go on a strict military diet where certain foods would be prohibited, and secondly, I wasn't going to give up on fried foods! This criterion seemed impossible to fulfill until a nutritionist I visited recommended I purchase an air fryer. I conducted my own research and, sure enough, this kitchen appliance was everything I needed! It was the health-conscious alternative to deep-fried foods. An air fryer uses hot, circulating air to fry foods until they achieve the same crispy and golden texture we love.

I started blogging about every new recipe I would make using my air fryer, and, slowly, I saw more and more interest in my dishes—and some people were even asking for the recipe. It reached a point where I couldn't keep up with the demand for my air fryer recipes.

That's when the idea of a cookbook developed: one book with all of my air fryer recipes for any and every occasion. Whether you are looking to prepare a quick 15-minute meal after work or preparing tasty snacks for game day, you will find the perfect recipe (and easy instructions to follow). I managed to get my health under control—and lose some weight in the process—without having to exclude any foods in my diet. The only thing that I willingly said "goodbye" to was grease (and I hope to never see it on my plate ever again).

Chapter 1 The Basics Guide of Air Fryer

The Mechanics of an Air Fryer

An air fryer is a kitchen countertop appliance that fries foods using superheated air. Food prepared in an air fryer comes out similar to deep-fried or roasted foods (depending on the particular recipe). After preparing my ingredients, I simply place them inside the perforated basket (every air fryer comes with one) and gently lower the basket into the air fryer where the food cooks. During my many years of cooking with an air fryer, I have found that my food cooks faster and more efficiently because of the intense environment of heat in the cylinder. What's more, food comes out crispy and golden without having to be submerged in oil. This is why my nutritionist recommended the air fryer as a healthy alternative to deep frying—at most, I have only used a tablespoon of oil in my air fryer recipes.

With an air fryer, I can enjoy guilt-free burgers every other week that are scrumptious and low-calorie. I also appreciate the temperature control on my air fryer dial, which allows me to prepare food on the go. Below is a quick explanation of each function found on a standard air fryer one might find online or in a department store (I use all of these functions in my recipes to cook delicious meals in a fraction of the time).

1. The temperature control dial allows you to select various frying temperatures that typically range from 175°F to 400°F (please note that these may vary depending on the air fryer model).

2. The control panel shows the red "Power" light that indicates the air fryer is on and the "Heat On" light that turns on when the desired cooking temperature is reached. The control panel also makes cooking a lot more convenient by giving you pre-set cooking functions to cook certain foods like poultry or fish. However, I still prefer manually setting my temperature so that I have more control of the final outcome!

3. The automatic timer allows you to set a duration for how long food will cook for, and the countdown begins as soon as the desired temperature is reached. Once the time has run out, the air fryer will turn off automatically. This is not the same with all models though, thus it's always best to manually place the temperature control dial and timer dial to zero once cooking is completed.

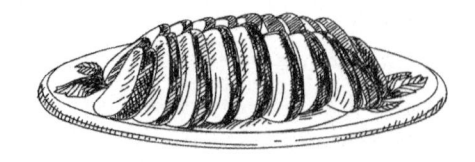

Why I Love Air Fryer Cooking

I must say that I am biased when it comes to air fryer cooking. This is because it has so many more benefits than other cooking methods. Below are a few things I love about my air fryer, which make it my ideal style of preparing hearty dishes.

An Air Fryer Is a Massive Time Saver

During the week, I struggle to allocate time for cooking in the kitchen. With so many tasks and demands all competing for my attention, easy and quick cooking is essential for me. Thankfully, I don't have to preheat my air fryer for hours before I can pack an entire meal in the basket and have it ready in minutes. Yes! It takes me the same amount of time to cook and plate my food as it does to preheat a conventional oven. The amount of time I save on cooking is usually spent on answering the last batch of emails of the day or simply catching up on my favorite Netflix series.

My Medical Reports Are Looking Better

I love cooking with my air fryer because of how much oil and fat that is excluded from the cooking process. Before I started using this savvy appliance, I indulged in deep-fried foods, being completely ignorant that I was putting my body at risk. The air fryer helped me reduce the amount of fat and oils I added to my foods. This simple yet effective adjustment allowed me to bring my cholesterol down and reduce the number of calories consumed with each meal.

Chapter 1 The Basics Guide of Air Fryer|3

Less Cleaning and Grease Stains in My Kitchen

I used to dread cooking with oil because of the hot splatters that would come out of the pan, especially when the temperature was high. Not only was I afraid of being burned with hot oil but I was also frustrated with the cleanup that usually awaited me once the meal had been cooked. Grease simply cannot be wiped away with a paper towel. It takes numerous attempts at wiping down countertops or stovetops to remove grease and the odor that is left behind. With my air fryer, cleanup is a breeze! I can prepare meals without using baking trays, pans, or grills. Just a few mixing bowls and a saucepan are what I typically need to prepare elaborate dishes—this also means zero grease stains to clean afterward.

The Best Option for Losing Weight Without a Strict Diet

Due to the cooking process used by an air fryer, it allowed me to lose some weight without having to go on a diet. As I mentioned earlier, strict eating plans are not my cup of tea, but that doesn't mean that my health needs to be compromised. I managed to lose weight by opting for healthier ingredients and preparing them with minimal fat or oil. The result was low-calorie dishes that were full of vitamins and minerals to help restore my body to good health. Friends of mine who were on diet plans started to use my recipes as part of their healthy eating. It made me happy to know that I can prepare healthy recipes that are diet-friendly but flexible enough for people to incorpo ate into their lifestyles.

I Didn't Need to Have Impressive Cooking Skills

I found that the benefit of i vesting in an intelligent kitchen appliance like the air fryer is that it did all of the cooking for me. This was a huge relief because when I lived at home, it was my mother or nonna who prepared all of our meals. Living alone for the first time meant that I needed to learn how to cook and prepare meals. Thankfully, air fryers are beginner-friendly and really easy to operate. It only took pressing a few buttons to get my meal going—the rest of the cooking process was carried out on my behalf.

A Guide to Picking the Perfect Air Fryer

When I was shopping for an air fryer online, I came across so many options! This made picking the perfect one an almost impossible task. Later on, I realized that I could choose an air fryer that was in my price range and offered all of the features I was looking for.

For instance, even with my tight budget, I had several options. I could opt for an air fryer with a smaller basket that still had all of the dials and buttons I needed. Of course, by increasing my budget by a couple of dollars, I could afford an air fryer with a larger basket (allowing me to add more ingredients at a time) that came with more buttons and a smart digital display. In the end, I didn't have to burn a hole in my wallet purchasing my first air fr er.

There were also 5 other components that I was on the lookout for when it came to purchasing my air fryer.

1. Size

Since air fryers are not small kitchen appliances, I had to first calculate how much kitchen space I had available for my air fryer. I had to look at the air fryer's dimensions, specifically focusing on the height because I wanted to place it beneath hanging cabinets. I also needed to make sure that my air fryer would have enough room on all sides of it so that it wouldn't knock against other appliances while cooking. My air fryer also needed enough ventilation (like being placed next to a window) because some foods, such as lamb or bacon, could make the fryer smoke. However, excessive smoking is not normal and the best solution when this happens is to simply switch the appliance off and contact the manufacturer.

2. Capacity

When I first recei ed my air fryer, I was surprised that the appliance was so large yet the inner basket was so small! Even though I knew that I had ordered a smaller unit, I didn't expect to only fit in a few ingredients in the basket before it was fully packed. The capacity of each air fryer model will vary, ranging from 3.7 quarts to 5.8 quarts. Thankfully, the 3.7 quarts air fryer was suitable for me because I lived alone. But it is also a big enough fryer for couples, too. Whenever I was tasked to prepare crispy snacks for a few friends, I would always prepare the food in batches (this is also a great cooking method to use when preparing family meals, otherwise opt for an extra-large air fryer).

3.Features

Air fryer features are something of a personal preference. Some people may prefer a manual dial, while others prefer a digital dial. The main difference between the two lies in the control panel. On digital air fryers, the control panel has added features like preheating the fryer, keeping the food warm after cooking, and a reminder to shake your basket to name a few. The higher in price you go, the more sophisticated the air fryers become. For instance, I noticed that some air fryers come with presets that allow you to simply press the "poultry" button and the fryer intuitively knows how long to cook the chicken for and the best temperature to achieve the desired results. These presets aren't mandatory because many air fryer recipes will give you instructions on how to manually set the temperature and the time.

4.Accessories

When buying my first air fr er, I needed to make sure that I could use certain accessories as part of my cooking process. For example, placing food in a baking or a small casserole dish would allow me to cook foods with a high liquid content like meats and vegetables in sauces. Small baking pans made to fit in an air fryer could also be used to bake bread and cakes. In essence, I was looking for an air fryer that would allow me to use smaller oven-safe accessories that were heat resistant.

5.Manufacturer and Warranty

One of the components I refused to compromise on was the brand of my air fryer. This is because different manufacturers offer different warranty programs. Generally, warranties on air fryers can range anywhere from 30 days to 2 years. Moreover, warranties may either cover the whole machine or different parts of the machine, such as the basket or heating element. Information about the warranty is available online and in the manufacturer's manual.

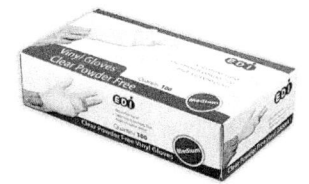

Kitchen Accessories and Techniques for Air Frying

Using an air fryer is not a complicated process. Yet, beginners may find that it takes some getting used to. For instance, the concept of using oven-safe dishes in an air fryer may be foreign for some or the fact that there are some basic techniques used exclusively for air frying. There's no need to panic, because below is a short summary of all the accessories and techniques that I use in my recipes.

1. Baking Pan

When using a baking pan for cooking, I tend to go for a 6 x 6 x 3 inch baking pan that fits snuggly in y air fryer (all of the recipes in this book were made with this particular baking pan). When using oven accessories for air frying, I always plan ahead. For instance, when my baking pan is unavailable for use, I grab an oven-safe dish that fits perfectly in y air fryer. I also have my aluminum sling ready for lowering and lifting my dish, as to avoid burning my fingers during the process.

2. Cooking Spray

On top of using an oil sprayer bottle, I always purchase cooking spray. This is another way of adding a coating of oil to foods. Not only does a cooking spray lightly coat food but it also helps prevent foods from sticking to the air fryer basket or baking pan. I also find cooking sp ay to be a great product to use for misting delicate foods or when extra-light olive oil would add an undesirable fl vor.

Chapter 1 The Basics Guide of Air Fryer|7

3. Dredging Station

One of the techniques I love to use is creating a dredging station. Normally, this is where I prepare an assembly line of ingredients needed for breading my food before it goes into the air fryer. Depending on the recipe, I line up 2 or 3 shallow containers filled with ingredients that I use for each stage of breading. Therefore, I usually start with flou , follow with whisked eggs, and then bread crumbs. Organizing all of my breading ingredients in this manner helps me speed up the process of getting my foods inside the fryer and ready to eat!

4. Food-Grade Gloves

Don't be surprised if some of the recipes in this book tell you to put on food-grade gloves when handling some ingredients, such as hot peppers. You can purchase food-grade gloves from restaurant supply stores or online. I prefer powder-free food-grade vinyl or latex gloves for my cooking. Gloves are only necessary when handling foods that can cause a burning sensation when contact is made with your eyes. However, if the recipe doesn't mention wearing gloves, you can proceed to mix food with your clean hands.

5. Muffin Cups

Some of the recipes that I have created will require muffin cups. Gene ally, each recipe will state the type of muffin paper that is needed. For instance, liquid batters hold well in foil cups and oven-safe silicone cups can hold just about any filling. Sometimes, you may need to layer a few cups together to create a sturdier cup before adding fillings. Once again, ou can judge by the consistency of your filling whether or not to double or triple the number of cups.

6. Oil for Misting

When adding oil to my foods, I use an oil sprayer bottle full of extra-light olive oil. I prefer using a spray bottle instead of directly adding oil to foods because the bottle offers me more flexibili y and control. I can decide based on the amount of pressure I exert, whether to give a heavy or light spray of oil to foods. I use extra-light olive oil because it has a higher smoke point than extra-virgin olive oil and its mild fl vor doesn't overpower the fl vor of foods (except some sweet or mildly seasoned dishes).

Kitchen Staples and Spices From the Pantry

My air fryer is an independent chef that takes the food I've prepped and turns it into a fl vorful masterpiece. However, I still need to carefully select the best ingredients and spices to create mouth-watering dishes. Below are some of the kitchen staples and spices I use frequently when cooking with my air fryer.

- **All-purpose flour** is great for breading recipes, baking, and thickening sauces. All-purpose flour can also be replaced with healthier alternatives, such as almond flou , for those individuals who have special dietary needs.

- **Brown sugar** is the perfect ingredient to use in dessert recipes or when preparing sauces and marinades.

- **Butter** is a great product to use for fl vor, but it can also be used as fat. Both salted and unsalted butter work well in recipes. Be careful not to substitute butter for margarine because this may change the results of the recipe.

- **Eggs** are used not only as the main ingredient (when making boiled eggs) but are also used in dessert recipes or when preparing an egg wash for breading. You will find that all of the recipes require large eggs.

- **Olive oil** will be used in most air frying recipes. It remains the healthier alternative to deep frying food in cooking oil.

- **Bread crumbs** are the reason why air fried foods come out crunchy. You can choose between fl vored or plain bread crumbs (or, you are welcome to season your bread crumbs at home).

- **Garlic** is one of my favorite spices to use during meal preparation. Make sure that you have a bottle of minced garlic ready in your refrigerator! If you don't have fresh garlic, you can also use either granulated or powdered garlic.

- **Sugar** is an essential ingredient in most dessert recipes. Granulated white sugar is the preferred option. Be careful when substituting sugar with honey because the fl vor of honey may change the results of the recipe.

Chapter 1 The Basics Guide of Air Fryer|9

- **Teriyaki sauce** is an absolutely delicious sauce to use as a marinade for poultry, seafood, or beef. My favorite brand is the Soy Vay marinade and sauce.
- **Ground black pepper** is a great spice to use when seeking another dimension of fl vor without overpowering your food.
- **Salt** comes in different varieties. The two main types I use are table salt and kosher salt. When I'm looking to add a bit more fl vor (especially on meats), I will use coarse sea salt. Remember that since kosher salt and sea salt have far larger grains than table salt, you will most likely use a reduced serving in your dishes.
- **Mustard** adds a wonderful fl vor component to food. When picking mustard, you can go for standard yellow mustard or Dijon mustard.
- **Paprika** is a great spice to use when making an egg or poultry dish.

Achieving the Perfect Time and Temperature

There are so many factors that can affect cooking time, including the size, volume, thickness, or temperature of the food. Even factors like wattage and the humidity in the air can impact cooking time. All of my recipes were tested in 1,425-watt air fryers. This means that if your air fryer has a higher or lower wattage, your food may cook faster or slower.

For most of the recipes, total cooking time shouldn't vary more than a couple of minutes, but to avoid overcooking, check your food regularly. A great trick is to check your food once it reaches the shortest cooking time displayed on the recipe. Assess whether it is fully cooked or needs more time. Don't be shy to press pause and open your air fryer drawer to check on your food. This may save you from having to eat overcooked or burnt food.

Eating raw or undercooked foods, such as eggs, meats, seafood, or poultry, can expose you to foodborne illnesses. The best way to ensure that your food is ready to eat is to cook it at the perfect temperature. For example, lamb, ground beef, pork, and veal should be cooked at temperatures that reach a minimum of 160°F. Other cuts of meat, including beef steaks, should be cooked at temperatures reaching at least 145°F. All poultry, including turkey and chicken, must be cooked at temperatures reaching a minimum of 165°F. The safest minimum temperatures for seafood can vary.

You can find the full list of minimum cooking tempe atures for many foods at https://www.foodsafety.gov/keep/charts/mintemp.html. When reheating leftovers in an air fryer, warm the food at a temperature of 350°F and continue doing so until your food reaches a temperature of 165°F. This is especially important when reheating potentially risky foods like chicken, beef, and pork.

Air Frying Cooking Timetable

Beef

Item	Temp (°F)	Time (mins)	Item	Temp (°F)	Time (mins)
Beef Eye Round Roast (4 lbs.)	400 °F	45 to 55	Meatballs (1-inch)	370 °F	7
Burger Patty (4 oz.)	370 °F	16 to 20	Meatballs (3-inch)	380 °F	10
Filet Mignon (8 oz.)	400 °F	18	Ribeye, bone-in (1-inch, 8 oz)	400 °F	10 to 15
Flank Steak (1.5 lbs.)	400 °F	12	Sirloin steaks (1-inch, 12 oz)	400 °F	9 to 14
Flank Steak (2 lbs.)	400 °F	20 to 28			

Chicken

Item	Temp (°F)	Time (mins)	Item	Temp (°F)	Time (mins)
Breasts, bone in (1 ¼ lb.)	370 °F	25	Legs, bone-in (1 ¾ lb.)	380 °F	30
Breasts, boneless (4 oz)	380 °F	12	Thighs, boneless (1 ½ lb.)	380 °F	18 to 20
Drumsticks (2 ½ lb.)	370 °F	20	Wings (2 lb.)	400 °F	12
Game Hen (halved 2 lb.)	390 °F	20	Whole Chicken	360 °F	75
Thighs, bone-in (2 lb.)	380 °F	22	Tenders	360 °F	8 to 10

Pork & Lamb

Item	Temp (°F)	Time (mins)	Item	Temp (°F)	Time (mins)
Bacon (regular)	400 °F	5 to 7	Pork Tenderloin	370 °F	15
Bacon (thick cut)	400 °F	6 to 10	Sausages	380 °F	15
Pork Loin (2 lb.)	360 °F	55	Lamb Loin Chops (1-inch thick)	400 °F	8 to 12
Pork Chops, bone in (1-inch, 6.5 oz)	400 °F	12	Rack of Lamb (1.5 – 2 lb.)	380 °F	22

Fish & Seafood

Item	Temp (°F)	Time (mins)	Item	Temp (°F)	Time (mins)
Calamari (8 oz)	400 °F	4	Tuna Steak	400 °F	7 to 10
Fish Fillet (1-inch, 8 oz)	400 °F	10	Scallops	400 °F	5 to 7
Salmon, fillet (6 oz)	380 °F	12	Shrimp	400 °F	5
Swordfish steak	400 °F	10			

Vegetables

INGREDIENT	AMOUNT	PREPARATION	OIL	TEMP	COOK TIME
Asparagus	2 bunches	Cut in half, trim stems	2 Tbsp	420°F	12-15 mins
Beets	1½ lbs	Peel, cut in ½-inch cubes	1 Tbsp	390°F	28-30 mins
Bell peppers (for roasting)	4 peppers	Cut in quarters, remove seeds	1 Tbsp	400°F	15-20 mins
Broccoli	1 large head	Cut in 1-2-inch florets	1 Tbsp	400°F	15-20 mins
Brussels sprouts	1 lb	Cut in half, remove stems	1 Tbsp	425°F	15-20 mins
Carrots	1 lb	Peel, cut in ¼-inch rounds	1 Tbsp	425°F	10-15 mins
Cauliflower	1 head	Cut in 1-2-inch florets	2 Tbsp	400°F	20-22 mins
Corn on the cob	7 ears	Whole ears, remove husks	1 Tbps	400°F	14-17 mins
Green beans	1 bag (12 oz)	Trim	1 Tbps	420°F	18-20 mins
Kale (for chips)	4 oz	Tear into pieces, remove stems	None	325°F	5-8 mins
Mushrooms	16 oz	Rinse, slice thinly	1 Tbps	390°F	25-30 mins
Potatoes, russet	1½ lbs	Cut in 1-inch wedges	1 Tbps	390°F	25-30 mins
Potatoes, russet	1 lb	Hand-cut fries, soak 30 mins in cold water, then pat dry	½ -3 Tbps	400°F	25-28 mins
Potatoes, sweet	1 lb	Hand-cut fries, soak 30 mins in cold water, then pat dry	1 Tbps	400°F	25-28 mins
Zucchini	1 lb	Cut in eighths lengthwise, then cut in half	1 Tbps	400°F	15-20 mins

Cleaning and Caring for an Air Fryer

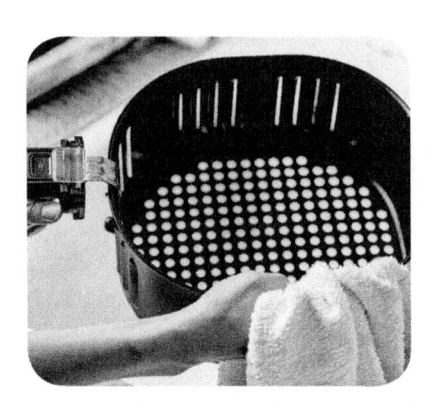

Air Fryers are safe appliances to have in the kitchen and they don't require much cleaning once cooking is complete. However, just like other gadgets in your kitchen, there are some general tips that you can follow to take care of your air fryer and ensure that it lasts for many years.

Tip 1: Do not touch the surface of your air fryer while it's on, otherwise you may get burned. Once cooking is complete, allow the air fryer to cool before handling it or removing your food or be sure to wear oven mitts or use a potholder when touching it.

Tip 2: Avoid spillages of liquids near the cord of your air fryer. Ideally, you should always keep the surfaces close to the cord and electrical socket completely dry to avoid electrical shocks or causing damage to the air fryer.

Tip 3: After purchasing your air fryer, clean it

12|Chapter 1 The Basics Guide of Air Fryer

with soapy water. Remove the basket, pan, and any other accessories and give them a thorough clean. Take a dampened paper towel and wipe down the inside and outside of the air fryer. Dry off all of the components before assembling the machine back together.

Tip 4: Clean the air fryer drawer and basket after every use. Leaving the drawer unwashed may cause food contamination or smelly odors. After washing the drawer and basket, you can place them back into the air fryer and turn the power on for 2 to 3 minutes for a quick and convenient dry.

Tip 5: Clean the air fryer heating element with a cleaning brush to remove any pieces of food that may be caught in it.

6 Beginner-Friendly Tips for Cooking Air-Fried Food

It doesn't take much effort to cook tender meats, crunchy fries, or roasted vegetables using an air fryer. There are a few tips that I have learned along the way that have helped me prepare restaurant-quality dishes on different occasions. Fortunately, this isn't a special talent that I have. Instead, it's a skill that you can also learn by following these simple tips:

Tip 1: Invest in an Oil Sprayer Bottle

Oil sprayer bottles come in handy when you need to add a small amount of oil to your food. Since many of the recipes in this cookbook require a small amount of oil, this small accessory may be used more often than you think!

Tip 2: Avoid Overpacking the Air Fryer Basket

It can be tempting to want to squeeze as many pieces of food as you can into a basket, but the results may be less than appetizing. The more space food has in a basket, the more evenly cooked and perfectly crisp it comes out. If you find that there isn't enough space left inside a basket, divide the food into 2 or 3 batches.

Tip 3: Check-In Regularly on Your Food

Even though the timer's job is to inform you when your food has cooked to completion, it may be useful to open the air fryer and check on your food. This will help to prevent overcooking and also give you a chance to flip or sha e food so that it cooks evenly.

Tip 4: Preheat Your Air Fryer Before Loading in Food

Although this step is not necessary, preheating your air fryer may save you even more time. It will ensure that by the time you are ready to place your food into the basket, the fryer has already achieved the desired temperature.

Tip 5: Prepare the Best Crunch With a Simple Breading Technique

Everyone loves deep-fried food for the crispy and golden texture that it produces. This same texture can be achieved using an air fryer by following a simple breading technique. Start by coating your food with flou , then egg, and then breadcrumbs. Press the breadcrumbs onto the food and make sure that your food is completely coated. Don't panic if some of the breadcrumbs fly way during cooking (this may be caused by the fan blowing inside of the air fryer).

Tip 6: Use Aluminum Foil as a Sling

A simple trick to use when transferring baking dishes in and out of the basket is an aluminum foil sling. To create the sling, fold aluminum foil into a strip of about 2 inches wide and 24 inches long. Place your cake pan or oven dish on the foil, and by folding the ends of your strip, you will be able to lift and lower your dish into the basket easily. After lowering your dish, carefully tuck the ends of the strip into the basket, and then place the basket into the air fryer. Once cooking time is complete, remove the basket from the air fryer and locate your foil strips. Once found, you can then easily lift the dish out of the basket and onto your kitchen countertop.

Prioritizing Health With Every Mouthful

My health and well-being are very important to me. After my hospital admission for high blood pressure, I was determined to adopt a new mindset about food. I found that healthier alternatives to foods were available, and this meant that I didn't have to cut out certain food groups from my diet. Here are some of the healthy cooking habits that I have embraced, which have helped me live a more vibrant life.

Oils and Fats

The best oils that I use for air frying have a high smoke point (the temperature at which they begin to smoke). Some of these oils include peanut oil, refined grapeseed oil, refined safflower oil, refined corn oil, a extra-light olive oil (which shouldn't be confused with extra-virgin olive oil that has a low smoke point). By far, the healthiest fat for cooking is olive oil because it has the ability to raise good cholesterol while reducing bad cholesterol. As olive oil contains monounsaturated fatty acids (MUFAs), cooking with it can reduce the risk of developing type 2 diabetes and reduce the risk of a stroke.

Sugar Substitutes

While many recipes use granulated white sugar, those with special dietary needs can use a few sugar substitutes for healthier low-carb dishes. For instance, one of the best sugar alternatives on the market today is known as Sukrin Gold. This product is 100% natural and made primarily with erythritol. It has an exceptionally sweet fl vor and contains hardly any calories. It is also safe for diabetics since it doesn't affect blood sugar and insulin levels. Other great sugar substitutes include granulated erythritol, stevia glycerite (which is a lot sweeter and has a far more distinct fl vor than erythritol), honey, maple syrup, or xylitol (which offers added health benefits li e preventing tooth decay, improving gut health, and helping your body fight infections)

Salt Substitutes

Many air frying recipes use table salt or sea salt to fl vor foods. Nevertheless, there are many salt substitutes on the market like sylvite, which is potassium chloride in mineral form. I must caution cooks when it comes to using salt substitutes as they may contain potassium, which is a mineral that can be dangerous when consumed by people who already have weakened kidneys. Since kidneys work to clear potassium from the blood, weak kidneys are not able to flush way potassium efficientl . This tends to lead to an overload of potassium in the blood and a condition known as hyperkalemia that can prove fatal if not treated immediately.

Low-Carb Options

I have also found healthy alternatives to some of the carbohydrate-rich foods that had been a part of my diet. For example, in place of pasta, I cut spaghetti squash into rings, remove all of the seeds and strings, and spray each ring lightly with olive oil and then add a sprinkle of salt and pepper. These rings then go into a pan for roasting. After roasting, I take a fork and scrape out the squash to yield a pasta-like texture. Zucchini is another low-carb summer vegetable that makes a healthy substitute for pasta. You can run it through a spiralizer (if you have one) or use a vegetable peeler to make your version of fettuccine. Cauliflower is my favorite go-to low-carb ingredient because it's so versatile. I steam it, mash it, or grate it with a food processor to make cauliflower rice.

Almond flour is a great substitute for all-purpose flour an can be used for breading or baking. Milled flaxseed is another effective flour substitute that is high in fiber and omega-3 fa y acids. After using milled flaxseed to ma e chocolate muffins, I found that it gave my muffins a more wholesome, whea -like fl vor, adding an even greater fl vor profile.

Top Anti-Inflammatory Foods

Inflammation is the body s natural response to injury and infection. It helps the body heal after experiencing cell or tissue damage and physical trauma. There are two classes of inflammation: acute and chronic. Acute inflammation is th good type because it kills bacteria, repairs tissue damage, and heals the body from injuries within a short period of time. Chronic inflammation, on the other hand, is prolonged, and because of this, it can cause a number of health issues, such as hypertension, inflammatory bowel disease, heart disease, obesity, and type 2 diabetes to name a few. The good news is that by simply consuming more anti-inflammatory foods, inflammation that already exists can be healed and the bod can gain better immunity against future flare-ups. Anti-infl mmatory foods will also help you experience natural energy and vitality. Below are 15 anti-inflammatory foods to incorpo ate into your diet today.

1. **Bell peppers**
2. **Broccoli**
3. **Kale**
4. **Spinach**
5. **Tomatoes**
6. **Blueberries**
7. **Salmon and other fatty fish**
8. **Nuts**
9. **Cinnamon**
10. **Garlic**
11. **Ginger**
12. **Rosemary**
13. **Turmeric**
14. **Extra-virgin olive oil**
15. **Green tea**

FAQs About Air Fryers

Below is a list of 3 commonly asked questions about air fryers. These questions and answers will put your fears to rest and make you feel more prepared for air fryer cooking!

Q: Why has my food come out dry, chewy, and not crispy?

A: Most likely, you went too light on the oil. Not only does oil provide fl vor to the food but it also enhances the texture and overall results. So, don't be shy to coat your ingredients with a sufficient amount.

Q: White or black smoke is coming out of my air fryer. What could be the problem?

A: If you happen to see white smoke coming out of your air fryer, it may indicate that there is too much fat or excess amounts of oil in your recipe. Black smoke is more of a concern because it indicates that there is something wrong with your air fryer machine. As soon as you notice black smoke, unplug your air fryer immediately and refrain from using it until you resolve the problem with a technician.

Q: Why won't my air fryer turn off?

A: If you have trouble switching your air fryer off, don't be alarmed. Most air fryers have a time delay when shutting down. For instance, once you switch the power button off, the fan may still continue to blow hot air for another 20 seconds. Patiently wait until the fan comes to a complete stop.

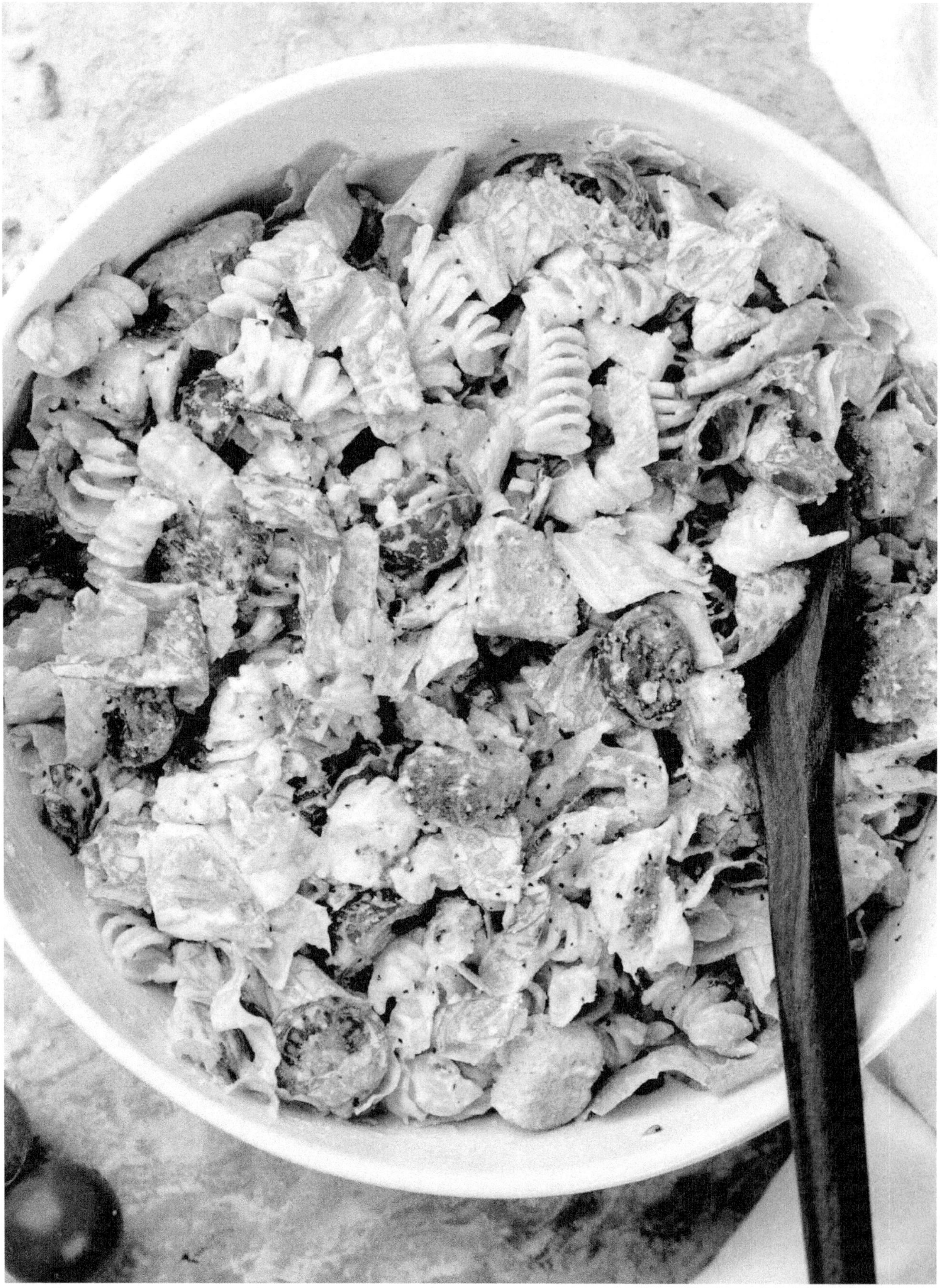

CHAPTER 2 *Staples Recipes*

Juicy Caesar Salad Dressing

Prep time: 5 minutes | Cook time: 0 minutes | Makes about ⅔ cup

½ cup extra-virgin olive oil
2 tablespoons freshly squeezed lemon juice
1 teaspoon anchovy paste
¼ teaspoon kosher salt or ⅛ teaspoon fine sal
¼ teaspoon minced or pressed garlic
1 egg, beaten

1. Add all the ingredients to a tall, narrow container.
2. Purée the mixture with an immersion blender until smooth.
3. Use immediately.

Vinegary Enchilada Sauce

Prep time: 15 minutes | Cook time: 0 minutes | Makes 2 cups

3 large ancho chiles, stems and seeds removed, torn into pieces
1½ cups very hot water
2 garlic cloves, peeled and lightly smashed
2 tablespoons wine vinegar
1½ teaspoons sugar
½ teaspoon dried oregano
½ teaspoon ground cumin
2 teaspoons kosher salt or 1 teaspoon fine sal

1. Mix together the chile pieces and hot water in a bowl and let stand for 10 to 15 minutes.
2. Pour the chiles and water into a blender jar. Fold in the garlic, vinegar, sugar, oregano, cumin, and salt and blend until smooth.
3. Use immediately.

Simple Flavor Packed Teriyaki Sauce

Prep time: 5 minutes | Cook time: 0 minutes | Makes ¾ cup

½ cup soy sauce
3 tablespoons honey
1 tablespoon rice wine or dry sherry
1 tablespoon rice vinegar
2 teaspoons minced fresh ginger
2 garlic cloves, smashed

1. Beat together all the ingredients in a small bowl.
2. Use immediately.

Milky air fryer Grits

Prep time: 3 minutes | Cook time: 1 hour 5 minutes | Makes about 4 cups

1 cup grits or polenta (not instant or quick cook)
2 cups chicken or vegetable stock
2 cups milk
2 tablespoons unsalted butter, cut into 4 pieces
1 teaspoon kosher salt or ½ teaspoon fine sal

1. Add the grits to the baking pan. Stir in the stock, milk, butter, and salt.
2. Select Bake, set the temperature to 325°F (163°C), and set the time for 1 hour and 5 minutes. Select Start to begin preheating.
3. Once the unit has preheated, place the pan into the air fryer.
4. After 15 minutes, remove the pan from the air fryer and stir the polenta. Return the pan to the air fryer and continue cooking.
5. After 30 minutes, remove the pan again and stir the polenta again. Return the pan to the air fryer and continue cooking for 15 to 20 minutes, or until the polenta is soft and creamy and the liquid is absorbed.
6. When done, remove the pan from the air fryer.
7. Serve immediately.

Easy Shawarma Spice Mix

Prep time: 5 minutes | Cook time: 0 minutes | Makes about 1 tablespoon

1 teaspoon smoked paprika
1 teaspoon cumin
¼ teaspoon turmeric
¼ teaspoon kosher salt or ⅛ teaspoon fine sal
¼ teaspoon cinnamon
¼ teaspoon allspice
¼ teaspoon red pepper fla es
¼ teaspoon freshly ground black pepper

1. Stir together all the ingredients in a small bowl.
2. Use immediately or place in an airtight container in the pantry.

Sauce Flavored Asian Dipping Sauce

Prep time: 15 minutes | Cook time: 0 minutes | Makes about 1 cup

¼ cup rice vinegar
¼ cup hoisin sauce
¼ cup low-sodium chicken or vegetable stock
3 tablespoons soy sauce
1 tablespoon minced or grated ginger
1 tablespoon minced or pressed garlic
1 teaspoon chili-garlic sauce or sriracha (or more to taste)

1. Stir together all the ingredients in a small bowl, or place in a jar with a tight-fitting lid and shake until well mixed.
2. Use immediately.

Milky Air Fryer Baked Rice

Prep time: 3 minutes | Cook time: 35 minutes | Makes about 4 cups

1 cup long-grain white rice, rinsed and drained
1 tablespoon unsalted butter, melted, or 1 tablespoon extra-virgin olive oil
2 cups water
1 teaspoon kosher salt or ½ teaspoon fine sal

1. Add the butter and rice to the baking pan and stir to coat. Pour in the water and sprinkle with the salt. Stir until the salt is dissolved.
2. Select Bake, set the temperature to 325ºF (163ºC), and set the time for 35 minutes. Select Start to begin preheating.
3. Once the unit has preheated, place the pan into the air fryer.
4. After 20 minutes, remove the pan from the air fryer. Stir the rice. Transfer the pan back to the air fryer and continue cooking for 10 to 15 minutes, or until the rice is mostly cooked through and the water is absorbed.
5. When done, remove the pan from the air fryer and cover with aluminum foil. Let stand for 10 minutes. Using a fork, gently fluff the rice.
6. Serve immediately.

Classic Marinara Sauce

Prep time: 15 minutes | Cook time: 30 minutes | Makes about 3 cups

¼ cup extra-virgin olive oil
3 garlic cloves, minced
1 small onion, chopped (about ½ cup)
2 tablespoons minced or puréed sun-dried tomatoes (optional)
1 (28-ounce / 794-g) can crushed tomatoes
½ teaspoon dried basil
½ teaspoon dried oregano
¼ teaspoon red pepper fla es
1 teaspoon kosher salt or ½ teaspoon fine salt, plus more as needed

1. Heat the oil in a medium saucepan over medium heat.
2. Add the garlic and onion and sauté for 2 to 3 minutes, or until the onion is softened. Add the sun-dried tomatoes (if desired) and cook for 1 minute until fragrant. Stir in the crushed tomatoes, scraping any brown bits from the bottom of the pot. Fold in the basil, oregano, red pepper fla es, and salt. Stir well.
3. Bring to a simmer. Cook covered for about 30 minutes, stirring occasionally.
4. Turn off the heat and allow the sauce to cool for about 10 minutes.
5. Taste and adjust the seasoning, adding more salt if needed.
6. Use immediately.

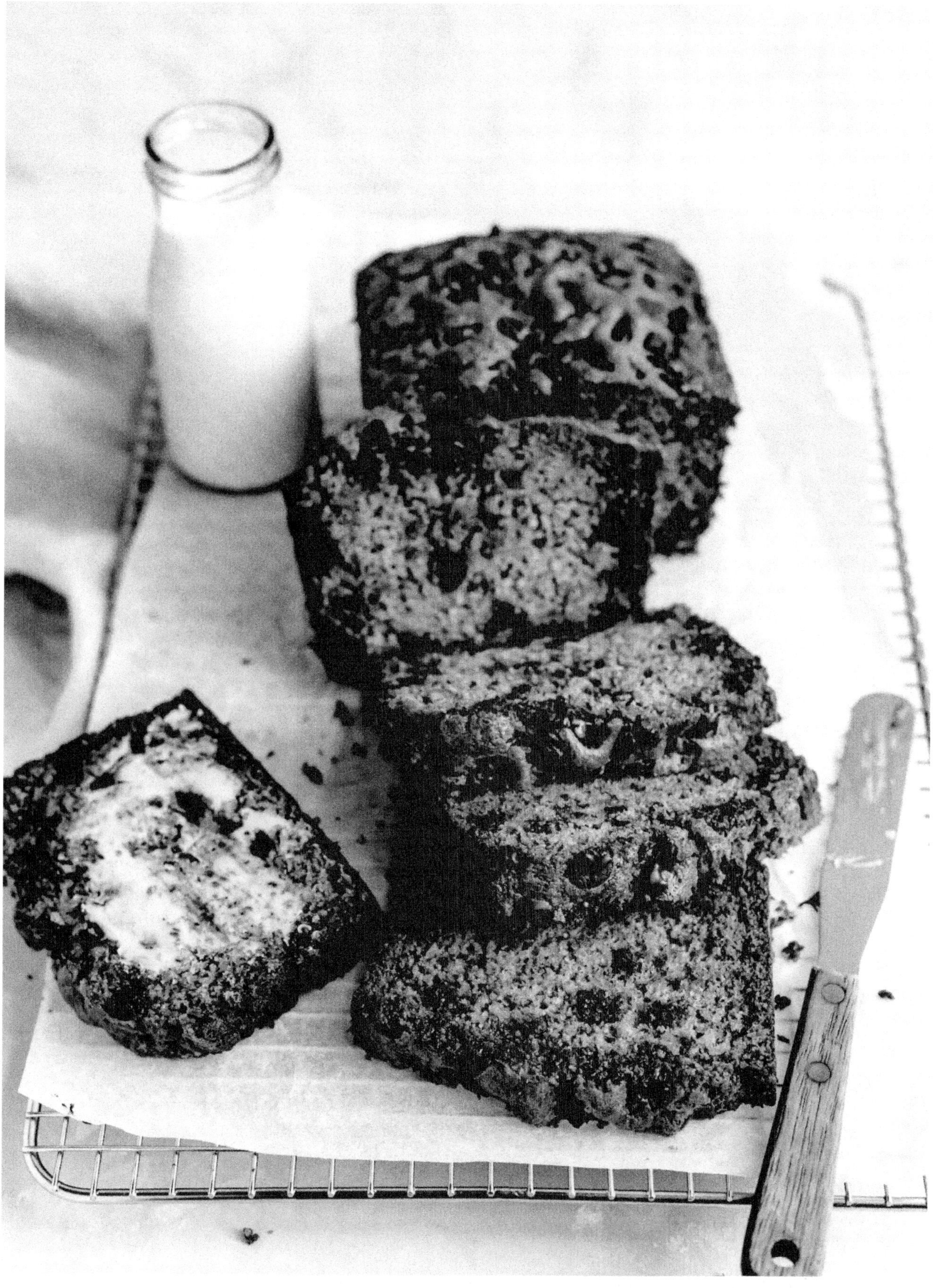

CHAPTER 3 *Healthy Breakfasts*

Grilled Breakfast Tater Tot Casserole

Prep time: 5 minutes | Cook time: 17 to 18 minutes | Serves 4

4 eggs
1 cup milk
Salt and pepper, to taste
12 ounces (340 g) ground chicken sausage
1 pound (454 g) frozen tater tots, thawed
¾ cup grated Cheddar cheese
Cooking spray

1. Whisk together the eggs and milk in a medium bowl. Season with salt and pepper to taste and stir until mixed. Set aside.
2. Place a skillet over medium-high heat and spritz with cooking spray. Place the ground sausage in the skillet and break it into smaller pieces with a spatula or spoon. Cook for 3 to 4 minutes until the sausage Starts to brown, stirring occasionally. Remove from heat and set aside.
3. Coat a baking pan with cooking spray. Arrange the tater tots in the baking pan.
4. Select Bake, set temperature to 400ºF (205ºC) and set time to 14 minutes. Select Start to begin preheating.
5. Once preheated, place the pan into the air fryer.
6. After 6 minutes, remove the pan from the air fryer. Stir the tater tots and add the egg mixture and cooked sausage. Return the pan to the air fryer and continue cooking.
7. After another 6 minutes, remove the pan from the air fryer. Scatter the cheese on top of the tater tots. Return the pan to the air fryer and continue to cook for 2 minutes more.
8. When done, the cheese should be bubbly and melted.
9. Let the mixture cool for 5 minutes and serve warm.

Milky Chocolate Banana Bread

Prep time: 10 minutes | Cook time: 30 minutes | Serves 4

¼ cup cocoa powder
6 tablespoons plus 2 teaspoons all-purpose flou , divided
½ teaspoon kosher salt
¼ teaspoon baking soda
1½ ripe bananas
1 large egg, whisked
¼ cup vegetable oil
½ cup sugar
3 tablespoons buttermilk or plain yogurt (not Greek)
½ teaspoon vanilla extract
6 tablespoons chopped white chocolate
6 tablespoons chopped walnuts

1. Mix together the cocoa powder, 6 tablespoons of the flou , salt, and baking soda in a medium bowl.
2. Mash the bananas with a fork in another medium bowl until smooth. Fold in the egg, oil, sugar, buttermilk, and vanilla, and whisk until thoroughly combined. Add the wet mixture to the dry mixture and stir until well incorporated.
3. Combine the white chocolate, walnuts, and the remaining 2 tablespoons of flour in a third bowl and toss to coat. Add this mixture to the batter and stir until well incorporated. Pour the batter into a baking pan and smooth the top with a spatula.
4. Select Bake, set temperature to 310ºF (154ºC) and set time to 30 minutes. Select Start to begin preheating.
5. Once the air fryer has preheated, place the pan into the air fryer.
6. When done, a toothpick inserted into the center of the bread should come out clean.
7. Remove from the air fryer and allow to cool on a wire rack for 10 minutes before serving.

Air Fried Eggs in Pepper Rings

Prep time: 5 minutes | Cook time: 7 minutes | Serves 4

1 large red, yellow, or orange bell pepper, cut into four ¾-inch rings
4 eggs
Salt and freshly ground black pepper, to taste
2 teaspoons salsa
Cooking spray

1. Coat a baking pan lightly with cooking spray.
2. Put 4 bell pepper rings in the prepared baking pan. Crack one egg into each bell pepper ring and sprinkle with salt and pepper. Top each egg with ½ teaspoon of salsa.
3. Select Air Fry, set temperature to 350°F (180°C) and set time to 7 minutes. Select Start to begin preheating.
4. Once preheated, place the pan into the air fryer.
5. When done, the eggs should be cooked to your desired doneness.
6. Remove the rings from the pan to a plate and serve warm.

Meaty Canadian Bacon Muffin Sandwiches

Prep time: 5 minutes | Cook time: 8 minutes | Serves 4

4 English muffins, split
8 slices Canadian bacon
4 slices cheese
Cooking spray

1. Make the sandwiches: Top each of 4 muffin hal es with 2 slices of Canadian bacon, 1 slice of cheese, and finish with the remaining muffin hal .
2. Put the sandwiches in the air fryer basket and spritz the tops with cooking spray.
3. Select Bake, set temperature to 370°F (188°C), and set time to 8 minutes. Select Start to begin preheating.
4. Once preheated, place the basket into the air fryer. Flip the sandwiches halfway through the cooking time.
5. When cooking is complete, remove the basket from the air fryer. Divide the sandwiches among four plates and serve warm.

Eggy Sausage and Cheese Quiche

Prep time: 5 minutes | Cook time: 25 minutes | Serves 4

12 large eggs
1 cup heavy cream
Salt and black pepper, to taste
12 ounces (340 g) sugar-free breakfast sausage
2 cups shredded Cheddar cheese
Cooking spray

1. Coat a casserole dish with cooking spray.
2. Beat together the eggs, heavy cream, salt and pepper in a large bowl until creamy. Stir in the breakfast sausage and Cheddar cheese.
3. Pour the sausage mixture into the prepared casserole dish.
4. Select Bake, set temperature to 375°F (190°C) and set time to 25 minutes. Select Start to begin preheating.
5. Once the air fryer has preheated, place the dish into the air fryer.
6. When done, the top of the quiche should be golden brown and the eggs will be set.
7. Remove from the air fryer and let sit for 5 to 10 minutes before serving.

Glazed Strawberry Toast

Prep time: 5 minutes | Cook time: 8 minutes | Makes 4 toasts

4 slices bread, ½-inch thick
1 cup sliced strawberries
1 teaspoon sugar
Cooking spray

1. On a clean work surface, lay the bread slices and spritz one side of each slice of bread with cooking spray.
2. Place the bread slices in the air fryer basket, sprayed side down. Top with the strawberries and a sprinkle of sugar.
3. Select Air Fry, set temperature to 375°F (190°C) and set time to 8 minutes. Select Start to begin preheating.
4. Once preheated, place the basket into the air fryer.
5. When cooking is complete, the toast should be well browned on each side. Remove from the air fryer to a plate and serve.

Chapter 3 Healthy Breakfasts | 23

Syrupy Breakfast Blueberry Cobbler

Prep time: 5 minutes | Cook time: 15 minutes | Serves 4

¾ teaspoon baking powder
1/3 cup whole-wheat pastry flou
Dash sea salt
1/3 cup unsweetened nondairy milk
2 tablespoons maple syrup
½ teaspoon vanilla
Cooking spray
½ cup blueberries
¼ cup granola
Nondairy yogurt, for topping (optional)

1. Spritz a baking pan with cooking spray.
2. Mix together the baking powder, flou , and salt in a medium bowl. Add the milk, maple syrup, and vanilla and whisk to combine.
3. Scrape the mixture into the prepared pan. Scatter the blueberries and granola on top.
4. Select Bake, set temperature to 347ºF (175ºC) and set time to 15 minutes. Select Start to begin preheating.
5. Once preheated, place the pan into the air fryer.
6. When done, the top should begin to brown and a knife inserted in the center should come out clean.
7. Let the cobbler cool for 5 minutes and serve with a drizzle of nondairy yogurt.

Eggy Spinach, Leek and Cheese Frittata

Prep time: 10 minutes | Cook time: 22 minutes | Serves 2

4 large eggs
4 ounces (113 g) baby bella mushrooms, chopped
1 cup (1 ounce / 28-g) baby spinach, chopped
½ cup (2 ounces / 57-g) shredded Cheddar cheese
1/3 cup (from 1 large) chopped leek, white part only
¼ cup halved grape tomatoes
1 tablespoon 2% milk
¼ teaspoon dried oregano
¼ teaspoon garlic powder
½ teaspoon kosher salt
Freshly ground black pepper, to taste
Cooking spray

1. Lightly spritz a baking dish with cooking spray.
2. Whisk the eggs in a large bowl until frothy. Add the mushrooms, baby spinach, cheese, leek, tomatoes, milk, oregano, garlic powder, salt, and pepper and stir until well blended. Pour the mixture into the prepared baking dish.
3. Select Bake, set temperature to 300ºF (150ºC) and set time to 22 minutes. Select Start to begin preheating.
4. Once the air fryer has preheated, place the dish into the air fryer.
5. When cooked, the center will be puffed up and the top will be golden brown.
6. Let the frittata cool for 5 minutes before slicing to serve.

Milky Buttermilk Biscuits

Prep time: 5 minutes | Cook time: 18 minutes | Makes 16 biscuits

2½ cups all-purpose flou
1 tablespoon baking powder
1 teaspoon kosher salt
1 teaspoon sugar
½ teaspoon baking soda
8 tablespoons (1 stick) unsalted butter, at room temperature
1 cup buttermilk, chilled

1. Stir together the flou , baking powder, salt, sugar, and baking powder in a large bowl.
2. Add the butter and stir to mix well. Pour in the buttermilk and stir with a rubber spatula just until incorporated.
3. Place the dough onto a lightly floured surface and roll the dough out to a disk, ½ inch thick. Cut out the biscuits with a 2-inch round cutter and re-roll any scraps until you have 16 biscuits.
4. Arrange the biscuits in the air fryer basket in a single layer.
5. Select Bake, set temperature to 325ºF (163ºC), and set time to 18 minutes. Select Start to begin preheating.
6. Once preheated, place the basket into the air fryer.
7. When cooked, the biscuits will be golden brown.
8. Remove from the air fryer to a plate and serve hot.

Air Fried Peppered Maple Bacon Knots

Prep time: 5 minutes | Cook time: 7 to 8 minutes | Serves 6

1 pound (454 g) maple smoked center-cut bacon
¼ cup maple syrup
¼ cup brown sugar
Coarsely cracked black peppercorns, to taste

1. On a clean work surface, tie each bacon strip in a loose knot.
2. Stir together the maple syrup and brown sugar in a bowl. Generously brush this mixture over the bacon knots.
3. Place the bacon knots in the air fryer basket and sprinkle with the coarsely cracked black peppercorns.
4. Select Air Fry, set temperature to 390°F (199°C), and set time to 8 minutes. Select Start to begin preheating.
5. Once preheated, place the basket into the air fryer.
6. After 5 minutes, remove the basket from the air fryer and flip the bacon knots. Return the basket to the air fryer and continue cooking for 2 to 3 minutes more.
7. When cooking is complete, the bacon should be crisp. Remove from the air fryer to a paper towel-lined plate. Let the bacon knots cool for a few minutes and serve warm.

Eggy Veggie Frittata

Prep time: 10 minutes | Cook time: 12 minutes | Serves 4

½ cup chopped red bell pepper
⅓ cup grated carrot
⅓ cup minced onion
1 teaspoon olive oil
1 egg
6 egg whites
⅓ cup 2% milk
1 tablespoon shredded Parmesan cheese

1. Mix together the red bell pepper, carrot, onion, and olive oil in a baking pan and stir to combine.
2. Select Bake, set temperature to 350°F (180°C) and set time to 12 minutes. Select Start to begin preheating.
3. Once preheated, place the pan into the air fryer.
4. After 3 minutes, remove the pan from the air fryer. Stir the vegetables. Return the pan to the air fryer and continue cooking.
5. Meantime, whisk together the egg, egg whites, and milk in a medium bowl until creamy.
6. After 3 minutes, remove the pan from the air fryer. Pour the egg mixture over the top and scatter with the Parmesan cheese. Return the pan to the air fryer and continue cooking for additional 6 minutes.
7. When cooking is complete, the eggs will be set and the top will be golden around the edges.
8. Allow the frittata to cool for 5 minutes before slicing and serving.

Sumptuous Breakfast Cheese Sandwiches

Prep time: 5 minutes | Cook time: 8 minutes | Serves 2

1 teaspoon butter, softened
4 slices bread
4 slices smoked country ham
4 slices Cheddar cheese
4 thick slices tomato

1. Spoon ½ teaspoon of butter onto one side of 2 slices of bread and spread it all over.
2. Assemble the sandwiches: Top each of 2 slices of unbuttered bread with 2 slices of ham, 2 slices of cheese, and 2 slices of tomato. Place the remaining 2 slices of bread on top, butter-side up.
3. Lay the sandwiches in the air fryer basket, buttered side down.
4. Select Bake, set temperature to 370°F (188°C), and set time to 8 minutes. Select Start to begin preheating.
5. Once preheated, place the basket into the air fryer. Flip the sandwiches halfway through the cooking time.
6. When cooking is complete, the sandwiches should be golden brown on both sides and the cheese should be melted. Remove from the air fryer. Allow to cool for 5 minutes before slicing to serve.

Chapter 3 Healthy Breakfasts |25

Syrupy Vanilla Granola

Prep time: 5 minutes | Cook time: 40 minutes | Serves 4

1 cup rolled oats
3 tablespoons maple syrup
1 tablespoon sunflower oi
1 tablespoon coconut sugar
¼ teaspoon vanilla
¼ teaspoon cinnamon
¼ teaspoon sea salt

1. Mix together the oats, maple syrup, sunflower oil, coconut suga , vanilla, cinnamon, and sea salt in a medium bowl and stir to combine. Transfer the mixture to a baking pan.
2. Select Bake, set temperature to 248°F (120°C) and set time to 40 minutes. Select Start to begin preheating.
3. Once preheated, place the pan into the air fryer. Stir the granola four times during cooking.
4. When cooking is complete, the granola will be mostly dry and lightly browned.
5. Let the granola stand for 5 to 10 minutes before serving.

Tasty Turkey Breakfast Sausage Patties

Prep time: 5 minutes | Cook time: 10 minutes | Serves 4

1 tablespoon chopped fresh thyme
1 tablespoon chopped fresh sage
1¼ teaspoons kosher salt
1 teaspoon chopped fennel seeds
¾ teaspoon smoked paprika
½ teaspoon onion powder
½ teaspoon garlic powder
⅛ teaspoon crushed red pepper fla es
⅛ teaspoon freshly ground black pepper
1 pound (454 g) 93% lean ground turkey
½ cup finely minced sweet apple (peeled)

1. Thoroughly combine the thyme, sage, salt, fennel seeds, paprika, onion powder, garlic powder, red pepper fla es, and black pepper in a medium bowl.
2. Add the ground turkey and apple and stir until well incorporated. Divide the mixture into 8 equal portions and shape into patties with your hands, each about ¼ inch thick and 3 inches in diameter.
3. Place the patties in the air fryer basket in a single layer.
4. Select Air Fry, set temperature to 400°F (205°C), and set time to 10 minutes. Select Start to begin preheating.
5. Once preheated, place the basket into the air fryer. Flip the patties halfway through the cooking time.
6. When cooking is complete, the patties should be nicely browned and cooked through. Remove from the air fryer to a plate and serve warm.

Cheesy Spinach and Bacon Roll-ups

Prep time: 5 minutes | Cook time: 8 to 9 minutes | Serves 4

4 flour tortillas (6- or 7-inch size)
4 slices Swiss cheese
1 cup baby spinach leaves
4 slices turkey bacon

Special Equipment:
4 toothpicks, soak in water for at least 30 minutes

1. On a clean work surface, top each tortilla with one slice of cheese and ¼ cup of spinach, then tightly roll them up.
2. Wrap each tortilla with a strip of turkey bacon and secure with a toothpick.
3. Arrange the roll-ups in the air fryer basket, leaving space between each roll-up.
4. Select Air Fry, set temperature to 390°F (199°C), and set time to 8 minutes. Select Start to begin preheating.
5. Once preheated, place the basket into the air fryer.
6. After 4 minutes, remove the basket from the air fryer. Flip the roll-ups with tongs and rearrange them for more even cooking. Return to the air fryer and continue cooking for another 4 minutes.
7. When cooking is complete, the bacon should be crisp. If necessary, continue cooking for 1 minute more. Remove the basket from the air fryer. Rest for 5 minutes and remove the toothpicks before serving.

Baked Egg in a Hole

Prep time: 5 minutes | Cook time: 5 minutes | Serves 1

1 slice bread
1 teaspoon butter, softened
1 egg
Salt and pepper, to taste
1 tablespoon shredded Cheddar cheese
2 teaspoons diced ham

1. On a flat work surface, cut a hole in the center of the bread slice with a 2½-inch-diameter biscuit cutter.
2. Spread the butter evenly on each side of the bread slice and transfer to a baking dish.
3. Crack the egg into the hole and season as desired with salt and pepper. Scatter the shredded cheese and diced ham on top.
4. Select Bake, set temperature to 330ºF (166ºC), and set time to 5 minutes. Select Start to begin preheating.
5. Once preheated, place the baking dish into the air fryer.
6. When cooking is complete, the bread should be lightly browned and the egg should be set. Remove from the air fryer and serve hot.

Sweet Milky Monkey Bread

Prep time: 5 minutes | Cook time: 8 minutes | Serves 4

1 (8-ounce / 227-g) can refrigerated biscuits
3 tablespoons melted unsalted butter
¼ cup white sugar
3 tablespoons brown sugar
½ teaspoon cinnamon
⅛ teaspoon nutmeg

1. On a clean work surface, cut each biscuit into 4 pieces.
2. In a shallow bowl, place the melted butter. In another shallow bowl, stir together the white sugar, brown sugar, cinnamon, and nutmeg until combined.
3. Dredge the biscuits, one at a time, in the melted butter, then roll them in the sugar mixture to coat well. Spread the biscuits evenly in a baking pan.
4. Select Bake, set temperature to 350ºF (180ºC) and set time to 8 minutes. Select Start to begin preheating.
5. Once the air fryer has preheated, place the pan into the air fryer.
6. When cooked, the biscuits should be golden brown.
7. Cool for 5 minutes before serving.

Baked Asparagus and Cheese Strata

Prep time: 10 minutes | Cook time: 17 minutes | Serves 4

6 asparagus spears, cut into 2-inch pieces
1 tablespoon water
2 slices whole-wheat bread, cut into ½-inch cubes
4 eggs
3 tablespoons whole milk
2 tablespoons chopped fla -leaf parsley
½ cup grated Havarti or Swiss cheese
Pinch salt
Freshly ground black pepper, to taste
Cooking spray

1. Add the asparagus spears and 1 tablespoon of water in a baking pan.
2. Select Bake, set temperature to 330ºF (166ºC) and set time to 4 minutes. Select Start to begin preheating.
3. Once preheated, place the pan into the air fryer.
4. When cooking is complete, the asparagus spears will be crisp-tender.
5. Remove the asparagus from the pan and drain on paper towels.
6. Spritz the pan with cooking spray. Place the bread and asparagus in the pan.
7. Whisk together the eggs and milk in a medium mixing bowl until creamy. Fold in the parsley, cheese, salt, and pepper and stir to combine. Pour this mixture into the baking pan.
8. Select Bake and set time to 13 minutes. Place the pan back to the air fryer. When done, the eggs will be set and the top will be lightly browned.
9. Let cool for 5 minutes before slicing and serving.

Milky Spinach and Bacon English Muffins

Prep time: 5 minutes | Cook time: 10 minutes | Serves 4

2 strips turkey bacon, cut in half crosswise
2 whole-grain English muffins, spli
1 cup fresh baby spinach, long stems removed
¼ ripe pear, peeled and thinly sliced
4 slices Provolone cheese

1. Put the turkey bacon strips in the air fryer basket.
2. Select Air Fry, set temperature to 390°F (199°C), and set time to 6 minutes. Select Start to begin preheating.
3. Once preheated, place the basket into the air fryer. Flip the strips halfway through the cooking time.
4. When cooking is complete, the bacon should be crisp.
5. Remove from the air fryer and drain on paper towels. Set aside.
6. Put the muffin hal es in the air fryer basket.
7. Select Air Fry and set time to 2 minutes. Return the basket to the air fryer. When done, the muffin hal es will be lightly browned.
8. Remove the basket from the air fryer. Top each muffin half with ¼ of the ba y spinach, several pear slices, a strip of turkey bacon, followed by a slice of cheese.
9. Select Bake, set temperature to 360°F (182°C), and set time to 2 minutes. Place the basket back to the air fryer. When done, the cheese will be melted.
10. Serve warm.

Oily Cinnamon Sweet Potato Chips

Prep time: 5 minutes | Cook time: 8 minutes | Makes 6 to 8 slices

1 small sweet potato, cut into ⅜ inch-thick slices
2 tablespoons olive oil
1 to 2 teaspoon ground cinnamon

1. Add the sweet potato slices and olive oil in a bowl and toss to coat. Fold in the cinnamon and stir to combine.
2. Lay the sweet potato slices in a single layer in the air fryer basket.
3. Select Air Fry, set temperature to 390°F (199°C), and set time to 8 minutes. Select Start to begin preheating.
4. Once preheated, place the basket into the air fryer. Stir the potato slices halfway through the cooking time.
5. When cooking is complete, the chips should be crisp. Remove the basket from the air fryer. Allow to cool for 5 minutes before serving.

Air Fried Ham and Cheese Toast

Prep time: 5 minutes | Cook time: 6 minutes | Serves: 1

1 slice bread
1 teaspoon butter, at room temperature
1 egg
Salt and freshly ground black pepper, to taste
2 teaspoons diced ham
1 tablespoon grated Cheddar cheese

1. On a clean work surface, use a 2½-inch biscuit cutter to make a hole in the center of the bread slice with about ½-inch of bread remaining.
2. Spread the butter on both sides of the bread slice. Crack the egg into the hole and season with salt and pepper to taste. Transfer the bread to the air fryer basket.
3. Select Air Fry, set temperature to 325°F (163°C), and set time to 6 minutes. Select Start to begin preheating.
4. Once preheated, place the basket into the air fryer.
5. After 5 minutes, remove the basket from the air fryer. Scatter the cheese and diced ham on top and continue cooking for an additional 1 minute.
6. When cooking is complete, the egg should be set and the cheese should be melted. Remove the toast from the air fryer to a plate and let cool for 5 minutes before serving.

Syrupy Banana and Oat Bread Pudding

Prep time: 10 minutes | Cook time: 16 minutes | Serves 4

2 medium ripe bananas, mashed
½ cup low-fat milk
2 tablespoons maple syrup
2 tablespoons peanut butter
1 teaspoon vanilla extract
1 teaspoon ground cinnamon
2 slices whole-grain bread, cut into bite-sized cubes
¼ cup quick oats
Cooking spray

1. Spritz a baking dish lightly with cooking spray.
2. Mix the bananas, milk, maple syrup, peanut butter, vanilla, and cinnamon in a large mixing bowl and stir until well incorporated.
3. Add the bread cubes to the banana mixture and stir until thoroughly coated. Fold in the oats and stir to combine.
4. Transfer the mixture to the baking dish. Wrap the baking dish in aluminum foil.
5. Select Air Fry, set temperature to 350°F (180°C) and set time to 16 minutes. Select Start to begin preheating.
6. Once the air fryer has preheated, place the baking dish into the air fryer.
7. After 10 minutes, remove the baking dish from the air fryer. Remove the foil. Return the baking dish to the air fryer and continue to cook another 6 minutes.
8. When done, the pudding should be set.
9. Let the pudding cool for 5 minutes before serving.

Baked Bourbon Vanilla French Toast

Prep time: 15 minutes | Cook time: 6 minutes | Serves 4

2 large eggs
2 tablespoons water
⅔ cup whole or 2% milk
1 tablespoon butter, melted
2 tablespoons bourbon
1 teaspoon vanilla extract
8 (1-inch-thick) French bread slices
Cooking spray

1. Line the air fryer basket with parchment paper and spray it with cooking spray.
2. Beat the eggs with the water in a shallow bowl until combined. Add the milk, melted butter, bourbon, and vanilla and stir to mix well.
3. Dredge 4 slices of bread in the batter, turning to coat both sides evenly. Transfer the bread slices onto the parchment paper.
4. Select Bake, set temperature to 320°F (160°C) and set time to 6 minutes. Select Start to begin preheating.
5. Once the air fryer has preheated, place the basket into the air fryer. Flip the slices halfway through the cooking time.
6. When cooking is complete, the bread slices should be nicely browned.
7. Remove from the air fryer to a plate and serve warm.

Milky Hash Brown Casserole

Prep time: 15 minutes | Cook time: 30 minutes | Serves 4

3½ cups frozen hash browns, thawed
1 teaspoon salt
1 teaspoon freshly ground black pepper
3 tablespoons butter, melted
1 (10.5-ounce / 298-g) can cream of chicken soup
½ cup sour cream
1 cup minced onion
½ cup shredded sharp Cheddar cheese
Cooking spray

1. Put the hash browns in a large bowl and season with salt and black pepper. Add the melted butter, cream of chicken soup, and sour cream and stir until well incorporated. Mix in the minced onion and cheese and stir well.
2. Spray a baking pan with cooking spray.
3. Spread the hash brown mixture evenly into the baking pan.
4. Select Bake, set temperature to 325°F (163°C) and set time to 30 minutes. Select Start to begin preheating.
5. Once the air fryer has preheated, place the pan into the air fryer.
6. When cooked, the hash brown mixture will be browned.
7. Cool for 5 minutes before serving.

Eggy Hash Brown Cups

Prep time: 10 minutes | Cook time: 9 minutes | Serves 6

4 eggs, beaten
2¼ cups frozen hash browns, thawed
1 cup diced ham
½ cup shredded Cheddar cheese
½ teaspoon Cajun seasoning
Cooking spray

1. Lightly spritz a 12-cup muffin tin with cooking spray.
2. Combine the beaten eggs, hash browns, diced ham, cheese, and Cajun seasoning in a medium bowl and stir until well blended.
3. Spoon a heaping 1½ tablespoons of egg mixture into each muffin cu .
4. Select Bake, set temperature to 350°F (180°C) and set time to 9 minutes. Select Start to begin preheating.
5. Once preheated, place the muffin tin into the air fryer.
6. When cooked, the muffins will be golden brown.
7. Allow to cool for 5 to 10 minutes on a wire rack and serve warm.

Eggy Crustless Broccoli Quiche

Prep time: 5 minutes | Cook time: 10 minutes | Serves 4

1 cup broccoli floret
¾ cup chopped roasted red peppers
1¼ cups grated Fontina cheese
6 eggs
¾ cup heavy cream
½ teaspoon salt
Freshly ground black pepper, to taste
Cooking spray

1. Spritz a baking pan with cooking spray
2. Add the broccoli florets and roasted red peppers to the pan and scatter the grated Fontina cheese on top.
3. In a bowl, beat together the eggs and heavy cream. Sprinkle with salt and pepper. Pour the egg mixture over the top of the cheese. Wrap the pan in foil.
4. Select Air Fry, set temperature to 325°F (163°C) and set time to 10 minutes. Select Start to begin preheating.
5. Once preheated, place the pan into the air fryer.
6. After 8 minutes, remove the pan from the air fryer. Remove the foil. Return the pan to the air fryer and continue to cook another 2 minutes.
7. When cooked, the quiche should be golden brown.
8. Rest for 5 minutes before cutting into wedges and serve warm.

Milky Western Omelet

Prep time: 5 minutes | Cook time: 20 minutes | Serves 2

¼ cup chopped bell pepper, green or red
¼ cup chopped onion
¼ cup diced ham
1 teaspoon butter
4 large eggs
2 tablespoons milk
⅛ teaspoon salt
¾ cup shredded sharp Cheddar cheese

1. Put the bell pepper, onion, ham, and butter in a baking pan and mix well.
2. Select Air Fry, set temperature to 390°F (199°C) and set time to 5 minutes. Select Start to begin preheating.
3. Once the air fryer has preheated, place the pan into the air fryer.
4. After 1 minute, remove the pan from the air fryer. Stir the mixture. Return the pan to the air fryer and continue to cook for another 4 minutes.
5. When done, the veggies should be softened.
6. Whisk together the eggs, milk, and salt in a bowl. Pour the egg mixture over the veggie mixture.
7. Select Bake, set temperature to 360°F (182°C) and set time to 15 minutes. Place the pan into the air fryer.
8. After 14 minutes, remove the pan from the air fryer. Scatter the omelet with the shredded cheese. Return the pan to the air fryer and continue to cook for another 1 minute.
9. When cooking is complete, the top will be lightly golden browned, the eggs will be set and the cheese will be melted.
10. Let the omelet cool for 5 minutes before serving.

Creamy Bacon and Egg Bread Cups

Prep time: 10 minutes | Cook time: 10 minutes | Serves 4

4 (3-by-4-inch) crusty rolls
4 thin slices Gouda or Swiss cheese mini wedges
5 eggs
2 tablespoons heavy cream
3 strips precooked bacon, chopped
½ teaspoon dried thyme
Pinch salt
Freshly ground black pepper, to taste

1. On a clean work surface, cut the tops off the rolls. Using your fingers, rem ve the insides of the rolls to make bread cups, leaving a ½-inch shell. Place a slice of cheese onto each roll bottom.
2. Whisk together the eggs and heavy cream in a medium bowl until well combined. Fold in the bacon, thyme, salt, and pepper and stir well.
3. Scrape the egg mixture into the prepared bread cups. Arrange the bread cups in the air fryer basket.
4. Select Bake, set temperature to 330°F (166°C) and set time to 10 minutes. Select Start to begin preheating.
5. Once preheated, place the basket into the air fryer.
6. When cooked, the eggs should be cooked to your preference.
7. Serve warm.

Cheesy Fried Cheese Grits

Prep time: 10 minutes | Cook time: 11 minutes | Serves 4

⅔ cup instant grits
1 teaspoon salt
1 teaspoon freshly ground black pepper
¾ cup whole or 2% milk
3 ounces (85 g) cream cheese, at room temperature
1 large egg, beaten
1 tablespoon butter, melted
1 cup shredded mild Cheddar cheese
Cooking spray

1. Mix the grits, salt, and black pepper in a large bowl. Add the milk, cream cheese, beaten egg, and melted butter and whisk to combine. Fold in the Cheddar cheese and stir well.
2. Spray a baking pan with cooking spray. Spread the grits mixture into the baking pan.
3. Select Air Fry, set temperature to 400°F (205°C) and set time to 11 minutes. Select Start to begin preheating.
4. Once preheated, place the pan into the air fryer. Stir the mixture halfway through the cooking time.
5. When done, a knife inserted in the center should come out clean.
6. Rest for 5 minutes and serve warm.

Cheesy Egg Florentine with Spinach

Prep time: 10 minutes | Cook time: 15 minutes | Serves 4

3 cups frozen spinach, thawed and drained
2 tablespoons heavy cream
¼ teaspoon kosher salt
⅛ teaspoon freshly ground black pepper
4 ounces (113 g) Ricotta cheese
2 garlic cloves, minced
½ cup panko bread crumbs
3 tablespoons grated Parmesan cheese
2 teaspoons unsalted butter, melted
4 large eggs

1. In a medium bowl, whisk together the spinach, heavy cream, salt, pepper, Ricotta cheese and garlic.
2. In a small bowl, whisk together the bread crumbs, Parmesan cheese and butter. Set aside.
3. Spoon the spinach mixture on the sheet pan and form four even circles.
4. Select Roast, set temperature to 375°F (190°C) and set time to 15 minutes. Select Start to begin preheating.
5. Once the unit has preheated, place the pan into the air fryer.
6. After 8 minutes, remove the pan from the air fryer. The spinach should be bubbling. With the back of a large spoon, make indentations in the spinach for the eggs. Crack the eggs into the indentations and sprinkle the panko mixture over the surface of the eggs. Return the pan to the air fryer to continue cooking.
7. When cooking is complete, remove the pan from the air fryer. Serve hot.

Chapter 3 Healthy Breakfasts | 31

Juicy Chicken Breakfast Sausages

Prep time: 15 minutes | Cook time: 10 minutes | Makes 8 patties

1 Granny Smith apple, peeled and finely choppe
2 tablespoons apple juice
2 garlic cloves, minced
1 egg white
⅓ cup minced onion
3 tablespoons ground almonds
⅛ teaspoon freshly ground black pepper
1 pound (454 g) ground chicken breast

1. Combine all the ingredients except the chicken in a medium mixing bowl and stir well.
2. Add the chicken breast to the apple mixture and mix with your hands until well incorporated.
3. Divide the mixture into 8 equal portions and shape into patties. Arrange the patties in the air fry basket.
4. Select Air Fry, set temperature to 330ºF (166ºC) and set time to 10 minutes. Select Start to begin preheating.
5. Once the air fryer has preheated, place the air fry basket into the air fryer.
6. When done, a meat thermometer inserted in the center of the chicken should reach at least 165ºF (74ºC).
7. Remove from the air fryer to a plate. Let the chicken cool for 5 minutes and serve warm.

Meaty Breakfast Casserole

Prep time: 10 minutes | Cook time: 16 minutes | Serves 4

6 slices bacon
6 eggs
Salt and pepper, to taste
Cooking spray
½ cup chopped green bell pepper
½ cup chopped onion
¾ cup shredded Cheddar cheese

1. Place the bacon in a skillet over medium-high heat and cook each side for about 4 minutes until evenly crisp. Remove from the heat to a paper towel-lined plate to drain. Crumble it into small pieces and set aside.
2. Whisk the eggs with the salt and pepper in a medium bowl.
3. Spritz a baking pan with cooking spray.
4. Place the whisked eggs, crumbled bacon, green bell pepper, and onion in the prepared pan.
5. Select Bake, set temperature to 400ºF (205ºC) and set time to 8 minutes. Select Start to begin preheating.
6. Once preheated, place the pan into the air fryer.
7. After 6 minutes, remove the pan from the air fryer. Scatter the Cheddar cheese all over. Return the pan to the air fryer and continue to cook another 2 minutes.
8. When cooking is complete, let sit for 5 minutes and serve on plates.

Fried Potatoes with Peppers and Onions

Prep time: 10 minutes | Cook time: 35 minutes | Serves 4

1 pound (454 g) red potatoes, cut into ½-inch dices
1 large red bell pepper, cut into ½-inch dices
1 large green bell pepper, cut into ½-inch dices
1 medium onion, cut into ½-inch dices
1½ tablespoons extra-virgin olive oil
1¼ teaspoons kosher salt
¾ teaspoon sweet paprika
¾ teaspoon garlic powder
Freshly ground black pepper, to taste

1. Mix together the potatoes, bell peppers, onion, oil, salt, paprika, garlic powder, and black pepper in a large mixing and toss to coat.
2. Transfer the potato mixture to the air fry basket.
3. Select Air Fry, set temperature to 350ºF (180ºC) and set time to 35 minutes. Select Start to begin preheating.
4. Once preheated, place the air fry basket into the air fryer. Stir the potato mixture three times during cooking.
5. When done, the potatoes should be nicely browned.
6. Remove from the air fryer to a plate and serve warm.

Cheesy Artichoke-Mushroom Frittata

Prep time: 10 minutes | Cook time: 15 minutes | Serves 6

8 eggs
½ teaspoon kosher salt
¼ cup whole milk
¾ cup shredded Mozzarella cheese, divided
2 tablespoons unsalted butter, melted
1 cup coarsely chopped artichoke hearts
¼ cup chopped onion
½ cup mushrooms
¼ cup grated Parmesan cheese
¼ teaspoon freshly ground black pepper

1. In a medium bowl, whisk together the eggs and salt. Let rest for a minute or two, then pour in the milk and whisk again. Stir in ½ cup of the Mozzarella cheese.
2. Grease the sheet pan with the butter. Stir in the artichoke hearts and onion and toss to coat with the butter.
3. Select Roast, set temperature to 375ºF (190ºC) and set time to 12 minutes. Select Start to begin preheating.
4. Once the unit has preheated, place the pan into the air fryer.
5. After 5 minutes, remove the pan. Spread the mushrooms over the vegetables. Pour the egg mixture on top. Stir gently just to distribute the vegetables evenly. Return the pan to the air fryer and continue cooking for 5 to 7 minutes, or until the edges are set. The center will still be quite liquid.
6. Select Broil, set temperature to Low and set time to 3 minutes. Place the pan into the air fryer.
7. After 1 minute, remove the pan and sprinkle the remaining ¼ cup of the Mozzarella and Parmesan cheese over the frittata. Return the pan to the air fryer and continue cooking for 2 minutes.
8. When cooking is complete, the cheese should be melted with the top completely set but not browned. Sprinkle the black pepper on top and serve.

Baked Mini Cinnamon Rolls

Prep time: 5 minutes | Cook time: 25 minutes | Makes 18 rolls

⅓ cup light brown sugar
2 teaspoons cinnamon
1 (9-by-9-inch) frozen puff pastry sheet, thawed
All-purpose flou , for dusting
6 teaspoons unsalted butter, melted, divided

1. In a small bowl, stir together the brown sugar and cinnamon.
2. On a clean work surface, lightly dust with the flour and l y the puff pastry sheet. Using a rolling pin, press the folds together and roll the dough out in one direction so that it measures about 9 by 11 inches. Cut it in half to form two squat rectangles of about 5½ by 9 inches.
3. Brush 2 teaspoons of the butter over each pastry half. Sprinkle with 2 tablespoons of the cinnamon sugar. Pat it down lightly with the palm of your hand to help it adhere to the butter.
4. Starting with the 9-inch side of one rectangle. Using your hands, carefully roll the dough into a cylinder. Repeat with the other rectangle. To make slicing easier, refrigerate the rolls for 10 to 20 minutes.
5. Using a sharp knife, slice each roll into nine 1-inch pieces. Transfer the rolls to the center of the sheet pan. They should be very close to each other, but not quite touching. Drizzle the remaining 2 teaspoons of the butter over the rolls and sprinkle with the remaining cinnamon sugar.
6. Select Bake, set temperature to 350ºF (180ºC) and set time to 25 minutes. Select Start to begin preheating.
7. Once the unit has preheated, place the pan into the air fryer.
8. When cooking is complete, remove the pan and check the rolls. They should be puffed up and golden brown.
9. Let the rolls rest for 5 minutes and transfer them to a wire rack to cool completely. Serve.

Baked Whole-Wheat Muffins with Blueberries

Prep time: 5 minutes | Cook time: 25 minutes | Makes 8 muffins

½ cup unsweetened applesauce
½ cup plant-based milk
½ cup maple syrup
1 teaspoon vanilla extract
2 cups whole-wheat flou
½ teaspoon baking soda
1 cup blueberries
Cooking spray

1. Spritz a 8-cup muffin pan with cooking spray.
2. In a large bowl, stir together the applesauce, milk, maple syrup and vanilla extract. Whisk in the flour and baking soda until no dry flour is left and the batter is smooth. Gently mix in the blueberries until they are evenly distributed throughout the batter.
3. Spoon the batter into the muffin cups, three-quarters full.
4. Select Bake, set temperature to 375ºF (190ºC) and set time to 25 minutes. Select Start to begin preheating.
5. Once preheated, place the pan into the air fryer.
6. When cooking is complete, remove the pan and check the muffins. ou can stick a knife into the center of a muffin and it should come out clean.
7. Let rest for 5 minutes before serving.

Coconut Brown Rice Porridge with Dates

Prep time: 5 minutes | Cook time: 23 minutes | Serves 1 or 2

½ cup cooked brown rice
1 cup canned coconut milk
¼ cup unsweetened shredded coconut
¼ cup packed dark brown sugar
4 large Medjool dates, pitted and roughly chopped
½ teaspoon kosher salt
¼ teaspoon ground cardamom
Heavy cream, for serving (optional)

1. Place all the ingredients except the heavy cream in a baking pan and stir until blended.
2. Select Bake, set temperature to 375ºF (190ºC) and set time to 23 minutes. Select Start to begin preheating.
3. Once the air fryer has preheated, place the pan into the air fryer. Stir the porridge halfway through the cooking time.
4. When cooked, the porridge will be thick and creamy.
5. Remove from the air fryer and ladle the porridge into bowls.
6. Serve hot with a drizzle of the cream, if desired.

Milky Maple Walnut Pancake

Prep time: 10 minutes | Cook time: 20 minutes | Serves 4

3 tablespoons melted butter, divided
1 cup flou
2 tablespoons sugar
1½ teaspoons baking powder
¼ teaspoon salt
1 egg, beaten
¾ cup milk
1 teaspoon pure vanilla extract
½ cup roughly chopped walnuts
Maple syrup or fresh sliced fruit, for serving

1. Grease a baking pan with 1 tablespoon of melted butter.
2. Mix together the flou , sugar, baking powder, and salt in a medium bowl. Add the beaten egg, milk, the remaining 2 tablespoons of melted butter, and vanilla and stir until the batter is sticky but slightly lumpy.
3. Slowly pour the batter into the greased baking pan and scatter with the walnuts.
4. Select Bake, set temperature to 330ºF (166ºC) and set time to 20 minutes. Select Start to begin preheating.
5. Once preheated, place the pan into the air fryer.
6. When cooked, the pancake should be golden brown and cooked through.
7. Let the pancake rest for 5 minutes and serve topped with the maple syrup or fresh fruit, if desired.

Sweet Cornmeal Pancake

Prep time: 10 minutes | Cook time: 6 minutes | Serves 4

1½ cups yellow cornmeal
½ cup all-purpose flou
2 tablespoons sugar
1 teaspoon salt
1 teaspoon baking powder
1 cup whole or 2% milk
1 large egg, lightly beaten
1 tablespoon butter, melted
Cooking spray

1. Line the air fryer basket with parchment paper.
2. Stir together the cornmeal, flou , sugar, salt, and baking powder in a large bowl. Mix in the milk, egg, and melted butter and whisk to combine.
3. Drop tablespoonfuls of the batter onto the parchment paper for each pancake. Spray the pancakes with cooking spray.
4. Select Bake, set temperature to 350ºF (180ºC) and set time to 6 minutes. Select Start to begin preheating.
5. Once the air fryer has preheated, place the basket into the air fryer. Flip the pancakes and spray with cooking spray again halfway through the cooking time.
6. When cooking is complete, remove the pancakes from the air fryer to a plate.
7. Cool for 5 minutes and serve immediately.

Milky Mixed Berry Dutch Baby Pancake

Prep time: 10 minutes | Cook time: 14 minutes | Serves 4

1 tablespoon unsalted butter, at room temperature
1 egg
2 egg whites
½ cup 2% milk
½ cup whole-wheat pastry flou
1 teaspoon pure vanilla extract
1 cup sliced fresh strawberries
½ cup fresh raspberries
½ cup fresh blueberries

1. Grease a baking pan with the butter.
2. Using a hand mixer, beat together the egg, egg whites, milk, pastry flou , and vanilla in a medium mixing bowl until well incorporated.
3. Pour the batter into the pan.
4. Select Bake, set temperature to 330ºF (166ºC) and set time to 14 minutes. Select Start to begin preheating.
5. Once the air fryer has preheated, place the pan into the air fryer.
6. When cooked, the pancake should puff up in the center and the edges should be golden brown
7. Allow the pancake to cool for 5 minutes and serve topped with the berries.

Aromatic French Toast Sticks

Prep time: 5 minutes | Cook time: 12 minutes | Serves 4

3 slices low-sodium whole-wheat bread, each cut into 4 strips
1 tablespoon unsalted butter, melted
1 tablespoon 2 percent milk
1 tablespoon sugar
1 egg, beaten
1 egg white
1 cup sliced fresh strawberries
1 tablespoon freshly squeezed lemon juice

1. Arrange the bread strips on a plate and drizzle with the melted butter.
2. In a bowl, whisk together the milk, sugar, egg and egg white.
3. Dredge the bread strips into the egg mixture and place on a wire rack to let the batter drip off. Arrange half the coated bread strips on the sheet pan.
4. Select Air Fry, set temperature to 380ºF (193ºC) and set time to 6 minutes. Select Start to begin preheating.
5. Once preheated, place the pan into the air fryer.
6. After 3 minutes, remove the pan from the air fryer. Use tongs to turn the strips over. Rotate the pan and return the pan to the air fryer to continue cooking.
7. When cooking is complete, the strips should be golden brown.
8. In a small bowl, mash the strawberries with a fork and stir in the lemon juice. Serve the French toast sticks with the strawberry sauce.

Oily Corned Beef Hash with Eggs

Prep time: 10 minutes | Cook time: 25 minutes | Serves 4

2 medium Yukon Gold potatoes, peeled and cut into ¼-inch cubes
1 medium onion, chopped
⅓ cup diced red bell pepper
3 tablespoons vegetable oil
½ teaspoon dried thyme
½ teaspoon kosher salt, divided
½ teaspoon freshly ground black pepper, divided
¾ pound (340 g) corned beef, cut into ¼-inch pieces
4 large eggs

1. In a large bowl, stir together the potatoes, onion, red pepper, vegetable oil, thyme, ¼ teaspoon of the salt and ¼ teaspoon of the pepper. Spread the vegetable mixture on the sheet pan in an even layer.
2. Select Roast, set temperature to 375ºF (190ºC) and set time to 25 minutes. Select Start to begin preheating.
3. Once the unit has preheated, place the pan into the air fryer.
4. After 15 minutes, remove the pan from the air fryer and add the corned beef. Stir the mixture to incorporate the corned beef. Return the pan to the air fryer and continue cooking.
5. After 5 minutes, remove the pan from the air fryer. Using a large spoon, create 4 circles in the hash to hold the eggs. Gently crack an egg into each circle. Season the eggs with the remaining ¼ teaspoon of the salt and ¼ teaspoon of the pepper. Return the pan to the air fryer. Continue cooking for 3 to 5 minutes, depending on how you like your eggs.
6. When cooking is complete, remove the pan from the air fryer. Serve immediately.

Tomato-Corn Frittata with Avocado Dressing

Prep time: 10 minutes | Cook time: 20 minutes | Serves 2 or 3

½ cup cherry tomatoes, halved
Kosher salt and freshly ground black pepper, to taste
6 large eggs, lightly beaten
½ cup fresh corn kernels
¼ cup milk
1 tablespoon finely chopped fresh dill
½ cup shredded Monterey Jack cheese

Avocado Dressing:
1 ripe avocado, pitted and peeled
2 tablespoons fresh lime juice
¼ cup olive oil
1 scallion, finely chopped
8 fresh basil leaves, finely choppe

1. Put the tomato halves in a colander and lightly season with salt. Set aside for 10 minutes to drain well. Pour the tomatoes into a large bowl and fold in the eggs, corn, milk, and dill. Sprinkle with salt and pepper and stir until mixed.
2. Pour the egg mixture into a baking pan.
3. Select Bake, set temperature to 300ºF (150ºC) and set time to 15 minutes. Select Start to begin preheating.
4. Once the air fryer has preheated, place the pan into the air fryer.
5. When done, remove the pan from the air fryer. Scatter the cheese on top.
6. Select Bake, set temperature to 315ºF (157ºC) and set time to 5 minutes. Return the pan to the air fryer.
7. Meanwhile, make the avocado dressing: Mash the avocado with the lime juice in a medium bowl until smooth. Mix in the olive oil, scallion, and basil and stir until well incorporated.
8. When cooking is complete, the frittata will be puffy and set. Let the frittata cool for 5 minutes and serve alongside the avocado dressing.

Cheesy Rice, Shrimp, and Spinach Frittata

Prep time: 15 minutes | Cook time: 16 minutes | Serves 4

4 eggs
Pinch salt
½ cup cooked rice
½ cup chopped cooked shrimp
½ cup baby spinach
½ cup grated Monterey Jack cheese
Nonstick cooking spray

1. Spritz a baking pan with nonstick cooking spray.
2. Whisk the eggs and salt in a small bowl until frothy.
3. Place the cooked rice, shrimp, and baby spinach in the baking pan. Pour in the whisked eggs and scatter the cheese on top.
4. Select Bake, set temperature to 320ºF (160ºC) and set time to 16 minutes. Select Start to begin preheating.
5. Once the air fryer has preheated, place the pan into the air fryer.
6. When cooking is complete, the frittata should be golden and puffy.
7. Let the frittata cool for 5 minutes before slicing to serve.

Cheesy Mini Brown Rice Quiches

Prep time: 10 minutes | Cook time: 14 minutes | Serves 6

4 ounces (113 g) diced green chilies
3 cups cooked brown rice
1 cup shredded reduced-fat Cheddar cheese, divided
½ cup egg whites
⅓ cup fat-free milk
¼ cup diced pimiento
½ teaspoon cumin
1 small eggplant, cubed
1 bunch fresh cilantro, finely chopped
Cooking spray

1. Spritz a 12-cup muffin pan with cooking spray.
2. In a large bowl, stir together all the ingredients, except for ½ cup of the cheese.
3. Scoop the mixture evenly into the muffin cups and sprinkle the remaining ½ cup of the cheese on top.
4. Select Bake, set temperature to 400ºF (205ºC) and set time to 14 minutes. Select Start to begin preheating.
5. Once the unit has preheated, place the pan into the air fryer.
6. When cooking is complete, remove the pan and check the quiches. They should be set.
7. Carefully transfer the quiches to a platter and serve immediately.

Olives, Kale, and Pecorino Baked Eggs

Prep time: 5 minutes | Cook time: 11 minutes | Serves 2

1 cup roughly chopped kale leaves, stems and center ribs removed
¼ cup grated pecorino cheese
¼ cup olive oil
1 garlic clove, peeled
3 tablespoons whole almonds
Kosher salt and freshly ground black pepper, to taste
4 large eggs
2 tablespoons heavy cream
3 tablespoons chopped pitted mixed olives

1. Place the kale, pecorino, olive oil, garlic, almonds, salt, and pepper in a small blender and blitz until well incorporated.
2. One at a time, crack the eggs in a baking pan. Drizzle the kale pesto on top of the egg whites. Top the yolks with the cream and swirl together the yolks and the pesto.
3. Select Bake, set temperature to 300ºF (150ºC) and set time to 11 minutes. Select Start to begin preheating.
4. Once preheated, place the pan into the air fryer.
5. When cooked, the top should begin to brown and the eggs should be set.
6. Allow the eggs to cool for 5 minutes. Scatter the olives on top and serve warm.

Baked Quesadillas with Blueberries

Prep time: 5 minutes | Cook time: 4 minutes | Serves 2

¼ cup nonfat Ricotta cheese
¼ cup plain nonfat Greek yogurt
2 tablespoons finely ground flaxseed
1 tablespoon granulated stevia
½ teaspoon cinnamon
¼ teaspoon vanilla extract
2 (8-inch) low-carb whole-wheat tortillas
½ cup fresh blueberries, divided

1. Line the sheet pan with the aluminum foil.
2. In a small bowl, whisk together the Ricotta cheese, yogurt, flaxseeds, stevia, cinnamon and vanilla.
3. Place the tortillas on the sheet pan. Spread half of the yogurt mixture on each tortilla, almost to the edges. Top each tortilla with ¼ cup of blueberries. Fold the tortillas in half.
4. Select Bake, set temperature to 400°F (205°C) and set time to 4 minutes. Select Start to begin preheating.
5. Once the unit has preheated, place the pan into the air fryer.
6. When cooking is complete, remove the pan from the air fryer. Serve immediately.

Air Fried Egg and Avocado Burrito

Prep time: 10 minutes | Cook time: 4 minutes | Serves 4

4 low-sodium whole-wheat flour tortilla

Filling:
1 hard-boiled egg, chopped
2 hard-boiled egg whites, chopped
1 ripe avocado, peeled, pitted, and chopped
1 red bell pepper, chopped
1 (1.2-ounce / 34-g) slice low-sodium, low-fat American cheese, torn into pieces
3 tablespoons low-sodium salsa, plus additional for serving (optional)

Special Equipment:
4 toothpicks (optional), soaked in water for at least 30 minutes

1. Make the filling: Combine the egg, egg whites, avocado, red bell pepper, cheese, and salsa in a medium bowl and stir until blended.
2. Assemble the burritos: Arrange the tortillas on a clean work surface and place ¼ of the prepared filling in the middle of each tortilla, leaving about 1½-inch on each end unfilled. old in the opposite sides of each tortilla and roll up. Secure with toothpicks through the center, if needed.
3. Transfer the burritos to the air fry basket.
4. Select Air Fry, set temperature to 390°F (199°C) and set time to 4 minutes. Select Start to begin preheating.
5. Once the air fryer has preheated, place the air fry basket into the air fryer.
6. When cooking is complete, the burritos should be crisp and golden brown.
7. Allow to cool for 5 minutes and serve with salsa, if desired.

Cheesy Avocado with Eggs

Prep time: 5 minutes | Cook time: 9 minutes | Serves 2

1 large avocado, halved and pitted
2 large eggs
2 tomato slices, divided
½ cup nonfat Cottage cheese, divided
½ teaspoon fresh cilantro, for garnish

1. Line the sheet pan with the aluminium foil.
2. Slice a thin piece from the bottom of each avocado half so they sit flat. Remove a small amount from each avocado half to make a bigger hole to hold the egg.
3. Arrange the avocado halves on the pan, hollow-side up. Break 1 egg into each half. Top each half with 1 tomato slice and ¼ cup of the Cottage cheese.
4. Select Bake, set temperature to 425°F (220°C) and set time to 9 minutes. Select Start to begin preheating.
5. Once the unit has preheated, place the pan into the air fryer.
6. When cooking is complete, remove the pan from the air fryer. Garnish with the fresh cilantro and serve.

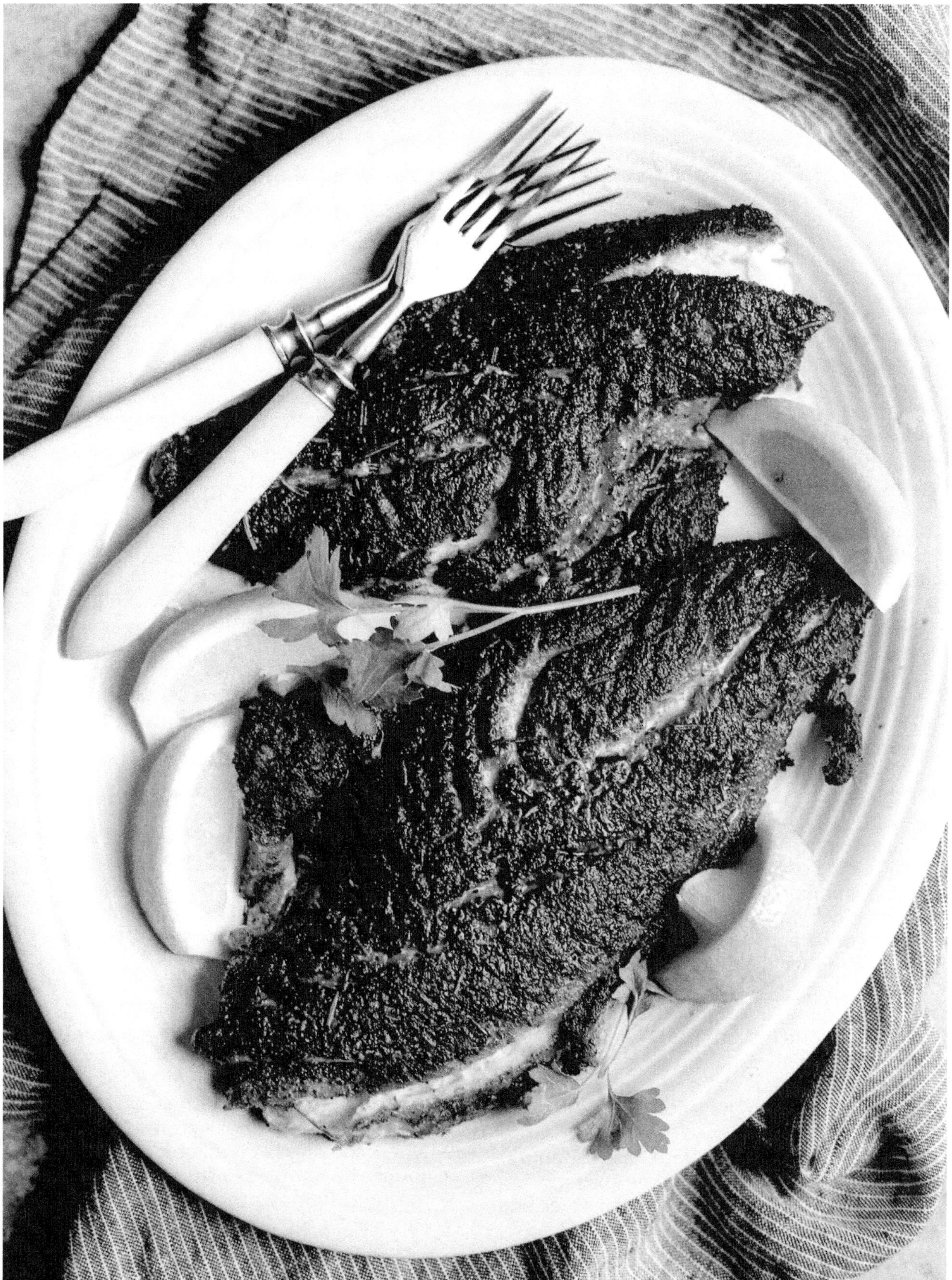

CHAPTER 4 *Fish and Seafood*

Oily Cauliflower Fritters

Prep time: 5 minutes | Cook time: 24 minutes | Serves 2

½ pound (227 g) sole fillet
½ pound (227 g) mashed cauliflower
½ cup red onion, chopped
1 bell pepper, finely chopped
1 egg, beaten
2 garlic cloves, minced
2 tablespoons fresh parsley, chopped
1 tablespoon olive oil
1 tablespoon coconut aminos
½ teaspoon scotch bonnet pepper, minced
½ teaspoon paprika
Salt and white pepper, to taste
Cooking spray

1. Spray the air fry basket with cooking spray. Place the sole fillets in the basket.
2. Select Air Fry, set temperature to 395°F (202°C), and set time to 10 minutes. Select Start to begin preheating.
3. Once preheated, place the basket into the air fryer. Flip the fillets halfway through.
4. When cooking is complete, transfer the fish fillets to a large bowl. Mash the fillets into flakes. Add the remaining ingredients and stir to combine.
5. Make the fritters: Scoop out 2 tablespoons of the fish mixture and shape into a patty about ½ inch thick with your hands. Repeat with the remaining fish mixture. Place the patties in the air fry basket.
6. Select Bake, set temperature to 380°F (193°C), and set time to 14 minutes. Select Start to begin preheating.
7. Once preheated, place the basket into the air fryer. Flip the patties halfway through.
8. When cooking is complete, they should be golden brown and cooked through. Remove the basket from the air fryer and cool for 5 minutes before serving.

Cheesy Tuna Patties

Prep time: 5 minutes | Cook time: 17 to 18 minutes | Serves 4

Tuna Patties:
1 pound (454 g) canned tuna, drained
1 egg, whisked
2 tablespoons shallots, minced
1 garlic clove, minced
1 cup grated Romano cheese
Sea salt and ground black pepper, to taste
1 tablespoon sesame oil

Cheese Sauce:
1 tablespoon butter
1 cup beer
2 tablespoons grated Colby cheese

1. Mix together the canned tuna, whisked egg, shallots, garlic, cheese, salt, and pepper in a large bowl and stir to incorporate.
2. Divide the tuna mixture into four equal portions and form each portion into a patty with your hands. Refrigerate the patties for 2 hours.
3. When ready, brush both sides of each patty with sesame oil, then place in the air fry basket.
4. Select Bake, set temperature to 360°F (182°C), and set time to 14 minutes. Select Start to begin preheating.
5. Once preheated, place the basket into the air fryer. Flip the patties halfway through the cooking time.
6. Meanwhile, melt the butter in a saucepan over medium heat.
7. Pour in the beer and whisk constantly, or until it begins to bubble. Add the grated Colby cheese and mix well. Continue cooking for 3 to 4 minutes, or until the cheese melts. Remove from the heat.
8. When cooking is complete, the patties should be lightly browned and cooked through. Remove the patties from the air fryer to a plate. Drizzle them with the cheese sauce and serve immediately.

Golden Breaded Fish Fillets

Prep time: 20 minutes | Cook time: 7 minutes | Serves 4

1 pound (454 g) fish fillet
1 tablespoon coarse brown mustard
1 teaspoon Worcestershire sauce
½ teaspoon hot sauce
Salt, to taste
Cooking spray
Crumb Coating:
¾ cup panko bread crumbs
¼ cup stone-ground cornmeal
¼ teaspoon salt

1. On your cutting board, cut the fish fillet crosswise into slices, about 1 inch wide.
2. In a small bowl, stir together the mustard, Worcestershire sauce, and hot sauce to make a paste and rub this paste on all sides of the fi lets. Season with salt to taste.
3. In a shallow bowl, thoroughly combine all the ingredients for the crumb coating and spread them on a sheet of wax paper.
4. Roll the fish fillets in the crumb mixtur until thickly coated. Spritz all sides of the fish with cooking sp ay, then arrange them in the air fry basket in a single layer.
5. Select Air Fry, set temperature to 400°F (205°C), and set time to 7 minutes. Select Start to begin preheating.
6. Once preheated, place the air fry basket into the air fryer.
7. When cooking is complete, the fish should fla e apart with a fork. Remove from the air fryer and serve warm.

Roasted Parmesan-Crusted Halibut Fillets

Prep time: 5 minutes | Cook time: 10 minutes | Serves 4

2 medium-sized halibut fillet
Dash of tabasco sauce
1 teaspoon curry powder
½ teaspoon ground coriander
½ teaspoon hot paprika
Kosher salt and freshly cracked mixed peppercorns, to taste
2 eggs
1½ tablespoons olive oil
½ cup grated Parmesan cheese

1. On a clean work surface, drizzle the halibut fillets with the tabasco sauce. Sprinkle with the curry powder, coriander, hot paprika, salt, and cracked mixed peppercorns. Set aside.
2. In a shallow bowl, beat the eggs until frothy. In another shallow bowl, combine the olive oil and Parmesan cheese.
3. One at a time, dredge the halibut fillets in the beaten eggs, shaking off any excess, then roll them over the Parmesan cheese until evenly coated.
4. Arrange the halibut fillets in the air fry basket in a single layer.
5. Select Roast, set temperature to 365°F (185°C), and set time to 10 minutes. Select Start to begin preheating.
6. Once preheated, place the basket into the air fryer.
7. When cooking is complete, the fish should be golden brown and crisp. Cool for 5 minutes before serving.

Lemon-Honey Snapper with Fruit

Prep time: 15 minutes | Cook time: 12 minutes | Serves 4

4 (4-ounce / 113-g) red snapper fillet
2 teaspoons olive oil
3 plums, halved and pitted
3 nectarines, halved and pitted
1 cup red grapes
1 tablespoon freshly squeezed lemon juice
1 tablespoon honey
½ teaspoon dried thyme

1. Arrange the red snapper fillets in the air fry basket and drizzle the olive oil over the top.
2. Select Air Fry, set temperature to 390°F (199°C), and set time to 12 minutes. Select Start to begin preheating.
3. Once preheated, place the basket into the air fryer.
4. After 4 minutes, remove the basket from the air fryer. Top the fillets with the plums and nectarines. Scatter the red grapes all over the fillets. Drizzle with the lemon juice and honey and sprinkle the thyme on top. Return the basket to the air fryer and continue cooking for 8 minutes, or until the fish is fla .
5. When cooking is complete, remove from the air fryer and serve warm.

Juicy Swordfish Steaks

Prep time: 10 minutes | Cook time: 8 minutes | Serves 4

4 (4-ounce / 113-g) swordfish steak
½ teaspoon toasted sesame oil
1 jalapeño pepper, finely mince
2 garlic cloves, grated
2 tablespoons freshly squeezed lemon juice
1 tablespoon grated fresh ginger
½ teaspoon Chinese five-spice powder
⅛ teaspoon freshly ground black pepper

1. On a clean work surface, place the swordfish steaks and brush both sides of the fish with the sesame oil
2. Combine the jalapeño, garlic, lemon juice, ginger, five-spice powder, and black pepper in a small bowl and stir to mix well. Rub the mixture all over the fish until completely coated. Allow to sit for 10 minutes.
3. When ready, arrange the swordfish steaks in the air fry basket.
4. Select Air Fry, set temperature to 380°F (193°C), and set time to 8 minutes. Select Start to begin preheating.
5. Once preheated, place the basket into the air fryer. Flip the steaks halfway through.
6. When cooking is complete, remove from the air fryer and cool for 5 minutes before serving.

Cheesy Salmon with Asparagus

Prep time: 10 minutes | Cook time: 15 minutes | Serves 4

4 (6-ounce / 170 g) salmon fillets, patted dry
1 teaspoon kosher salt, divided
1 tablespoon honey
2 tablespoons unsalted butter, melted
2 teaspoons Dijon mustard
2 pounds (907 g) asparagus, trimmed
Lemon wedges, for serving

1. Season both sides of the salmon fillets with ½ teaspoon of kosher salt.
2. Whisk together the honey, 1 tablespoon of butter, and mustard in a small bowl. Set aside.
3. Arrange the asparagus on a sheet pan. Drizzle the remaining 1 tablespoon of butter all over and season with the remaining ½ teaspoon of salt, tossing to coat. Move the asparagus to the outside of the sheet pan.
4. Put the salmon fillets on the sheet pan, skin-side down. Brush the fillets generously with the honey mixture.
5. Select Roast, set temperature to 375°F (190°C), and set time to 15 minutes. Select Start to begin preheating.
6. Once the air fryer has preheated, place the pan into the air fryer. Toss the asparagus once halfway through the cooking time.
7. When done, transfer the salmon fillets and asparagus to a plate. Serve warm with a squeeze of lemon juice.

Easy Fried Salmon Patties

Prep time: 5 minutes | Cook time: 11 minutes | Makes 6 patties

1 (14.75-ounce / 418-g) can Alaskan pink salmon, drained and bones removed
½ cup bread crumbs
1 egg, whisked
2 scallions, diced
1 teaspoon garlic powder
Salt and pepper, to taste
Cooking spray

1. Stir together the salmon, bread crumbs, whisked egg, scallions, garlic powder, salt, and pepper in a large bowl until well incorporated.
2. Divide the salmon mixture into six equal portions and form each into a patty with your hands.
3. Arrange the salmon patties in the air fry basket and spritz them with cooking spray.
4. Select Air Fry, set temperature to 400°F (205°C), and set time to 10 minutes. Select Start to begin preheating.
5. Once preheated, place the basket into the air fryer. Flip the patties once halfway through.
6. When cooking is complete, the patties should be golden brown and cooked through. Remove the patties from the air fryer and serve on a plate.

Air Fried Crispy Fish Sticks

Prep time: 10 minutes | Cook time: 6 minutes | Serves 8

8 ounces (227 g) fish fillets (pollock o cod), cut into ½ × 3 inches strips
Salt, to taste (optional)
½ cup plain bread crumbs
Cooking spray

1. Season the fish strips with salt to taste, if desired.
2. Place the bread crumbs on a plate, then roll the fish in the bread crumbs until well coated. Spray all sides of the fish with cooking spray. Transfer to the air fry basket in a single layer.
3. Select Air Fry, set temperature to 400ºF (205ºC), and set time to 6 minutes. Select Start to begin preheating.
4. Once preheated, place the basket into the air fryer.
5. When cooked, the fish sticks should be golden brown and crispy. Remove from the air fryer to a plate and serve hot.

Oily Basil Salmon with Tomatoes

Prep time: 10 minutes | Cook time: 15 minutes | Serves 4

4 (6-ounce / 170-g) salmon fillets, patted dry
1 teaspoon kosher salt, divided
2 pints cherry or grape tomatoes, halved if large, divided
3 tablespoons extra-virgin olive oil, divided
2 garlic cloves, minced
1 small red bell pepper, deseeded and chopped
2 tablespoons chopped fresh basil, divided

1. Season both sides of the salmon with ½ teaspoon of kosher salt.
2. Put about half of the tomatoes in a large bowl, along with the remaining ½ teaspoon of kosher salt, 2 tablespoons of olive oil, garlic, bell pepper, and 1 tablespoon of basil. Toss to coat and then transfer to the sheet pan.
3. Arrange the salmon fillets on the sheet pan, skin-side down. Brush them with the remaining 1 tablespoon of olive oil.
4. Select Roast, set temperature to 375ºF (190ºC), and set time to 15 minutes. Select Start to begin preheating.
5. Once preheated, place the pan into the air fryer.
6. After 7 minutes, remove the pan and fold in the remaining tomatoes. Return the pan to the air fryer and continue cooking.
7. When cooked, remove the pan from the air fryer. Serve sprinkled with the remaining 1 tablespoon of basil.

Cheesy Parmesan-Crusted Salmon Patties

Prep time: 10 minutes | Cook time: 13 minutes | Serves 4

1 pound (454 g) salmon, chopped into ½-inch pieces
2 tablespoons coconut flou
2 tablespoons grated Parmesan cheese
1½ tablespoons milk
½ white onion, peeled and finely chopped
½ teaspoon butter, at room temperature
½ teaspoon chipotle powder
½ teaspoon dried parsley fla es
⅓ teaspoon ground black pepper
⅓ teaspoon smoked cayenne pepper
1 teaspoon fine sea salt

1. Put all the ingredients for the salmon patties in a bowl and stir to combine well.
2. Scoop out 2 tablespoons of the salmon mixture and shape into a patty with your palm, about ½ inch thick. Repeat until all the mixture is used. Transfer to the refrigerator for about 2 hours until firm
3. When ready, arrange the salmon patties in the air fry basket.
4. Select Bake, set temperature to 395ºF (202ºC), and set time to 13 minutes. Select Start to begin preheating.
5. Once preheated, place the basket into the air fryer. Flip the patties halfway through the cooking time.
6. When cooking is complete, the patties should be golden brown. Remove from the air fryer and cool for 5 minutes before serving.

Vinegary Hoisin Tuna

Prep time: 15 minutes | Cook time: 5 minutes | Serves 4

½ cup hoisin sauce
2 tablespoons rice wine vinegar
2 teaspoons sesame oil
2 teaspoons dried lemongrass
1 teaspoon garlic powder
¼ teaspoon red pepper flakes
½ small onion, quartered and thinly sliced
8 ounces (227 g) fresh tuna, cut into 1-inch cubes
Cooking spray
3 cups cooked jasmine rice

1. In a small bowl, whisk together the hoisin sauce, vinegar, sesame oil, lemongrass, garlic powder, and red pepper flakes.
2. Add the sliced onion and tuna cubes and gently toss until the fish is evenly coated.
3. Arrange the coated tuna cubes in the air fry basket in a single layer.
4. Select Air Fry, set temperature to 390ºF (199ºC), and set time to 5 minutes. Select Start to begin preheating.
5. Once preheated, place the basket into the air fryer. Flip the fish halfway through the cooking time.
6. When cooking is complete, the fish should begin to flake. Continue cooking for 1 minute, if necessary. Remove from the air fryer and serve over hot jasmine rice.

Mustard-Crusted Sole Fillets

Prep time: 5 minutes | Cook time: 10 minutes | Serves 4

5 teaspoons low-sodium yellow mustard
1 tablespoon freshly squeezed lemon juice
4 (3.5-ounce / 99-g) sole fillet
2 teaspoons olive oil
½ teaspoon dried marjoram
½ teaspoon dried thyme
⅛ teaspoon freshly ground black pepper
1 slice low-sodium whole-wheat bread, crumbled

1. Whisk together the mustard and lemon juice in a small bowl until thoroughly mixed and smooth. Spread the mixture evenly over the sole fillets, then transfer the fillets to the air fry basket.
2. In a separate bowl, combine the olive oil, marjoram, thyme, black pepper, and bread crumbs and stir to mix well. Gently but firmly press the mixture onto the top of fillets, coating them completely.
3. Select Bake, set temperature to 320ºF (160ºC), and set time to 10 minutes. Select Start to begin preheating.
4. Once preheated, place the basket into the air fryer.
5. When cooking is complete, the fish should reach an internal temperature of 145ºF (63ºC) on a meat thermometer. Remove the basket from the air fryer and serve on a plate.

Yummy Oily Teriyaki Salmon

Prep time: 15 minutes | Cook time: 15 minutes | Serves 4

¾ cup Teriyaki sauce, divided
4 (6-ounce / 170-g) skinless salmon fillets
4 heads baby bok choy, root ends trimmed off and cut in half lengthwise through the root
1 teaspoon sesame oil
1 tablespoon vegetable oil
1 tablespoon toasted sesame seeds

1. Set aside ¼ cup of Teriyaki sauce and pour the remaining sauce into a resealable plastic bag. Put the salmon into the bag and seal, squeezing as much air out as possible. Allow the salmon to marinate for at least 10 minutes.
2. Arrange the bok choy halves on the sheet pan. Drizzle the oils over the vegetables, tossing to coat. Drizzle about 1 tablespoon of the reserved Teriyaki sauce over the bok choy, then push them to the sides of the sheet pan.
3. Put the salmon fillets in the middle of the sheet pan.
4. Select Roast, set temperature to 375ºF (190ºC), and set time to 15 minutes. Select Start to begin preheating.
5. Once the air fryer has preheated, place the pan into the air fryer.
6. When done, remove the pan and brush the salmon with the remaining Teriyaki sauce. Serve garnished with the sesame seeds.

44 | Chapter 4 Fish and Seafood

Herbed Salmon with Roasted Asparagus

Prep time: 5 minutes | Cook time: 12 minutes | Serves 2

2 teaspoons olive oil, plus additional for drizzling
2 (5-ounce / 142-g) salmon fillets, with skin
Salt and freshly ground black pepper, to taste
1 bunch asparagus, trimmed
1 teaspoon dried tarragon
1 teaspoon dried chives
Fresh lemon wedges, for serving

1. Rub the olive oil all over the salmon fillets. Sprinkle with salt and pepper to taste.
2. Put the asparagus on a foil-lined baking sheet and place the salmon fillets on to , skin-side down.
3. Select Roast, set temperature to 425ºF (220ºC), and set time to 12 minutes. Select Start to begin preheating.
4. Once preheated, place the pan into the air fryer.
5. When cooked, the fillets should register 145ºF (63ºC) on an instant-read thermometer. Remove from the air fryer and cut the salmon fillets in half crosswise, then use a metal spatula to lift flesh from skin and t ansfer to a serving plate. Discard the skin and drizzle the salmon fillets with additional oli e oil. Scatter with the herbs.
6. Serve the salmon fillets with roasted asparagus spears and lemon wedges on the side.

Oily Fish Tacos

Prep time: 10 minutes | Cook time: 10 to 15 minutes | Serves 6

1 tablespoon avocado oil
1 tablespoon Cajun seasoning
4 (5 to 6 ounce / 142 to 170 g) tilapia fillet
1 (14-ounce / 397-g) package coleslaw mix
12 corn tortillas
2 limes, cut into wedges

1. Line a baking pan with parchment paper.
2. In a shallow bowl, stir together the avocado oil and Cajun seasoning to make a marinade. Place the tilapia fillets into the bowl, turning to coat evenly.
3. Put the fillets in the baking pan in a single layer.
4. Select Air Fry, set temperature to 375ºF (190ºC), and set time to 10 minutes. Select Start to begin preheating.
5. Once preheated, slide the pan into the air fryer.
6. When cooked, the fish should be fla . If necessary, continue cooking for 5 minutes more. Remove the fish from the air fryer to a plate.
7. Assemble the tacos: Spoon some of the coleslaw mix into each tortilla and top each with ⅓ of a tilapia fillet. Squee e some lime juice over the top of each taco and serve immediately.

Air Fried Milky Cod Fillets

Prep time: 15 minutes | Cook time: 12 minutes | Serves 4

4 cod fillet
¼ teaspoon fine sea salt
1 teaspoon cayenne pepper
¼ teaspoon ground black pepper, or more to taste
½ cup fresh Italian parsley, coarsely chopped
½ cup non-dairy milk
4 garlic cloves, minced
1 Italian pepper, chopped
1 teaspoon dried basil
½ teaspoon dried oregano
Cooking spray

1. Lightly spritz a baking dish with cooking spray.
2. Season the fillets with salt, c yenne pepper, and black pepper.
3. Pulse the remaining ingredients in a food processor, then transfer the mixture to a shallow bowl. Coat the fillets with the mixture.
4. Select Air Fry, set temperature to 375ºF (190ºC), and set time to 12 minutes. Select Start to begin preheating.
5. Once preheated, place the baking dish into the air fryer.
6. When cooking is complete, the fish will be flak . Remove from the air fryer and serve on a plate.

Ginger Flavored Tuna Lettuce Wraps

Prep time: 10 minutes | Cook time: 4 to 7 minutes | Serves 4

1 pound (454 g) fresh tuna steak, cut into 1-inch cubes
2 garlic cloves, minced
1 tablespoon grated fresh ginger
½ teaspoon toasted sesame oil
4 low-sodium whole-wheat tortillas
2 cups shredded romaine lettuce
1 red bell pepper, thinly sliced
¼ cup low-fat mayonnaise

1. Combine the tuna cubes, garlic, ginger, and sesame oil in a medium bowl and toss until well coated. Allow to sit for 10 minutes.
2. When ready, place the tuna cubes in the air fry basket.
3. Select Air Fry, set temperature to 390°F (199°C), and set time to 6 minutes. Select Start to begin preheating.
4. Once preheated, place the basket into the air fryer.
5. When cooking is complete, the tuna cubes should be cooked through and golden brown. Remove the tuna cubes from the air fryer to a plate.
6. Make the wraps: Place the tortillas on a flat work surface and top each tortilla evenly with the cooked tuna, lettuce, bell pepper, and finish with the m yonnaise. Roll them up and serve immediately.

Honeyed Halibut Steaks with Parsley

Prep time: 5 minutes | Cook time: 10 minutes | Serves 4

1 pound (454 g) halibut steaks
¼ cup vegetable oil
2½ tablespoons Worcester sauce
2 tablespoons honey
2 tablespoons vermouth
1 tablespoon freshly squeezed lemon juice
1 tablespoon fresh parsley leaves, coarsely chopped
Salt and pepper, to taste
1 teaspoon dried basil

1. Put all the ingredients in a large mixing dish and gently stir until the fish is coated evenly. Transfer the fish to the air fry basket.
2. Select Roast, set temperature to 390°F (199°C), and set time to 10 minutes. Select Start to begin preheating.
3. Once preheated, place the basket into the air fryer. Flip the fish halfway through cooking time.
4. When cooking is complete, the fish should reach an internal temperature of at least 145°F (63°C) on a meat thermometer. Remove from the air fryer and let the fish cool for 5 minutes before serving.

Baked Golden Beer-Battered Cod

Prep time: 5 minutes | Cook time: 15 minutes | Serves 4

2 eggs
1 cup malty beer
1 cup all-purpose flou
½ cup cornstarch
1 teaspoon garlic powder
Salt and pepper, to taste
4 (4-ounce / 113-g) cod fillet
Cooking spray

1. In a shallow bowl, beat together the eggs with the beer. In another shallow bowl, thoroughly combine the flour and cornstarch. Sprinkle with the garlic powder, salt, and pepper.
2. Dredge each cod fillet in the flou mixture, then in the egg mixture. Dip each piece of fish in the flour mixture second time.
3. Spritz the air fry basket with cooking spray. Arrange the cod fillets in the basket in a single layer.
4. Select Air Fry, set temperature to 400°F (205°C), and set time to 15 minutes. Select Start to begin preheating.
5. Once preheated, place the basket into the air fryer. Flip the fillets half ay through the cooking time.
6. When cooking is complete, the cod should reach an internal temperature of 145°F (63°C) on a meat thermometer and the outside should be crispy. Let the fish cool for 5 minutes and ser e.

Milky Cajun and Lemon Pepper Cod

Prep time: 5 minutes | Cook time: 12 minutes | Makes 2 cod fillets

1 tablespoon Cajun seasoning
1 teaspoon salt
½ teaspoon lemon pepper
½ teaspoon freshly ground black pepper
2 (8-ounce / 227-g) cod fillets, cut to fi into the air fry basket
Cooking spray
2 tablespoons unsalted butter, melted
1 lemon, cut into 4 wedges

1. Spritz the air fry basket with cooking spray.
2. Thoroughly combine the Cajun seasoning, salt, lemon pepper, and black pepper in a small bowl. Rub this mixture all over the cod fillets until completely coated.
3. Put the fillets in the air fry bas et and brush the melted butter over both sides of each fillet
4. Select Bake, set temperature to 360ºF (182ºC), and set time to 12 minutes. Select Start to begin preheating.
5. Once preheated, place the basket into the air fryer. Flip the fillets half ay through the cooking time.
6. When cooking is complete, the fish should fla e apart with a fork. Remove the fillets from the air fr er and serve with fresh lemon wedges.

Juicy Salmon Bowl

Prep time: 15 minutes | Cook time: 12 minutes | Serves 4

12 ounces (340 g) salmon fillets, cut into 1½-inch cubes
1 red onion, chopped
1 jalapeño pepper, minced
1 red bell pepper, chopped
¼ cup low-sodium salsa
2 teaspoons peanut oil or safflower oi
2 tablespoons low-sodium tomato juice
1 teaspoon chili powder

1. Mix together the salmon cubes, red onion, jalapeño, red bell pepper, salsa, peanut oil, tomato juice, chili powder in a medium metal bowl and stir until well incorporated.
2. Select Bake, set temperature to 370ºF (188ºC), and set time to 12 minutes. Select Start to begin preheating.
3. Once preheated, place the metal bowl into the air fryer. Stir the ingredients once halfway through the cooking time.
4. When cooking is complete, the salmon should be cooked through and the veggies should be fork-tender. Serve warm.

Baked Tilapia with Garlic Aioli

Prep time: 5 minutes | Cook time: 15 minutes | Serves 4

Tilapia:
4 tilapia fillet
1 tablespoon extra-virgin olive oil
1 teaspoon garlic powder
1 teaspoon paprika
1 teaspoon dried basil
A pinch of lemon-pepper seasoning

Garlic Aioli:
2 garlic cloves, minced
1 tablespoon mayonnaise
Juice of ½ lemon
1 teaspoon extra-virgin olive oil
Salt and pepper, to taste

1. On a clean work surface, brush both sides of each fillet with the oli e oil. Sprinkle with the garlic powder, paprika, basil, and lemon-pepper seasoning. Place the fillets in the air fry bas et.
2. Select Bake, set temperature to 400ºF (205ºC), and set time to 15 minutes. Select Start to begin preheating.
3. Once preheated, place the basket into the air fryer. Flip the fillets half ay through.
4. Meanwhile, make the garlic aioli: Whisk together the garlic, mayo, lemon juice, olive oil, salt, and pepper in a small bowl until smooth.
5. When cooking is complete, the fish should fla e apart with a fork and no longer translucent in the center. Remove the fish from the air fr er and serve with the garlic aioli on the side.

Aromatic Baked Cod Fillet

Prep time: 10 minutes | Cook time: 12 minutes | Serves 4

1 teaspoon olive oil
4 cod fillets
¼ teaspoon fine sea salt
¼ teaspoon ground black pepper, or more to taste
1 teaspoon cayenne pepper
½ cup fresh Italian parsley, coarsely chopped
½ cup nondairy milk
1 Italian pepper, chopped
4 garlic cloves, minced
1 teaspoon dried basil
½ teaspoon dried oregano

1. Lightly coat the sides and bottom of a baking dish with the olive oil. Set aside.
2. In a large bowl, sprinkle the fillets with salt, black pepper, and cayenne pepper.
3. In a food processor, pulse the remaining ingredients until smoothly puréed.
4. Add the purée to the bowl of fillets and toss to coat, then transfer to the prepared baking dish.
5. Select Bake, set temperature to 380°F (193°C), and set time to 12 minutes. Select Start to begin preheating.
6. Once preheated, place the baking dish into the air fryer.
7. When cooking is complete, the fish should flake when pressed lightly with a fork. Remove from the air fryer and serve warm.

Butter-Juicy Salmon Steak

Prep time: 5 minutes | Cook time: 10 minutes | Serves 4

4 tablespoons butter, melted
2 cloves garlic, minced
Sea salt and ground black pepper, to taste
¼ cup dry white wine
1 tablespoon lime juice
1 teaspoon smoked paprika
½ teaspoon onion powder
4 salmon steaks
Cooking spray

1. Place all the ingredients except the salmon and oil in a shallow dish and stir to mix well.
2. Add the salmon steaks, turning to coat well on both sides. Transfer the salmon to the refrigerator to marinate for 30 minutes.
3. When ready, put the salmon steaks in the air fry basket, discarding any excess marinade. Spray the salmon steaks with cooking spray.
4. Select Air Fry, set temperature to 360°F (182°C), and set time to 10 minutes. Select Start to begin preheating.
5. Once preheated, place the basket into the air fryer. Flip the salmon steaks halfway through.
6. When cooking is complete, remove from the air fryer and divide the salmon steaks among four plates. Serve warm.

Scallops with Broccoli and Bean

Prep time: 15 minutes | Cook time: 9 minutes | Serves 4

1 cup frozen peas
1 cup green beans
1 cup frozen chopped broccoli
2 teaspoons olive oil
½ teaspoon dried oregano
½ teaspoon dried basil
12 ounces (340 g) sea scallops, rinsed and patted dry

1. Put the peas, green beans, and broccoli in a large bowl. Drizzle with the olive oil and toss to coat well. Transfer the vegetables to the air fry basket.
2. Select Air Fry, set temperature to 400°F (205°C), and set time to 5 minutes. Select Start to begin preheating.
3. Once preheated, place the basket into the air fryer.
4. When cooking is complete, the vegetables should be fork-tender. Transfer the vegetables to a serving bowl. Scatter with the oregano and basil and set aside.
5. Place the scallops in the air fry basket.
6. Select Air Fry, set temperature to 400°F (205°C), and set time to 4 minutes. Select Start to begin preheating.
7. Once preheated, place the basket into the air fryer.
8. When cooking is complete, the scallops should be firm and just opaque in the center. Remove from the air fryer to the bowl of vegetables and toss well. Serve warm.

Lemony Red Snapper Fillet

Prep time: 13 minutes | Cook time: 10 minutes | Serves 4

1 teaspoon olive oil
1½ teaspoons black pepper
¼ teaspoon garlic powder
¼ teaspoon thyme
⅛ teaspoon cayenne pepper
4 (4-ounce / 113-g) red snapper fillets, skin on
4 thin slices lemon
Nonstick cooking spray

1. Spritz the air fry basket with nonstick cooking spray.
2. In a small bowl, stir together the olive oil, black pepper, garlic powder, thyme, and cayenne pepper. Rub the mixture all over the fillets until completely coated
3. Lay the fillets, skin-side down, in the air fry basket and top each fillet with a slice of lemon.
4. Select Bake, set temperature to 390ºF (199ºC), and set time to 10 minutes. Select Start to begin preheating.
5. Once preheated, place the basket into the air fryer. Flip the fillets half ay through.
6. When cooking is complete, the fish should be cooked through. Let the fish cool for 5 minutes and serve.

Roasted Scallops with Snow Peas

Prep time: 10 minutes | Cook time: 8 minutes | Serves 4

1 pound (454 g) sea scallops
3 tablespoons hoisin sauce
½ cup toasted sesame seeds
6 ounces (170 g) snow peas, trimmed
3 teaspoons vegetable oil, divided
1 teaspoon soy sauce
1 teaspoon sesame oil
1 cup roasted mushrooms

1. Brush the scallops with the hoisin sauce. Put the sesame seeds in a shallow dish. Roll the scallops in the sesame seeds until evenly coated.
2. Combine the snow peas with 1 teaspoon of vegetable oil, the sesame oil, and soy sauce in a medium bowl and toss to coat.
3. Grease the sheet pan with the remaining 2 teaspoons of vegetable oil. Put the scallops in the middle of the pan and arrange the snow peas around the scallops in a single layer.
4. Select Roast, set temperature to 375ºF (190ºC), and set time to 8 minutes. Select Start to begin preheating.
5. Once the air fryer has preheated, place the pan into the air fryer.
6. After 5 minutes, remove the pan and flip the scallops. Fold in the mushrooms and stir well. Return the pan to the air fryer and continue cooking.
7. When done, remove the pan from the air fryer and cool for 5 minutes. Serve warm.

Crispy Breadcrumb Scallops

Prep time: 5 minutes | Cook time: 7 minutes | Serves 4

1 egg
3 tablespoons flou
1 cup bread crumbs
1 pound (454 g) fresh scallops
2 tablespoons olive oil
Salt and black pepper, to taste

1. In a bowl, lightly beat the egg. Place the flour and bread crumbs into sepa ate shallow dishes.
2. Dredge the scallops in the flour and shake off any excess. Dip the flou - coated scallops in the beaten egg and roll in the bread crumbs.
3. Brush the scallops generously with olive oil and season with salt and pepper, to taste. Transfer the scallops to the air fry basket.
4. Select Air Fry, set temperature to 360ºF (182ºC), and set time to 7 minutes. Select Start to begin preheating.
5. Once preheated, place the basket into the air fryer. Flip the scallops halfway through the cooking time.
6. When cooking is complete, the scallops should reach an internal temperature of just 145ºF (63ºC) on a meat thermometer. Remove the basket from the air fryer. Let the scallops cool for 5 minutes and serve.

Garlic-Butter Shrimp with Sausage

Prep time: 10 minutes | Cook time: 15 minutes | Serves 4

1 pound (454 g) small red potatoes, halved
2 ears corn, shucked and cut into rounds, 1 to 1½ inches thick
2 tablespoons Old Bay or similar seasoning
½ cup unsalted butter, melted
1 (12- to 13-ounce / 340- to 369-g) package kielbasa or other smoked sausages
3 garlic cloves, minced
1 pound (454 g) medium shrimp, peeled and deveined

1. Place the potatoes and corn in a large bowl.
2. Stir together the butter and Old Bay seasoning in a small bowl. Drizzle half the butter mixture over the potatoes and corn, tossing to coat. Spread out the vegetables on a sheet pan.
3. Select Roast, set temperature to 350ºF (180ºC), and set time to 15 minutes. Select Start to begin preheating.
4. Once the air fryer has preheated, place the pan into the air fryer.
5. Meanwhile, cut the sausages into 2-inch lengths, then cut each piece in half lengthwise. Put the sausages and shrimp in a medium bowl and set aside.
6. Add the garlic to the bowl of remaining butter mixture and stir well.
7. After 10 minutes, remove the sheet pan and pour the vegetables into the large bowl. Drizzle with the garlic butter and toss until well coated. Arrange the vegetables, sausages, and shrimp on the sheet pan.
8. Return to the air fryer and continue cooking. After 5 minutes, check the shrimp for doneness. The shrimp should be pink and opaque. If they are not quite cooked through, roast for an additional 1 minute.
9. When done, remove from the air fryer and serve on a plate.

Savory Tilapia Fillet

Prep time: 10 minutes | Cook time: 12 minutes | Serves 4

1 tablespoon olive oil
1 tablespoon lemon juice
1 teaspoon minced garlic
½ teaspoon chili powder
4 tilapia fillet

1. Line a baking pan with parchment paper.
2. In a shallow bowl, stir together the olive oil, lemon juice, garlic, and chili powder to make a marinade. Put the tilapia fillets in the bowl, turning to coat evenly.
3. Place the fillets in the baking pan in a single layer.
4. Select Air Fry, set temperature to 375ºF (190ºC), and set time to 12 minutes. Select Start to begin preheating.
5. Once preheated, slide the pan into the air fryer.
6. When cooked, the fish will fl e apart with a fork. Remove from the air fryer to a plate and serve hot.

Breadcrumb-Crusted Fish Sticks

Prep time: 10 minutes | Cook time: 8 minutes | Makes 8 fish sticks

8 ounces (227 g) fish fillets (pollock o cod), cut into ½×3-inch strips
Salt, to taste
(optional)
½ cup plain bread crumbs
Cooking spray

1. Season the fish strips with salt to taste, if desired.
2. Place the bread crumbs on a plate. Roll the fish strips in the bread crumbs to coat. Spritz the fish strips with cooking spray.
3. Arrange the fish strips in the air fry basket in a single layer.
4. Select Air Fry, set temperature to 390ºF (199ºC), and set time to 8 minutes. Select Start to begin preheating.
5. Once preheated, place the basket into the air fryer.
6. When cooking is complete, they should be golden brown. Remove from the air fryer and cool for 5 minutes before serving.

Air Fried Paprika Shrimp

Prep time: 5 minutes | Cook time: 10 minutes | Serves 4

1 pound (454 g) tiger shrimp
2 tablespoons olive oil
½ tablespoon old bay seasoning
¼ tablespoon smoked paprika
¼ teaspoon cayenne pepper
A pinch of sea salt

1. Toss all the ingredients in a large bowl until the shrimp are evenly coated.
2. Arrange the shrimp in the air fry basket.
3. Select Air Fry, set temperature to 380°F (193°C), and set time to 10 minutes. Select Start to begin preheating.
4. Once preheated, place the basket into the air fryer.
5. When cooking is complete, the shrimp should be pink and cooked through. Remove from the air fryer and serve hot.

Buttery Catfish Cakes with Cheese

Prep time: 5 minutes | Cook time: 15 minutes | Serves 4

2 catfish fille
3 ounces (85 g) butter
1 cup shredded Parmesan cheese
1 cup shredded Swiss cheese
½ cup buttermilk
1 teaspoon baking powder
1 teaspoon baking soda
1 teaspoon Cajun seasoning

1. Bring a pot of salted water to a boil. Add the catfish fillets to the boiling ater and let them boil for 5 minutes until they become opaque.
2. Remove the fillets from the pot to a mixing bowl and fla e them into small pieces with a fork.
3. Add the remaining ingredients to the bowl of fish and stir until well incorporated.
4. Divide the fish mixture into 12 equal portions and shape each portion into a patty. Place the patties in the air fry basket.
5. Select Air Fry, set temperature to 380°F (193°C), and set time to 15 minutes. Select Start to begin preheating.
6. Once preheated, place the basket into the air fryer. Flip the patties halfway through the cooking time.
7. When cooking is complete, the patties should be golden brown and cooked through. Remove from the air fryer. Let the patties sit for 5 minutes and serve.

Aromatic Coconut-Crusted Prawns

Prep time: 15 minutes | Cook time: 8 minutes | Serves 4

12 prawns, cleaned and deveined
1 teaspoon fresh lemon juice
½ teaspoon cumin powder
Salt and ground black pepper, to taste
1 medium egg
⅓ cup beer
½ cup flou , divided
1 tablespoon curry powder
1 teaspoon baking powder
½ teaspoon grated fresh ginger
1 cup fla ed coconut

1. In a large bowl, toss the prawns with the lemon juice, cumin powder, salt, and pepper until well coated. Set aside.
2. In a shallow bowl, whisk together the egg, beer, ¼ cup of flou , curry powder, baking powder, and ginger until combined.
3. In a separate shallow bowl, put the remaining ¼ cup of flou , and on a plate, place the fla ed coconut.
4. Dip the prawns in the flou , then in the egg mixture, finally roll in the fl ed coconut to coat well. Transfer the prawns to a baking sheet.
5. Select Air Fry, set temperature to 350°F (180°C), and set time to 8 minutes. Select Start to begin preheating.
6. Once preheated, place the baking sheet into the air fryer.
7. After 5 minutes, remove from the air fryer and flip the p awns. Return to the air fryer and continue cooking for 3 minutes more.
8. When cooking is complete, remove from the air fryer and serve warm.

Chapter 4 Fish and Seafood |51

Air-Fried Pecan-Crusted Catfish

Prep time: 5 minutes | Cook time: 12 minutes | Serves 4

½ cup pecan meal
1 teaspoon fine sea salt
¼ teaspoon ground black pepper
4 (4-ounce / 113-g) catfish fille
Avocado oil spray

For Garnish (Optional):
Fresh oregano
Pecan halves

1. Spray the air fry basket with avocado oil spray.
2. Combine the pecan meal, sea salt, and black pepper in a large bowl. Dredge each catfish fillet in the meal mixture turning until well coated. Spritz the fillets with avocado oil spray, then transfer to the air fry basket.
3. Select Air Fry, set temperature to 375°F (190°C), and set time to 12 minutes. Select Start to begin preheating.
4. Once preheated, place the basket into the air fryer. Flip the fillets half ay through the cooking time.
5. When cooking is complete, the fish should be cooked through and no longer translucent. Remove from the air fryer and sprinkle the oregano sprigs and pecan halves on top for garnish, if desired. Serve immediately.

Aromatic Parmesan Fish Fillets

Prep time: 8 minutes | Cook time: 17 minutes | Serves 4

⅓ cup grated Parmesan cheese
½ teaspoon fennel seed
½ teaspoon tarragon
⅓ teaspoon mixed peppercorns
2 eggs, beaten
4 (4-ounce / 113-g) fish fillets, ha ed
2 tablespoons dry white wine
1 teaspoon seasoned salt

1. Place the grated Parmesan cheese, fennel seed, tarragon, and mixed peppercorns in a food processor and pulse for about 20 seconds until well combined. Transfer the cheese mixture to a shallow dish.
2. Place the beaten eggs in another shallow dish.
3. Drizzle the dry white wine over the top of fish fillets. Dredge each fillet in t beaten eggs on both sides, shaking off any excess, then roll them in the cheese mixture until fully coated. Season with the salt.
4. Arrange the fillets in the air fry bas et.
5. Select Air Fry, set temperature to 345°F (174°C), and set time to 17 minutes. Select Start to begin preheating.
6. Once preheated, place the basket into the air fryer. Flip the fillets once half ay through the cooking time.
7. When cooking is complete, the fish should be cooked through no longer translucent. Remove from the air fryer and cool for 5 minutes before serving.

Savory Roasted Shrimp

Prep time: 15 minutes | Cook time: 8 minutes | Serves 2

1 pound (454 g) shrimp, deveined
1½ tablespoons olive oil
1½ tablespoons balsamic vinegar
1 tablespoon coconut aminos
½ tablespoon fresh parsley, roughly chopped
Sea salt fla es, to taste
1 teaspoon Dijon mustard
½ teaspoon smoked cayenne pepper
½ teaspoon garlic powder
Salt and ground black peppercorns, to taste
1 cup shredded goat cheese

1. Except for the cheese, stir together all the ingredients in a large bowl until the shrimp are evenly coated.
2. Place the shrimp in the air fry basket.
3. Select Roast, set temperature to 385°F (196°C), and set time to 8 minutes. Select Start to begin preheating.
4. Once preheated, place the basket into the air fryer.
5. When cooking is complete, the shrimp should be pink and cooked through. Remove from the air fryer and serve with the shredded goat cheese sprinkled on top.

Cheesy Shrimp Salad with Caesar

Prep time: 10 minutes | Cook time: 15 minutes | Serves 4

½ baguette, cut into 1-inch cubes (about 2½ cups)
4 tablespoons extra-virgin olive oil, divided
¼ teaspoon granulated garlic
¼ teaspoon kosher salt
¾ cup Caesar dressing, divided
2 romaine lettuce hearts, cut in half lengthwise and ends trimmed
1 pound (454 g) medium shrimp, peeled and deveined
2 ounces (57 g) Parmesan cheese, coarsely grated

1. Make the croutons: Put the bread cubes in a medium bowl and drizzle 3 tablespoons of olive oil over top. Season with granulated garlic and salt and toss to coat. Transfer to the air fry basket in a single layer.
2. Select Air Fry, set temperature to 400°F (205°C), and set time to 4 minutes. Select Start to begin preheating.
3. Once the air fryer has preheated, place the basket into the air fryer. Toss the croutons halfway through the cooking time.
4. When done, remove the air fry basket from the air fryer and set aside.
5. Brush 2 tablespoons of Caesar dressing on the cut side of the lettuce. Set aside.
6. Toss the shrimp with the ¼ cup of Caesar dressing in a large bowl until well coated. Set aside.
7. Coat the sheet pan with the remaining 1 tablespoon of olive oil. Arrange the romaine halves on the coated pan, cut side down. Brush the tops with the remaining 2 tablespoons of Caesar dressing.
8. Select Roast, set temperature to 375°F (190°C), and set time to 10 minutes. Select Start to begin preheating.
9. Once the air fryer has preheated, place the pan into the air fryer.
10. After 5 minutes, remove the pan from the air fryer and flip the romaine hal es. Spoon the shrimp around the lettuce. Return the pan to the air fryer and continue cooking.
11. When done, remove the sheet pan from the air fryer. If they are not quite cooked through, roast for another 1 minute.
12. On each of four plates, put a romaine half. Divide the shrimp among the plates and top with croutons and grated Parmesan cheese. Serve immediately.

Parmesan-Crusted Hake with Garlic Sauce

Prep time: 5 minutes | Cook time: 10 minutes | Serves 3

Fish:
6 tablespoons mayonnaise
1 tablespoon fresh lime juice
1 teaspoon Dijon mustard
1 cup grated Parmesan cheese
Salt, to taste
¼ teaspoon ground black pepper, or more to taste
3 hake fillets, patted dry
Nonstick cooking spray

Garlic Sauce:
¼ cup plain Greek yogurt
2 tablespoons olive oil
2 cloves garlic, minced
½ teaspoon minced tarragon leaves

1. Mix the mayo, lime juice, and mustard in a shallow bowl and whisk to combine. In another shallow bowl, stir together the grated Parmesan cheese, salt, and pepper.
2. Dredge each fillet in the m yo mixture, then roll them in the cheese mixture until they are evenly coated on both sides.
3. Spray the air fry basket with nonstick cooking spray. Place the fillets in the basket.
4. Select Air Fry, set temperature to 395°F (202°C), and set time to 10 minutes. Select Start to begin preheating.
5. Once preheated, place the basket into the air fryer. Flip the fillets half ay through the cooking time.
6. Meanwhile, in a small bowl, whisk all the ingredients for the sauce until well incorporated.
7. When cooking is complete, the fish should fla e apart with a fork. Remove the fillets from the air fr er and serve warm alongside the sauce.

Aromatic Air-Fried Scallop

Prep time: 10 minutes | Cook time: 12 minutes | Serves 2

1/3 cup shallots, chopped
1½ tablespoons olive oil
1½ tablespoons coconut aminos
1 tablespoon Mediterranean seasoning mix
½ tablespoon balsamic vinegar
½ teaspoon ginger, grated
1 clove garlic, chopped
1 pound (454 g) scallops, cleaned
Cooking spray
Belgian endive, for garnish

1. Place all the ingredients except the scallops and Belgian endive in a small skillet over medium heat and stir to combine. Let this mixture simmer for about 2 minutes.
2. Remove the mixture from the skillet to a large bowl and set aside to cool.
3. Add the scallops, coating them all over, then transfer to the refrigerator to marinate for at least 2 hours.
4. When ready, place the scallops in the air fry basket in a single layer and spray with cooking spray.
5. Select Air Fry, set temperature to 345ºF (174ºC), and set time to 10 minutes. Select Start to begin preheating.
6. Once preheated, place the basket into the air fryer. Flip the scallops halfway through the cooking time.
7. When cooking is complete, the scallops should be tender and opaque. Remove from the air fryer and serve garnished with the Belgian endive.

Roasted Crab with Onion and Tomato

Prep time: 15 minutes | Cook time: 13 minutes | Serves 4

1½ cups peeled and cubed eggplant
2 large tomatoes, chopped
1 red bell pepper, chopped
1 onion, chopped
1 tablespoon olive oil
½ teaspoon dried basil
½ teaspoon dried thyme
Pinch salt
Freshly ground black pepper, to taste
1½ cups cooked crab meat

1. In a metal bowl, stir together the eggplant, tomatoes, bell pepper, onion, olive oil, basil and thyme. Season with salt and pepper.
2. Select Roast, set temperature to 400ºF (205ºC), and set time to 13 minutes. Select Start to begin preheating.
3. Once preheated, place the metal bowl into the air fryer in the air fryer.
4. After 9 minutes, remove the bowl from the air fryer. Add the crab meat and stir well and continue roasting for another 4 minutes, or until the vegetables are softened and the ratatouille is bubbling.
5. When cooking is complete, remove from the air fryer and serve warm.

Baked Flounder Fillets

Prep time: 8 minutes | Cook time: 12 minutes | Serves 2

2 flounder fillets patted dry
1 egg
½ teaspoon Worcestershire sauce
¼ cup almond flou
¼ cup coconut flou
½ teaspoon coarse sea salt
½ teaspoon lemon pepper
¼ teaspoon chili powder
Cooking spray

1. In a shallow bowl, beat together the egg with Worcestershire sauce until well incorporated.
2. In another bowl, thoroughly combine the almond flou , coconut flou , sea salt, lemon pepper, and chili powder.
3. Dredge the fillets in the egg mixture, shaking off any excess, then roll in the flour mixture to coat well
4. Spritz the air fry basket with cooking spray. Place the fillets in the pan
5. Select Bake, set temperature to 390ºF (199ºC), and set time to 12 minutes. Select Start to begin preheating.
6. Once preheated, place the basket into the air fryer.
7. After 7 minutes, remove from the air fryer and flip the fillets and s ay with cooking spray. Return the basket to the air fryer and continue cooking for 5 minutes, or until the fish is fla .
8. When cooking is complete, remove from the air fryer and serve warm.

Coconut Milky Fish Curry with Tomato

Prep time: 10 minutes | Cook time: 22 minutes | Serves 4

2 tablespoons sunflower oil, divide
1 pound (454 g) fish, chopped
1 ripe tomato, pureéd
2 red chilies, chopped
1 shallot, minced
1 garlic clove, minced
1 cup coconut milk
1 tablespoon coriander powder
1 teaspoon red curry paste
½ teaspoon fenugreek seeds
Salt and white pepper, to taste

1. Coat the air fry basket with 1 tablespoon of sunflower oil. Place the fish in the ai fry basket.
2. Select Air Fry, set temperature to 380ºF (193ºC), and set time to 10 minutes. Select Start to begin preheating.
3. Once preheated, place the basket into the air fryer. Flip the fish halfway through the cooking time.
4. When cooking is complete, transfer the cooked fish to a baking pan greased with the remaining 1 tablespoon of sunflower oil. Stir in the remaining ingredients.
5. Select Air Fry, set temperature to 350ºF (180ºC), and set time to 12 minutes. Select Start to begin preheating.
6. Once preheated, place the pan into the air fryer.
7. When cooking is complete, they should be heated through. Cool for 5 to 8 minutes before serving.

Breadcrumb-Crusted Catfish Nuggets

Prep time: 10 minutes | Cook time: 7 to 8 minutes | Serves 4

2 medium catfish fil ets, cut into chunks (approximately 1 × 2 inch)
Salt and pepper, to taste
2 eggs
2 tablespoons skim milk
½ cup cornstarch
1 cup panko bread crumbs
Cooking spray

1. In a medium bowl, season the fish chunks with salt and pepper to taste.
2. In a small bowl, beat together the eggs with milk until well combined.
3. Place the cornstarch and bread crumbs into separate shallow dishes.
4. Dredge the fish chunks one at a time in the cornstarch, coating well on both sides, then dip in the egg mixture, shaking off any excess, finally press well into the bread crumbs. Spritz the fish chunks with cooking spray.
5. Arrange the fish chunks in the air fry basket in a single layer.
6. Select Air Fry, set temperature to 390ºF (199ºC), and set time to 8 minutes. Select Start to begin preheating.
7. Once preheated, place the basket into the air fryer. Flip the fish chunks half ay through the cooking time.
8. When cooking is complete, they should be no longer translucent in the center and golden brown. Remove the fish chunks from the air fryer to a plate. Serve warm.

Aromatic Shrimp with Parsley

Prep time: 10 minutes | Cook time: 5 minutes | Serves 4

18 shrimp, shelled and deveined
2 garlic cloves, peeled and minced
2 tablespoons extra-virgin olive oil
2 tablespoons freshly squeezed lemon juice
½ cup fresh parsley, coarsely chopped
1 teaspoon onion powder
1 teaspoon lemon-pepper seasoning
½ teaspoon hot paprika
½ teaspoon salt
¼ teaspoon cumin powder

1. Toss all the ingredients in a mixing bowl until the shrimp are well coated.
2. Cover and allow to marinate in the refrigerator for 30 minutes.
3. When ready, transfer the shrimp to the air fry basket.
4. Select Air Fry, set temperature to 400ºF (205ºC), and set time to 5 minutes. Select Start to begin preheating.
5. Once preheated, place the basket into the air fryer.
6. When cooking is complete, the shrimp should be pink on the outside and opaque in the center. Remove from the air fryer and serve warm.

Air Fried Bacon-Wrapped Scallops

Prep time: 5 minutes | Cook time: 10 minutes | Serves 4

8 slices bacon, cut in half
16 sea scallops, patted dry
Cooking spray
Salt and freshly ground black pepper, to taste
16 toothpicks, soaked in water for at least 30 minutes

1. On a clean work surface, wrap half of a slice of bacon around each scallop and secure with a toothpick.
2. Lay the bacon-wrapped scallops in the air fry basket in a single layer.
3. Spritz the scallops with cooking spray and sprinkle the salt and pepper to season.
4. Select Air Fry, set temperature to 370°F (188°C), and set time to 10 minutes. Select Start to begin preheating.
5. Once preheated, place the basket into the air fryer. Flip the scallops halfway through the cooking time.
6. When cooking is complete, the bacon should be cooked through and the scallops should be firm. emove the scallops from the air fryer to a plate Serve warm.

Buttery Shrimp with Cherry Tomato

Prep time: 15 minutes | Cook time: 5 minutes | Serves 4

1½ pounds (680 g) jumbo shrimp, cleaned, shelled and deveined
1 pound (454 g) cherry tomatoes
2 tablespoons butter, melted
1 tablespoons Sriracha sauce
Sea salt and ground black pepper, to taste
1 teaspoon dried parsley fla es
½ teaspoon dried basil
½ teaspoon dried oregano
½ teaspoon mustard seeds
½ teaspoon marjoram

Special Equipment:
4 to 6 wooden skewers, soaked in water for 30 minutes

1. Put all the ingredients in a large bowl and toss to coat well.
2. Make the kebabs: Thread, alternating jumbo shrimp and cherry tomatoes, onto the wooden skewers. Place the kebabs in the air fry basket.
3. Select Air Fry, set temperature to 400°F (205°C), and set time to 5 minutes. Select Start to begin preheating.
4. Once preheated, place the basket into the air fryer.
5. When cooking is complete, the shrimp should be pink and the cherry tomatoes should be softened. Remove from the air fryer. Let the shrimp and cherry tomato kebabs cool for 5 minutes and serve hot.

Breaded Calamari Ring with Lemon

Prep time: 5 minutes | Cook time: 12 minutes | Serves 4

2 large eggs
2 garlic cloves, minced
½ cup cornstarch
1 cup bread crumbs
1 pound (454 g) calamari rings
Cooking spray
1 lemon, sliced

1. In a small bowl, whisk the eggs with minced garlic. Place the cornstarch and bread crumbs into separate shallow dishes.
2. Dredge the calamari rings in the cornstarch, then dip in the egg mixture, shaking off any excess, finally roll them in the bread crumbs to coat well. Let the calamari rings sit for 10 minutes in the refrigerator.
3. Spritz the air fry basket with cooking spray. Transfer the calamari rings to the basket.
4. Select Air Fry, set temperature to 390°F (199°C), and set time to 12 minutes. Select Start to begin preheating.
5. Once preheated, place the basket into the air fryer. Stir the calamari rings once halfway through the cooking time.
6. When cooking is complete, remove the basket from the air fryer. Serve the calamari rings with the lemon slices sprinkled on top.

Rice Shrimp Patties

Prep time: 15 minutes | Cook time: 12 minutes | Serves 4

½ pound (227 g) raw shrimp, shelled, deveined, and chopped finel
2 cups cooked sushi rice
¼ cup chopped red bell pepper
¼ cup chopped celery
¼ cup chopped green onion
2 teaspoons Worcestershire sauce
½ teaspoon salt
½ teaspoon garlic powder
½ teaspoon Old Bay seasoning
½ cup plain bread crumbs
Cooking spray

1. Put all the ingredients except the bread crumbs and oil in a large bowl and stir to incorporate.
2. Scoop out the shrimp mixture and shape into 8 equal-sized patties with your hands, no more than ½-inch thick. Roll the patties in the bread crumbs on a plate and spray both sides with cooking spray. Place the patties in the air fry basket.
3. Select Air Fry, set temperature to 390°F (199°C), and set time to 12 minutes. Select Start to begin preheating.
4. Once preheated, place the basket into the air fryer. Flip the patties halfway through the cooking time.
5. When cooking is complete, the outside should be crispy brown. Remove the basket from the air fryer. Divide the patties among four plates and serve warm.

Aromatic Air Fried Shrimp

Prep time: 10 minutes | Cook time: 8 minutes | Serves 4

1 pound (454 g) shrimp, deveined
4 tablespoons olive oil
1½ tablespoons lemon juice
1½ tablespoons fresh parsley, roughly chopped
2 cloves garlic, finely minced
1 teaspoon crushed red pepper fla es, or more to taste
Garlic pepper, to taste
Sea salt fla es, to taste

1. Toss all the ingredients in a large bowl until the shrimp are coated on all sides.
2. Arrange the shrimp in the air fry basket.
3. Select Air Fry, set temperature to 385°F (196°C), and set time to 8 minutes. Select Start to begin preheating.
4. Once preheated, place the basket into the air fryer.
5. When cooking is complete, the shrimp should be pink and cooked through. Remove from the air fryer and serve warm.

Panko Crab Sticks with Mayo Sauce

Prep time: 5 minutes | Cook time: 12 minutes | Serves 4

Crab Sticks:
2 eggs
1 cup flou
⅓ cup panko bread crumbs
1 tablespoon old bay seasoning
1 pound (454 g) crab sticks
Cooking spray

Mayo Sauce:
½ cup mayonnaise
1 lime, juiced
2 garlic cloves, minced

1. In a bowl, beat the eggs. In a shallow bowl, place the flou . In another shallow bowl, thoroughly combine the panko bread crumbs and old bay seasoning.
2. Dredge the crab sticks in the flou , shaking off any excess, then in the beaten eggs, finally press them in the bread crumb mixture to coat well.
3. Arrange the crab sticks in the air fry basket and spray with cooking spray.
4. Select Air Fry, set temperature to 390°F (199°C), and set time to 12 minutes. Select Start to begin preheating.
5. Once preheated, place the basket into the air fryer. Flip the crab sticks halfway through the cooking time.
6. Meanwhile, make the sauce by whisking together the mayo, lime juice, and garlic in a small bowl.
7. When cooking is complete, remove the basket from the air fryer. Serve the crab sticks with the mayo sauce on the side.

Tangy Shrimp

Prep time: 40 minutes | Cook time: 12 minutes | Serves 4

⅓ cup orange juice
3 teaspoons minced garlic
1 teaspoon Old Bay seasoning
¼ to ½ teaspoon cayenne pepper
1 pound (454 g) medium shrimp, thawed, deveined, peeled, with tails off, and patted dry
Cooking spray

1. Stir together the orange juice, garlic, Old Bay seasoning, and cayenne pepper in a medium bowl. Add the shrimp to the bowl and toss to coat well.
2. Cover the bowl with plastic wrap and marinate in the refrigerator for 30 minutes.
3. Spritz the air fry basket with cooking spray. Place the shrimp in the pan and spray with cooking spray.
4. Select Air Fry, set temperature to 400°F (205°C), and set time to 12 minutes. Select Start to begin preheating.
5. Once preheated, place the basket into the air fryer. Flip the shrimp halfway through the cooking time.
6. When cooked, the shrimp should be opaque and crisp. Remove from the air fryer and serve hot.

Shrimp Paella with Artichoke Heart

Prep time: 5 minutes | Cook time: 16 minutes | Serves 4

1 (10-ounce / 284-g) package frozen cooked rice, thawed
1 (6-ounce / 170-g) jar artichoke hearts, drained and chopped
¼ cup vegetable broth
½ teaspoon dried thyme
½ teaspoon turmeric
1 cup frozen cooked small shrimp
½ cup frozen baby peas
1 tomato, diced

1. Mix together the cooked rice, chopped artichoke hearts, vegetable broth, thyme, and turmeric in a baking pan and stir to combine.
2. Select Bake, set temperature to 340°F (171°C), and set time to 16 minutes. Select Start to begin preheating.
3. Once preheated, place the pan into the air fryer.
4. After 9 minutes, remove from the air fryer and add the shrimp, baby peas, and diced tomato to the baking pan. Mix well. Return the pan to the air fryer and continue cooking for 7 minutes more, or until the shrimp are done and the paella is bubbling.
5. When cooking is complete, remove the pan from the air fryer. Cool for 5 minutes before serving.

Buttery Scampi

Prep time: 5 minutes | Cook time: 8 minutes | Serves 4

Sauce:
¼ cup unsalted butter
2 tablespoons fish stock or chicken broth
2 cloves garlic, minced
2 tablespoons chopped fresh basil leaves
1 tablespoon lemon juice
1 tablespoon chopped fresh parsley, plus more for garnish
1 teaspoon red pepper fla es

Shrimp:
1 pound (454 g) large shrimp, peeled and deveined, tails removed
Fresh basil sprigs, for garnish

1. Put all the ingredients for the sauce in a baking pan and stir to incorporate.
2. Select Air Fry, set temperature to 350°F (180°C), and set time to 8 minutes. Select Start to begin preheating.
3. Once preheated, place the baking pan into the air fryer.
4. After 3 minutes, remove from the air fryer and add the shrimp to the baking pan, flipping to coat in the sauce. eturn the pan to the air fryer and continue cooking for 5 minutes until the shrimp are pink and opaque. Stir the shrimp twice during cooking.
5. When cooking is complete, remove the pan from the air fryer. Serve garnished with the parsley and basil sprigs.

Savory King Prawn

Prep time: 10 minutes | Cook time: 8 minutes | Serves 2

12 king prawns, rinsed
1 tablespoon coconut oil
Salt and ground black pepper, to taste
1 teaspoon onion powder
1 teaspoon garlic paste
1 teaspoon curry powder
½ teaspoon piri piri powder
½ teaspoon cumin powder

1. Combine all the ingredients in a large bowl and toss until the prawns are completely coated. Place the prawns in the air fry basket.
2. Select Air Fry, set temperature to 360°F (182°C), and set time to 8 minutes. Select Start to begin preheating.
3. Once preheated, place the basket into the air fryer. Flip the prawns halfway through the cooking time.
4. When cooking is complete, the prawns will turn pink. Remove from the air fryer and serve hot.

Fired Shrimp with Mayonnaise Sauce

Prep time: 5 minutes | Cook time: 7 minutes | Serves 4

Shrimp
12 jumbo shrimp
½ teaspoon garlic salt
¼ teaspoon freshly cracked mixed peppercorns

Sauce:
4 tablespoons mayonnaise
1 teaspoon grated lemon rind
1 teaspoon Dijon mustard
1 teaspoon chipotle powder
½ teaspoon cumin powder

1. In a medium bowl, season the shrimp with garlic salt and cracked mixed peppercorns.
2. Place the shrimp in the air fry basket.
3. Select Air Fry, set temperature to 395°F (202°C), and set time to 7 minutes. Select Start to begin preheating.
4. Once preheated, place the basket into the air fryer.
5. After 5 minutes, remove from the air fryer and flip the shrim . Return the basket to the air fryer and continue cooking for 2 minutes more, or until they are pink and no longer opaque.
6. Meanwhile, stir together all the ingredients for the sauce in a small bowl until well mixed.
7. When cooking is complete, remove the shrimp from the air fryer and serve alongside the sauce.

Crispy Crab Cakes with Bell Peppers

Prep time: 5 minutes | Cook time: 10 minutes | Serves 4

8 ounces (227 g) jumbo lump crab meat
1 egg, beaten
Juice of ½ lemon
⅓ cup bread crumbs
¼ cup diced green bell pepper
¼ cup diced red bell pepper
¼ cup mayonnaise
1 tablespoon Old Bay seasoning
1 teaspoon flou
Cooking spray

1. Make the crab cakes: Place all the ingredients except the flour and oil in a large bowl and stir until well incorporated.
2. Divide the crab mixture into four equal portions and shape each portion into a patty with your hands. Top each patty with a sprinkle of ¼ teaspoon of flou .
3. Arrange the crab cakes in the air fry basket and spritz them with cooking spray.
4. Select Air Fry, set temperature to 375°F (190°C), and set time to 10 minutes. Select Start to begin preheating.
5. Once preheated, place the basket into the air fryer. Flip the crab cakes halfway through.
6. When cooking is complete, the cakes should be cooked through. Remove the basket from the air fryer. Divide the crab cakes among four plates and serve.

Chapter 4 Fish and Seafood |59

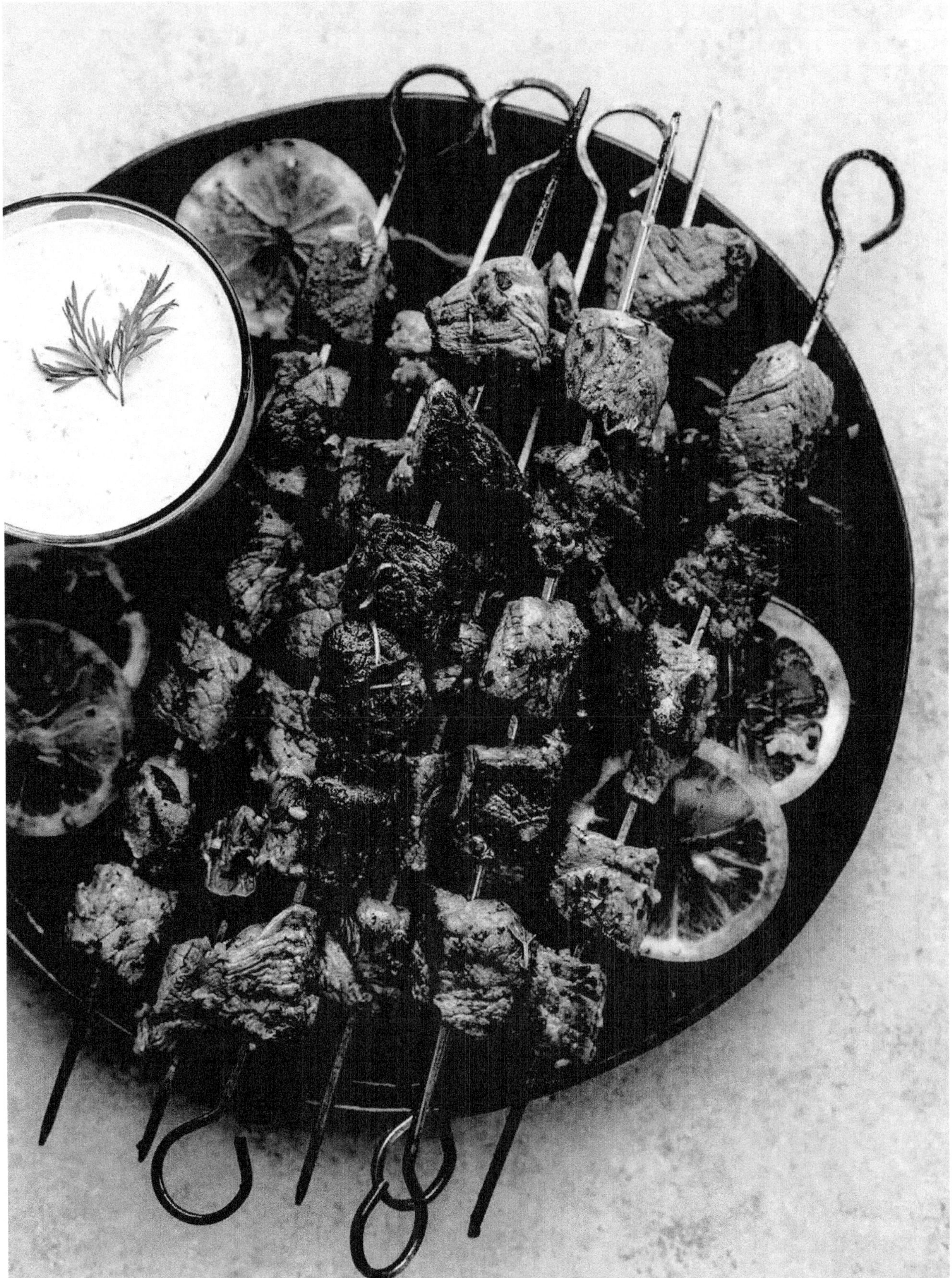

CHAPTER 5 *Red Meats*

Meat and Rice Stuffed Bell Peppers

Prep time: 20 minutes | Cook time: 18 minutes | Serves 4

¾ pound (340 g) lean ground beef
4 ounces (113 g) lean ground pork
¼ cup onion, minced
1 (15-ounce / 425-g) can crushed tomatoes
1 teaspoon Worcestershire sauce
1 teaspoon barbecue seasoning
1 teaspoon honey
½ teaspoon dried basil
½ cup cooked brown rice
½ teaspoon garlic powder
½ teaspoon oregano
½ teaspoon salt
2 small bell peppers, cut in half, stems removed, deseeded
Cooking spray

1. Spritz a baking pan with cooking spray.
2. Arrange the beef, pork, and onion in the baking pan.
3. Select Bake, set temperature to 360ºF (182ºC) and set time to 8 minutes. Press Start to begin preheating.
4. Once preheated, place the pan into the air fryer. Break the ground meat into chunks halfway through the cooking.
5. When cooking is complete, the ground meat should be lightly browned.
6. Meanwhile, combine the tomatoes, Worcestershire sauce, barbecue seasoning, honey, and basil in a saucepan. Stir to mix well.
7. Transfer the cooked meat mixture to a large bowl and add the cooked rice, garlic powder, oregano, salt, and ¼ cup of the tomato mixture. Stir to mix well.
8. Stuff the pepper halves with the mixture, then arrange the pepper halves in the air fry basket.
9. Select Air Fry. Set time to 10 minutes. Place the basket into the air fryer.
10. When cooking is complete, the peppers should be lightly charred.
11. Serve the stuffed peppers with the remaining tomato sauce on top.

Baked Apple-Glazed Pork

Prep time: 15 minutes | Cook time: 19 minutes | Serves 4

1 sliced apple
1 small onion, sliced
2 tablespoons apple cider vinegar, divided
½ teaspoon thyme
½ teaspoon rosemary
¼ teaspoon brown sugar
3 tablespoons olive oil, divided
¼ teaspoon smoked paprika
4 pork chops
Salt and ground black pepper, to taste

1. Combine the apple slices, onion, 1 tablespoon of vinegar, thyme, rosemary, brown sugar, and 2 tablespoons of olive oil in a baking pan. Stir to mix well.
2. Select Bake, set temperature to 350ºF (180ºC) and set time to 4 minutes. Press Start to begin preheating.
3. Once preheated, place the pan into the air fryer. Stir the mixture halfway through.
4. Meanwhile, combine the remaining vinegar and olive oil, and paprika in a large bowl. Sprinkle with salt and ground black pepper. Stir to mix well. Dredge the pork in the mixture and toss to coat well. Place the pork in the air fry basket.
5. When cooking is complete, remove the baking pan from the air fryer and place in the air fry basket.
6. Select Air Fry and set time to 10 minutes. Place the basket into the air fryer. Flip the pork chops halfway through.
7. When cooking is complete, the pork should be lightly browned.
8. Remove the pork from the air fryer and baste with baked apple mixture on both sides. Put the pork back to the air fryer and air fry for an additional 5 minutes. Flip halfway through.
9. Serve immediately.

Cheesy Beef Rolls

Prep time: 15 minutes | Cook time: 10 minutes | Makes 10 rolls

½ pound (227 g) cooked corned beef, chopped
½ cup drained and chopped sauerkraut
1 (8-ounce / 227-g) package cream cheese, softened
½ cup shredded Swiss cheese
20 slices prosciutto
Cooking spray

Thousand Island Sauce:
¼ cup chopped dill pickles
¼ cup tomato sauce
¾ cup mayonnaise
Fresh thyme leaves, for garnish
2 tablespoons sugar
⅛ teaspoon fine sea salt
Ground black pepper, to taste

1. Spritz the air fry basket with cooking spray.
2. Combine the beef, sauerkraut, cream cheese, and Swiss cheese in a large bowl. Stir to mix well.
3. Unroll a slice of prosciutto on a clean work surface, then top with another slice of prosciutto crosswise. Scoop up 4 tablespoons of the beef mixture in the center.
4. Fold the top slice sides over the filling as the ends of the roll, then roll up the long sides of the bottom prosciutto and make it into a roll shape. Overlap the sides by about 1 inch. Repeat with remaining filling and prosciutt .
5. Arrange the rolls in the prepared basket, seam side down, and spritz with cooking spray.
6. Select Air Fry. Set temperature to 400°F (205°C) and set time to 10 minutes. Press Start to begin preheating.
7. Once preheated, place the basket into the air fryer. Flip the rolls halfway through.
8. When cooking is complete, the rolls should be golden and crispy.
9. Meanwhile, combine the ingredients for the sauce in a small bowl. Stir to mix well.
10. Serve the rolls with the dipping sauce.

Savory Lamb Loin Chops

Prep time: 10 minutes | Cook time: 13 minutes | Serves 4

For the Lamb:
4 lamb loin chops
2 tablespoons vegetable oil
1 clove garlic, minced
½ teaspoon kosher salt
½ teaspoon black pepper

For the Horseradish Cream Sauce:
1 to 1½ tablespoons prepared horseradish
1 tablespoon Dijon mustard
½ cup mayonnaise
2 teaspoons sugar
Cooking spray

1. Spritz the air fry basket with cooking spray.
2. Place the lamb chops on a plate. Rub with the oil and sprinkle with the garlic, salt and black pepper. Let sit to marinate for 30 minutes at room temperature.
3. Make the horseradish cream sauce: Mix the horseradish, mustard, mayonnaise, and sugar in a bowl until well combined. Set half of the sauce aside until ready to serve.
4. Arrange the marinated chops in the air fry basket.
5. Select Air Fry. Set temperature to 325°F (163°C) and set time to 10 minutes. Press Start to begin preheating.
6. Once preheated, place the basket into the air fryer. Flip the lamb chops halfway through.
7. When cooking is complete, the lamb should be lightly browned.
8. Transfer the chops from the air fryer to the bowl of the horseradish sauce. Roll to coat well.
9. Put the coated chops back in the air fry basket into the air fryer. Select Air Fry. Set the temperature to 400°F (205°C) and the time to 3 minutes.
10. When cooking is complete, the internal temperature should reach 145°F (63°C) on a meat thermometer (for medium-rare). Flip the lamb halfway through.
11. Serve hot with the horseradish cream sauce.

Beef Meatballs with Marinara Sauce

Prep time: 5 minutes | Cook time: 8 minutes | Serves 4

1 pound (454 g) lean ground sirloin beef
2 tablespoons seasoned bread crumbs
¼ teaspoon kosher salt
1 large egg, beaten
1 cup marinara sauce, for serving
Cooking spray

1. Spritz the air fry basket with cooking spray.
2. Mix all the ingredients, except for the marinara sauce, into a bowl until well blended. Shape the mixture into sixteen meatballs.
3. Arrange the meatballs in the prepared basket and mist with cooking spray.
4. Select Air Fry. Set temperature to 360°F (182°C) and set time to 8 minutes. Press Start to begin preheating.
5. Once preheated, place the basket into the air fryer. Flip the meatballs halfway through.
6. When cooking is complete, the meatballs should be well browned.
7. Divide the meatballs among four plates and serve warm with the marinara sauce.

Bacon-Wrapped Filets Mignons

Prep time: 10 minutes | Cook time: 13 minutes | Serves 8

1 ounce (28 g) dried porcini mushrooms
½ teaspoon granulated white sugar
½ teaspoon salt
½ teaspoon ground white pepper
8 (4-ounce / 113-g) filets mignons or beef tenderloin steaks
8 thin-cut bacon strips

1. Put the mushrooms, sugar, salt, and white pepper in a spice grinder and grind to combine.
2. On a clean work surface, rub the filets mignons with the mushroom mixture, then wrap each filet with a bacon strip. Secure with toothpicks if necessary.
3. Arrange the bacon-wrapped filets mignons in the air fry basket, seam side down.
4. Select Air Fry. Set temperature to 400°F (205°C) and set time to 13 minutes. Press Start to begin preheating.
5. Once preheated, place the basket into the air fryer. Flip the filets half ay through.
6. When cooking is complete, the filets should be medium rare.
7. Serve immediately.

Air Fried Beef Satay

Prep time: 30 minutes | Cook time: 5 minutes | Serves 4

8 ounces (227 g) London broil, sliced into 8 strips
2 teaspoons curry powder
½ teaspoon kosher salt
Cooking spray

Peanut Dipping sauce:
2 tablespoons creamy peanut butter
1 tablespoon reduced-sodium soy sauce
2 teaspoons rice vinegar
1 teaspoon honey
1 teaspoon grated ginger

Special Equipment:
4 bamboo skewers, cut into halves and soaked in water for 20 minutes to keep them from burning while cooking

1. Spritz the air fry basket with cooking spray.
2. In a bowl, place the London broil strips and sprinkle with the curry powder and kosher salt to season. Thread the strips onto the soaked skewers.
3. Arrange the skewers in the prepared basket and spritz with cooking spray.
4. Select Air Fry. Set temperature to 360°F (182°C) and set time to 5 minutes. Press Start to begin preheating.
5. Once preheated, place the basket into the air fryer. Flip the beef halfway through the cooking time.
6. When cooking is complete, the beef should be well browned.
7. In the meantime, stir together the peanut butter, soy sauce, rice vinegar, honey, and ginger in a bowl to make the dipping sauce.
8. Transfer the beef to the serving dishes and let rest for 5 minutes. Serve with the peanut dipping sauce on the side.

Air Fried Carne Asada

Prep time: 5 minutes | Cook time: 15 minutes | Serves 4

3 chipotle peppers in adobo, chopped
1/3 cup chopped fresh oregano
1/3 cup chopped fresh parsley
4 cloves garlic, minced
Juice of 2 limes
1 teaspoon ground cumin seeds
1/3 cup olive oil
1 to 1½ pounds (454 g to 680 g) flank steak
Salt, to taste

1. Combine the chipotle, oregano, parsley, garlic, lime juice, cumin, and olive oil in a large bowl. Stir to mix well.
2. Dunk the flank steak in the mixture and press to coat well. Wrap the bowl in plastic and marinate under room temperature for at least 30 minutes.
3. Discard the marinade and place the steak in the air fry basket. Sprinkle with salt.
4. Select Air Fry. Set temperature to 390ºF (199ºC) and set time to 15 minutes. Press Start to begin preheating.
5. Once preheated, place the basket into the air fryer. Flip the steak halfway through the cooking time.
6. When cooking is complete, the steak should be medium-rare or reach your desired doneness.
7. Remove the steak from the air fryer and slice to serve.

Buttery New York Strip

Prep time: 5 minutes | Cook time: 14 minutes | Serves 4

2 pounds (907 g) New York Strip
1 teaspoon cayenne pepper
1 tablespoon honey
1 tablespoon Dijon mustard
½ stick butter, softened
Sea salt and freshly ground black pepper, to taste
Cooking spray

1. Spritz the air fry basket with cooking spray.
2. Sprinkle the New York Strip with cayenne pepper, salt, and black pepper on a clean work surface.
3. Arrange the New York Strip in the prepared basket and spritz with cooking spray.
4. Select Air Fry. Set temperature to 400ºF (205ºC) and set time to 14 minutes. Press Start to begin preheating.
5. Once preheated, place the basket into the air fryer. Flip the New York Strip halfway through.
6. When cooking is complete, the strips should be browned.
7. Meanwhile, combine the honey, mustard, and butter in a small bowl. Stir to mix well.
8. Transfer the air fried New York Strip onto a plate and baste with the honey-mustard butter before serving.

Air Fried Venison

Prep time: 10 minutes | Cook time: 10 minutes | Serves 4

2 eggs
¼ cup milk
1 cup whole wheat flou
½ teaspoon salt
¼ teaspoon ground
black pepper
1 pound (454 g) venison backstrap, sliced
Cooking spray

1. Spritz the air fry basket with cooking spray.
2. Whisk the eggs with milk in a large bowl. Combine the flour with salt and ground black pepper in a shallow dish.
3. Dredge the venison in the flour first, the into the egg mixture. Shake the excess off and roll the venison back over the flour to coat well
4. Arrange the venison in the pan and spritz with cooking spray.
5. Select Air Fry. Set temperature to 360ºF (182ºC) and set time to 10 minutes. Press Start to begin preheating.
6. Once preheated, place the basket into the air fryer. Flip the venison halfway through.
7. When cooking is complete, the internal temperature of the venison should reach at least 145ºF (63ºC) for medium rare.
8. Serve immediately.

Homemade Salsa Beef Meatballs

Prep time: 10 minutes | Cook time: 10 minutes | Serves 4

1 pound (454 g) ground beef (85% lean)
½ cup salsa
¼ cup diced green or red bell peppers
1 large egg, beaten
¼ cup chopped onions
½ teaspoon chili powder
1 clove garlic, minced
½ teaspoon ground cumin
1 teaspoon fine sea salt
Lime wedges, for serving
Cooking spray

1. Spritz the air fry basket with cooking spray.
2. Combine all the ingredients in a large bowl. Stir to mix well.
3. Divide and shape the mixture into 1-inch balls. Arrange the balls in the basket and spritz with cooking spray.
4. Select Air Fry. Set temperature to 350ºF (180ºC) and set time to 10 minutes. Press Start to begin preheating.
5. Once preheated, place the basket into the air fryer. Flip the balls with tongs halfway through.
6. When cooking is complete, the balls should be well browned.
7. Transfer the balls on a plate and squeeze the lime wedges over before serving.

Panko Crusted Calf's Liver Strips

Prep time: 15 minutes | Cook time: 5 minutes | Serves 4

1 pound (454 g) sliced calf's liver, cut into ½-inch wide strips
2 eggs
2 tablespoons milk
½ cup whole wheat flou
2 cups panko bread crumbs
Salt and ground black pepper, to taste
Cooking spray

1. Spritz the air fry basket with cooking spray.
2. Rub the calf's liver strips with salt and ground black pepper on a clean work surface.
3. Whisk the eggs with milk in a large bowl. Pour the flour in a shallow dish. our the panko on a separate shallow dish.
4. Dunk the liver strips in the flou , then in the egg mixture. Shake the excess off and roll the strips over the panko to coat well.
5. Arrange the liver strips in the basket and spritz with cooking spray.
6. Select Air Fry. Set temperature to 390ºF (199ºC) and set time to 5 minutes. Press Start to begin preheating.
7. Once preheated, place the basket into the air fryer. Flip the strips halfway through.
8. When cooking is complete, the strips should be browned.
9. Serve immediately.

Air Fried Lamb Kofta

Prep time: 25 minutes | Cook time: 10 minutes | Serves 4

1 pound (454 g) ground lamb
1 tablespoon ras el hanout (North African spice)
½ teaspoon ground coriander
1 teaspoon onion powder
1 teaspoon garlic powder
1 teaspoon cumin
2 tablespoons mint, chopped
Salt and ground black pepper, to taste

Special Equipment:
4 bamboo skewers

1. Combine the ground lamb, ras el hanout, coriander, onion powder, garlic powder, cumin, mint, salt, and ground black pepper in a large bowl. Stir to mix well.
2. Transfer the mixture into sausage molds and sit the bamboo skewers in the mixture. Refrigerate for 15 minutes.
3. Spritz the air fry basket with cooking spray. Place the lamb skewers in the pan and spritz with cooking spray.
4. Select Air Fry. Set temperature to 380ºF (193ºC) and set time to 10 minutes. Press Start to begin preheating.
5. Once preheated, place the basket into the air fryer. Flip the lamb skewers halfway through.
6. When cooking is complete, the lamb should be well browned.
7. Serve immediately.

Chapter 5 Red Meats

Easy Thai Curry Beef Meatballs

Prep time: 5 minutes | Cook time: 15 minutes | Serves 4

1 pound (454 g) ground beef
1 tablespoon sesame oil
2 teaspoons chopped lemongrass
1 teaspoon red Thai curry paste
1 teaspoon Thai seasoning blend
Juice and zest of ½ lime
Cooking spray

1. Spritz the air fry basket with cooking spray.
2. In a medium bowl, combine all the ingredients until well blended.
3. Shape the meat mixture into 24 meatballs and arrange them in the basket.
4. Select Air Fry. Set temperature to 380ºF (193ºC) and set time to 15 minutes. Press Start to begin preheating.
5. Once preheated, place the basket into the air fryer. Flip the meatballs halfway through.
6. When cooking is complete, the meatballs should be browned.
7. Transfer the meatballs to plates. Let cool for 5 minutes before serving.

Baked Beef and Tomato Sauce Meatloaf

Prep time: 15 minutes | Cook time: 25 minutes | Serves 4

1½ pounds (680 g) ground beef
1 cup tomato sauce
½ cup bread crumbs
2 egg whites
½ cup grated Parmesan cheese
1 diced onion
2 tablespoons chopped parsley
2 tablespoons minced ginger
2 garlic cloves, minced
½ teaspoon dried basil
1 teaspoon cayenne pepper
Salt and ground black pepper, to taste
Cooking spray

1. Spritz a meatloaf pan with cooking spray.
2. Combine all the ingredients in a large bowl. Stir to mix well.
3. Pour the meat mixture in the prepared meatloaf pan and press with a spatula to make it firm
4. Select Bake, set temperature to 360ºF (182ºC) and set time to 25 minutes. Press Start to begin preheating.
5. Once preheated, place the pan into the air fryer.
6. When cooking is complete, the beef should be well browned.
7. Serve immediately.

Air Fried Lahmacun (Turkish Pizza)

Prep time: 20 minutes | Cook time: 10 minutes | Serves 4

4 (6-inch) flour tortilla

For the Meat Topping:
4 ounces (113 g) ground lamb or 85% lean ground beef
¼ cup finely chopped green bell pepper
¼ cup chopped fresh parsley
1 small plum tomato, deseeded and chopped
2 tablespoons chopped yellow onion
1 garlic clove, minced
2 teaspoons tomato paste
¼ teaspoon sweet paprika
¼ teaspoon ground cumin
⅛ to ¼ teaspoon red pepper fla es
⅛ teaspoon ground allspice
⅛ teaspoon kosher salt
⅛ teaspoon black pepper

For Serving:
¼ cup chopped fresh mint
1 teaspoon extra-virgin olive oil
1 lemon, cut into wedges

1. Combine all the ingredients for the meat topping in a medium bowl until well mixed.
2. Lay the tortillas on a clean work surface. Spoon the meat mixture on the tortillas and spread all over.
3. Place the tortillas in the air fry basket.
4. Select Air Fry. Set temperature to 400ºF (205ºC) and set time to 10 minutes. Press Start to begin preheating.
5. Once preheated, place the basket into the air fryer.
6. When cooking is complete, the edge of the tortilla should be golden and the meat should be lightly browned.
7. Transfer them to a serving dish. Top with chopped fresh mint and drizzle with olive oil. Squeeze the lemon wedges on top and serve.

Baked Beef Steak

Prep time: 15 minutes | Cook time: 14 minutes | Serves 4

1 pound (454 g) beef steak, thinly sliced	2 cups beef broth
8 ounces (227 g) mushrooms, sliced	1 cup sour cream
	4 tablespoons butter, melted
1 whole onion, chopped	2 cups cooked egg noodles

1. Combine the mushrooms, onion, beef broth, sour cream and butter in a bowl until well blended. Add the beef steak to another bowl.
2. Spread the mushroom mixture over the steak and let marinate for 10 minutes.
3. Pour the marinated steak in a baking pan.
4. Select Bake, set temperature to 400°F (205°C) and set time to 14 minutes. Press Start to begin preheating.
5. Once preheated, place the pan into the air fryer. Flip the steak halfway through the cooking time.
6. When cooking is complete, the steak should be browned and the vegetables should be tender.
7. Serve hot with the cooked egg noodles.

Rump Steak with Broccoli

Prep time: 5 minutes | Cook time: 13 minutes | Serves 4

½ pound (227 g) rump steak	into floret
⅓ cup teriyaki marinade	2 red capsicums, sliced
1½ teaspoons sesame oil	Fine sea salt and ground black pepper, to taste
½ head broccoli, cut	Cooking spray

1. Toss the rump steak in a large bowl with teriyaki marinade. Wrap the bowl in plastic and refrigerate to marinate for at least an hour.
2. Spritz the air fry basket with cooking spray.
3. Discard the marinade and transfer the steak in the pan. Spritz with cooking spray.
4. Select Air Fry. Set temperature to 400°F (205°C) and set time to 13 minutes. Press Start to begin preheating.
5. Once preheated, place the basket into the air fryer. Flip the steak halfway through.
6. When cooking is complete, the steak should be well browned.
7. Meanwhile, heat the sesame oil in a nonstick skillet over medium heat. Add the broccoli and capsicum. Sprinkle with salt and ground black pepper. Sauté for 5 minutes or until the broccoli is tender.
8. Transfer the air fried rump steak on a plate and top with the sautéed broccoli and capsicum. Serve hot.

Air Fried Veal Loin

Prep time: 1 hour 10 minutes | Cook time: 12 minutes | Makes 3 veal chops

1½ teaspoons crushed fennel seeds	1½ teaspoons salt
1 tablespoon minced fresh rosemary leaves	½ teaspoon red pepper fla es
	2 tablespoons olive oil
1 tablespoon minced garlic	3 (10-ounce / 284-g) bone-in veal loin, about ½ inch thick
1½ teaspoons lemon zest	

1. Combine all the ingredients, except for the veal loin, in a large bowl. Stir to mix well.
2. Dunk the loin in the mixture and press to submerge. Wrap the bowl in plastic and refrigerate for at least an hour to marinate.
3. Arrange the veal loin in the air fry basket.
4. Select Air Fry. Set temperature to 400°F (205°C) and set time to 12 minutes. Press Start to begin preheating.
5. Once preheated, place the basket into the air fryer. Flip the veal halfway through.
6. When cooking is complete, the internal temperature of the veal should reach at least 145°F (63°C) for medium rare.
7. Serve immediately.

Air Fried Steak and Spinach Rolls

Prep time: 50 minutes | Cook time: 9 minutes | Serves 4

2 teaspoons dried Italian seasoning
2 cloves garlic, minced
1 tablespoon vegetable oil
1 teaspoon kosher salt
1 teaspoon ground black pepper
1 pound (454 g) flank steak, ¼ to ½ inch thick
1 (10-ounce / 284-g) package frozen spinach, thawed and squeezed dry
½ cup diced jarred roasted red pepper
1 cup shredded Mozzarella cheese
Cooking spray

1. Combine the Italian seasoning, garlic, vegetable oil, salt, and ground black pepper in a large bowl. Stir to mix well.
2. Dunk the steak in the seasoning mixture and toss to coat well. Wrap the bowl in plastic and marinate under room temperature for at least 30 minutes.
3. Spritz the air fry basket with cooking spray.
4. Remove the marinated steak from the bowl and unfold on a clean work surface, then spread the top of the steak with a layer of spinach, a layer of red pepper and a layer of cheese. Leave a ¼-inch edge uncovered.
5. Roll the steak up to wrap the filling, then secure with 3 toothpicks. Cut the roll in half and transfer the rolls in the prepared basket, seam side down.
6. Select Air Fry. Set temperature to 400°F (205°C) and set time to 9 minutes. Press Start to begin preheating.
7. Once preheated, place the basket into the air fryer. Flip the rolls halfway through the cooking.
8. When cooking is complete, the steak should be lightly browned and the internal temperature reaches at least 145°F (63°C).
9. Remove the rolls from the air fryer and slice to serve.

Savory Steak with Mushroom Gravy

Prep time: 20 minutes | Cook time: 33 minutes | Serves 2

For the Mushroom Gravy:
¾ cup sliced button mushrooms
¼ cup thinly sliced onions
¼ cup unsalted butter, melted
½ teaspoon fine sea salt
¼ cup beef broth

For the Steaks:
½ pound (227 g) ground beef (85% lean)
1 tablespoon dry mustard
2 tablespoons tomato paste
¼ teaspoon garlic powder
½ teaspoon onion powder
½ teaspoon fine sea salt
¼ teaspoon ground black pepper
Chopped fresh thyme leaves, for garnish

1. Toss the mushrooms and onions with butter in a baking pan to coat well, then sprinkle with salt.
2. Select Bake, set temperature to 390°F (199°C) and set time to 8 minutes. Press Start to begin preheating.
3. Once preheated, place the pan into the air fryer. Stir the mixture halfway through the cooking.
4. When cooking is complete, the mushrooms should be tender.
5. Pour the broth in the baking pan and set time to 10 more minutes to make the gravy.
6. Meanwhile, combine all the ingredients for the steaks, except for the thyme leaves, in a large bowl. Stir to mix well. Shape the mixture into two oval steaks.
7. Arrange the steaks over the gravy and set time to 15 minutes. When cooking is complete, the patties should be browned. Flip the steaks halfway through.
8. Transfer the steaks onto a plate and pour the gravy over. Sprinkle with fresh thyme and serve immediately.

Aromatic Steaks with Cucumber and Snap Pea Salad

Prep time: 15 minutes | Cook time: 15 minutes | Serves 4

1 (1½-pound / 680-g) boneless top sirloin steak, trimmed and halved crosswise
1½ teaspoons chili powder
1½ teaspoons ground cumin
¾ teaspoon ground coriander
⅛ teaspoon cayenne pepper
⅛ teaspoon ground cinnamon
1¼ teaspoons plus ⅛ teaspoon salt, divided
½ teaspoon plus ⅛ teaspoon ground black pepper, divided
1 teaspoon plus 1½ tablespoons extra-virgin olive oil, divided
3 tablespoons mayonnaise
1½ tablespoons white wine vinegar
1 tablespoon minced fresh dill
1 small garlic clove, minced
8 ounces (227 g) sugar snap peas, strings removed and cut in half on bias
½ English cucumber, halved lengthwise and sliced thin
2 radishes, trimmed, halved and sliced thin
2 cups baby arugula

1. In a bowl, mix chili powder, cumin, coriander, cayenne pepper, cinnamon, 1¼ teaspoons salt and ½ teaspoon pepper until well combined.
2. Add the steaks to another bowl and pat dry with paper towels. Brush with 1 teaspoon oil and transfer to the bowl of spice mixture. Roll over to coat thoroughly.
3. Arrange the coated steaks in the air fry basket, spaced evenly apart.
4. Select Air Fry. Set temperature to 400ºF (205ºC) and set time to 15 minutes. Press Start to begin preheating.
5. Once preheated, place the basket into the air fryer. Flip the steak halfway through to ensure even cooking.
6. When cooking is complete, an instant-read thermometer inserted in the thickest part of the meat should register at least 145ºF (63ºC).
7. Transfer the steaks to a clean work surface and wrap with aluminum foil. Let stand while preparing salad.
8. Make the salad: In a large bowl, stir together 1½ tablespoons olive oil, mayonnaise, vinegar, dill, garlic, ⅛ teaspoon salt, and ⅛ teaspoon pepper. Add snap peas, cucumber, radishes and arugula. Toss to blend well.
9. Slice the steaks and serve with the salad.

Cheesy Stuffed Beef Tenderloin

Prep time: 10 minutes | Cook time: 10 minutes | Serves 4

1½ pounds (680 g) beef tenderloin, pounded to ¼ inch thick
3 teaspoons sea salt
1 teaspoon ground black pepper
2 ounces (57 g) creamy goat cheese
½ cup crumbled feta cheese
¼ cup finely chopped onions
2 cloves garlic, minced
Cooking spray

1. Spritz the air fry basket with cooking spray.
2. Unfold the beef tenderloin on a clean work surface. Rub the salt and pepper all over the beef tenderloin to season.
3. Make the filling for the stuffed beef tenderloins: Combine the goat cheese, feta, onions, and garlic in a medium bowl. Stir until well blended.
4. Spoon the mixture in the center of the tenderloin. Roll the tenderloin up tightly like rolling a burrito and use some kitchen twine to tie the tenderloin.
5. Arrange the tenderloin in the air fry basket.
6. Select Air Fry. Set temperature to 400ºF (205ºC) and set time to 10 minutes. Press Start to begin preheating.
7. Once preheated, place the basket into the air fryer. Flip the tenderloin halfway through.
8. When cooking is complete, the instant-read thermometer inserted in the center of the tenderloin should register 135ºF (57ºC) for medium-rare.
9. Transfer to a platter and serve immediately.

Crusted Beef Steaks

Prep time: 5 minutes | Cook time: 10 minutes | Serves 4

4 beef steaks
2 teaspoons caraway seeds
2 teaspoons garlic powder
Sea salt and cayenne pepper, to taste
1 tablespoon melted butter
⅓ cup almond flou
2 eggs, beaten

1. Add the beef steaks to a large bowl and toss with the caraway seeds, garlic powder, salt and pepper until well coated.
2. Stir together the melted butter and almond flour in a bowl. Whisk the eggs in a different bowl.
3. Dredge the seasoned steaks in the eggs, then dip in the almond and butter mixture.
4. Arrange the coated steaks in the air fry basket.
5. Select Air Fry. Set temperature to 355°F (179°C) and set time to 10 minutes. Press Start to begin preheating.
6. Once preheated, place the basket into the air fryer. Flip the steaks once halfway through to ensure even cooking.
7. When cooking is complete, the internal temperature of the beef steaks should reach at least 145°F (63°C) on a meat thermometer.
8. Transfer the steaks to plates. Let cool for 5 minutes and serve hot.

Air Fried London Broil

Prep time: 8 hours 5 minutes | Cook time: 25 minutes | Serves 6

2 tablespoons Worcestershire sauce
2 tablespoons minced onion
¼ cup honey
⅔ cup ketchup
2 tablespoons apple cider vinegar
½ teaspoon paprika
¼ cup olive oil
1 teaspoon salt
1 teaspoon freshly ground black pepper
2 pounds (907 g) London broil, top round (about 1-inch thick)

1. Combine all the ingredients, except for the London broil, in a large bowl. Stir to mix well.
2. Pierce the meat with a fork generously on both sides, then dunk the meat in the mixture and press to coat well.
3. Wrap the bowl in plastic and refrigerate to marinate for at least 8 hours.
4. Discard the marinade and transfer the London broil to the air fry basket.
5. Select Air Fry. Set temperature to 400°F (205°C) and set time to 25 minutes. Press Start to begin preheating.
6. Once preheated, place the basket into the air fryer. Flip the meat halfway through the cooking time.
7. When cooking is complete, the meat should be well browned.
8. Transfer the cooked London broil on a plate and allow to cool for 5 minutes before slicing to serve.

Air Fried Beef Kofta

Prep time: 10 minutes | Cook time: 13 minutes | Makes 12 koftas

1½ pounds (680 g) lean ground beef
1 teaspoon onion powder
¾ teaspoon ground cinnamon
¾ teaspoon ground dried turmeric
1 teaspoon ground cumin
¾ teaspoon salt
¼ teaspoon cayenne
12 (3½- to 4-inch-long) cinnamon sticks
Cooking spray

1. Spritz the air fry basket with cooking spray.
2. Combine all the ingredients, except for the cinnamon sticks, in a large bowl. Toss to mix well.
3. Divide and shape the mixture into 12 balls, then wrap each ball around each cinnamon stick and leave a quarter of the length uncovered.
4. Arrange the beef-cinnamon sticks in the prepared basket and spritz with cooking spray.
5. Select Air Fry. Set temperature to 375°F (190°C) and set time to 13 minutes. Press Start to begin preheating.
6. Once preheated, place the basket into the air fryer. Flip the sticks halfway through the cooking.
7. When cooking is complete, the beef should be browned.
8. Serve immediately.

Baked Zucchini Ground Beef

Prep time: 5 minutes | Cook time: 12 minutes | Serves 4

1½ pounds (680 g) ground beef
1 pound (454 g) chopped zucchini
2 tablespoons extra-virgin olive oil
1 teaspoon dried oregano
1 teaspoon dried basil
1 teaspoon dried rosemary
2 tablespoons fresh chives, chopped

1. In a large bowl, combine all the ingredients, except for the chives, until well blended.
2. Place the beef and zucchini mixture in the baking pan.
3. Select Bake, set temperature to 400°F (205°C) and set time to 12 minutes. Press Start to begin preheating.
4. Once preheated, place the pan into the air fryer.
5. When cooking is complete, the beef should be browned and the zucchini should be tender.
6. Divide the beef and zucchini mixture among four serving dishes. Top with fresh chives and serve hot.

Crispy Golden Schnitzel

Prep time: 5 minutes | Cook time: 14 minutes | Serves 2

½ cup pork rinds
½ tablespoon fresh parsley
½ teaspoon fennel seed
½ teaspoon mustard
⅓ tablespoon cider vinegar
1 teaspoon garlic salt
⅓ teaspoon ground black pepper
2 eggs
2 pork schnitzel, halved
Cooking spray

1. Spritz the air fry basket with cooking spray.
2. Put the pork rinds, parsley, fennel seeds, and mustard in a food processor. Pour in the vinegar and sprinkle with salt and ground black pepper. Pulse until well combined and smooth.
3. Pour the pork rind mixture in a large bowl. Whisk the eggs in a separate bowl.
4. Dunk the pork schnitzel in the whisked eggs, then dunk in the pork rind mixture to coat well. Shake the excess off.
5. Arrange the schnitzel in the basket and spritz with cooking spray.
6. Select Air Fry. Set temperature to 350°F (180°C) and set time to 14 minutes. Press Start to begin preheating.
7. Once preheated, place the basket into the air fryer.
8. After 7 minutes, remove the basket from the air fryer. Flip the schnitzel. Return the basket to the air fryer and continue cooking.
9. When cooking is complete, the schnitzel should be golden and crispy.
10. Serve immediately.

Breaded Golden Wasabi Spam

Prep time: 5 minutes | Cook time: 12 minutes | Serves 3

⅔ cup all-purpose flou
2 large eggs
1½ tablespoons wasabi paste
2 cups panko bread crumbs
6 ½-inch-thick spam slices
Cooking spray

1. Spritz the air fry basket with cooking spray.
2. Pour the flour in a shallow plate. Whisk the eggs with wasabi in a large bowl. Pour the panko in a separate shallow plate.
3. Dredge the spam slices in the flour first then dunk in the egg mixture, and then roll the spam over the panko to coat well. Shake the excess off.
4. Arrange the spam slices in the basket and spritz with cooking spray.
5. Select Air Fry. Set temperature to 400°F (205°C) and set time to 12 minutes. Press Start to begin preheating.
6. Once preheated, place the basket into the air fryer. Flip the spam slices halfway through.
7. When cooking is complete, the spam slices should be golden and crispy.
8. Serve immediately.

Easy Lamb Chops with Asparagus

Prep time: 10 minutes | Cook time: 15 minutes | Serves 4

4 asparagus spears, trimmed
2 tablespoons olive oil, divided
1 pound (454 g) lamb chops
1 garlic clove, minced
2 teaspoons chopped fresh thyme, for serving
Salt and ground black pepper, to taste

1. Spritz the air fry basket with cooking spray.
2. On a large plate, brush the asparagus with 1 tablespoon olive oil, then sprinkle with salt. Set aside.
3. On a separate plate, brush the lamb chops with remaining olive oil and sprinkle with salt and ground black pepper.
4. Arrange the lamb chops in the basket.
5. Select Air Fry. Set temperature to 400ºF (205ºC) and set time to 15 minutes. Press Start to begin preheating.
6. Once preheated, place the basket into the air fryer. Flip the lamb chops and add the asparagus and garlic halfway through.
7. When cooking is complete, the lamb should be well browned and the asparagus should be tender.
8. Serve them on a plate with thyme on top.

Golden Lamb Chops

Prep time: 5 minutes | Cook time: 25 minutes | Serves 4

1 cup all-purpose flou
2 teaspoons dried sage leaves
2 teaspoons garlic powder
1 tablespoon mild paprika
1 tablespoon salt
4 (6-ounce / 170-g) bone-in lamb shoulder chops, fat trimmed
Cooking spray

1. Spritz the air fry basket with cooking spray.
2. Combine the flou , sage leaves, garlic powder, paprika, and salt in a large bowl. Stir to mix well. Dunk in the lamb chops and toss to coat well.
3. Arrange the lamb chops in the basket and spritz with cooking spray.
4. Select Air Fry. Set temperature to 375ºF (190ºC) and set time to 25 minutes. Press Start to begin preheating.
5. Once preheated, place the basket into the air fryer. Flip the chops halfway through.
6. When cooking is complete, the chops should be golden brown and reaches your desired doneness.
7. Serve immediately.

Crispy Bacon-Wrapped Sausage

Prep time: 1 hour 15 minutes | Cook time: 32 minutes | Serves 4

8 pork sausages
8 bacon strips

Relish:
8 large tomatoes, chopped
1 small onion, peeled
1 clove garlic, peeled
1 tablespoon white wine vinegar
3 tablespoons
chopped parsley
1 teaspoon smoked paprika
2 tablespoons sugar
Salt and ground black pepper, to taste

1. Purée the tomatoes, onion, and garlic in a food processor until well mixed and smooth.
2. Pour the purée in a saucepan and drizzle with white wine vinegar. Sprinkle with salt and ground black pepper. Simmer over medium heat for 10 minutes.
3. Add the parsley, paprika, and sugar to the saucepan and cook for 10 more minutes or until it has a thick consistency. Keep stirring during the cooking. Refrigerate for an hour to chill.
4. Wrap the sausage with bacon strips and secure with toothpicks, then place them in the air fry basket.
5. Select Air Fry. Set temperature to 350ºF (180ºC) and set time to 12 minutes. Press Start to begin preheating.
6. Once preheated, place the basket into the air fryer. Flip the bacon-wrapped sausage halfway through.
7. When cooking is complete, the bacon should be crispy and browned.
8. Transfer the bacon-wrapped sausage on a plate and baste with the relish or just serve with the relish alongside.

Cheesy Beef and Pork Sausage Meatloaf

Prep time: 10 minutes | Cook time: 25 minutes | Serves 4

¾ pound (340 g) ground chuck
4 ounces (113 g) ground pork sausage
2 eggs, beaten
1 cup Parmesan cheese, grated
1 cup chopped shallot
3 tablespoons plain milk
1 tablespoon oyster sauce
1 tablespoon fresh parsley
1 teaspoon garlic paste
1 teaspoon chopped porcini mushrooms
½ teaspoon cumin powder
Seasoned salt and crushed red pepper flakes, to taste

1. In a large bowl, combine all the ingredients until well blended.
2. Place the meat mixture in the baking pan. Use a spatula to press the mixture to fill the pan
3. Select Bake, set temperature to 360°F (182°C) and set time to 25 minutes. Press Start to begin preheating.
4. Once preheated, place the pan into the air fryer.
5. When cooking is complete, the meatloaf should be well browned.
6. Let the meatloaf rest for 5 minutes. Transfer to a serving dish and slice. Serve warm.

Bacon-Wrapped Hot Dogs

Prep time: 5 minutes | Cook time: 10 minutes | Serves 5

10 thin slices of bacon
5 pork hot dogs, halved
1 teaspoon cayenne pepper

Sauce:
¼ cup mayonnaise
4 tablespoons low-carb ketchup
1 teaspoon rice vinegar
1 teaspoon chili powder

1. Arrange the slices of bacon on a clean work surface. One by one, place the halved hot dog on one end of each slice, season with cayenne pepper and wrap the hot dog with the bacon slices and secure with toothpicks as needed.
2. Place wrapped hot dogs in the air fry basket.
3. Select Air Fry. Set temperature to 390°F (199°C) and set time to 10 minutes. Press Start to begin preheating.
4. Once preheated, place the basket into the air fryer. Flip the bacon-wrapped hot dogs halfway through.
5. When cooking is complete, the bacon should be crispy and browned.
6. Make the sauce: Stir all the ingredients for the sauce in a small bowl. Wrap the bowl in plastic and set in the refrigerator until ready to serve.
7. Transfer the hot dogs to a platter and serve hot with the sauce.

Crispy Pork Tenderloin

Prep time: 5 minutes | Cook time: 10 minutes | Serves 6

2 large egg whites
1½ tablespoons Dijon mustard
2 cups crushed pretzel crumbs
1½ pounds (680 g) pork tenderloin, cut into ¼-pound (113-g) sections
Cooking spray

1. Spritz the air fry basket with cooking spray.
2. Whisk the egg whites with Dijon mustard in a bowl until bubbly. Pour the pretzel crumbs in a separate bowl.
3. Dredge the pork tenderloin in the egg white mixture and press to coat. Shake the excess off and roll the tenderloin over the pretzel crumbs.
4. Arrange the well-coated pork tenderloin in the basket and spritz with cooking spray.
5. Select Air Fry. Set temperature to 350°F (180°C) and set time to 10 minutes. Press Start to begin preheating.
6. Once preheated, place the basket into the air fryer.
7. After 5 minutes, remove the basket from the air fryer. Flip the pork. Return the basket to the air fryer and continue cooking.
8. When cooking is complete, the pork should be golden brown and crispy.
9. Serve immediately.

Golden Lemony Pork Chop

Prep time: 15 minutes | Cook time: 15 minutes | Serves 4

4 thin boneless pork loin chops
2 tablespoons lemon juice
½ cup flou
¼ teaspoon marjoram
1 teaspoon salt
1 cup panko bread crumbs
2 eggs
Lemon wedges, for serving
Cooking spray

1. On a clean work surface, drizzle the pork chops with lemon juice on both sides.
2. Combine the flour with marjo am and salt on a shallow plate. Pour the bread crumbs on a separate shallow dish. Beat the eggs in a large bowl.
3. Dredge the pork chops in the flou , then dunk in the beaten eggs to coat well. Shake the excess off and roll over the bread crumbs. Arrange the pork chops in the air fry basket and spritz with cooking spray.
4. Select Air Fry. Set temperature to 400°F (205°C) and set time to 15 minutes. Press Start to begin preheating.
5. Once preheated, place the basket into the air fryer.
6. After 7 minutes, remove the basket from the air fryer. Flip the pork. Return the basket to the air fryer and continue cooking.
7. When cooking is complete, the pork should be crispy and golden.
8. Squeeze the lemon wedges over the fried chops and serve immediately.

Chuck and Sausage Sandwiches

Prep time: 15 minutes | Cook time: 24 minutes | Serves 4

1 large egg
¼ cup whole milk
24 saltines, crushed but not pulverized
1 pound (454 g) ground chuck
1 pound (454 g) Italian sausage, casings removed
4 tablespoons grated Parmesan cheese, divided
1 teaspoon kosher salt
4 sub rolls, split
1 cup Marinara sauce
¾ cup shredded Mozzarella cheese

1. In a large bowl, whisk the egg into the milk, then stir in the crackers. Let sit for 5 minutes to hydrate.
2. With your hands, break the ground chuck and sausage into the milk mixture, alternating beef and sausage. When you've added half of the meat, sprinkle 2 tablespoons of the grated Parmesan and the salt over it, then continue breaking up the meat until it's all in the bowl. Gently mix everything together. Try not to overwork the meat, but get it all combined.
3. Form the mixture into balls about the size of a golf ball. You should get about 24 meatballs. Flatten the balls slightly to prevent them from rolling, then place them on a baking pan, about 2 inches apart.
4. Select Roast, set temperature to 400ºF (205ºC), and set time to 20 minutes. Press Start to begin preheating.
5. Once preheated, place the pan into the air fryer.
6. After 10 minutes, remove the pan from the air fryer and turn over the meatballs. Return the pan to the air fryer and continue cooking.
7. When cooking is complete, remove the pan from the air fryer. Place the meatballs on a rack. Wipe off the baking pan.
8. Open the rolls, cut-side up, on the baking pan. Place 3 to 4 meatballs on the base of each roll, and top each sandwich with ¼ cup of marinara sauce. Divide the Mozzarella among the top halves of the buns and sprinkle the remaining Parmesan cheese over the Mozzarella.
9. Select Broil, set temperature to High, and set time to 4 minutes. Press Start to begin preheating.
10. Once preheated, place the pan into the air fryer. Check the sandwiches after 2 minutes; the Mozzarella cheese should be melted and bubbling slightly.
11. When cooking is complete, remove the pan from the air fryer. Close the sandwiches and serve.

Teriyaki Pork Skewers

Prep time: 10 minutes | Cook time: 12 minutes | Serves 4

¼ teaspoon kosher salt or ⅛ teaspoon fine sal
1 medium pork tenderloin (about 1 pound / 454 g), cut into 1½-inch chunks
1 green bell pepper, seeded and cut into 1-inch pieces
1 red bell pepper, seeded and cut into 1-inch pieces
2 cups fresh pineapple chunks
¾ cup Teriyaki Sauce or store-bought variety, divided

Special Equipment:
12 (9- to 12-inch) wooden skewers, soaked in water for about 30 minutes

1. Sprinkle the pork cubes with the salt.
2. Thread the pork, bell peppers, and pineapple onto a skewer. Repeat until all skewers are complete. Brush the skewers generously with about half of the Teriyaki Sauce. Place them on the sheet pan.
3. Select Roast, set temperature to 375°F (190°C), and set time to 10 minutes. Select Start to begin preheating.
4. Once the unit has preheated, place the pan into the air fryer.
5. After about 5 minutes, remove the pan from the air fryer. Turn over the skewers and brush with the remaining half of Teriyaki Sauce. Transfer the pan back to the air fryer and continue cooking until the vegetables are tender and browned in places and the pork is browned and cooked through.
6. Remove the pan from the air fryer and serve.

Bangers and Cauliflower Mash

Prep time: 5 minutes | Cook time: 27 minutes | Serves 6

1 pound (454 g) cauliflowe , chopped
6 pork sausages, chopped
½ onion, sliced
3 eggs, beaten
⅓ cup Colby cheese
1 teaspoon cumin powder
½ teaspoon tarragon
½ teaspoon sea salt
½ teaspoon ground black pepper
Cooking spray

1. Spritz the baking pan with cooking spray.
2. In a saucepan over medium heat, boil the cauliflower until tende . Place the boiled cauliflower in a food processor and pulse until puréed. Transfer to a large bowl and combine with remaining ingredients until well blended.
3. Pour the cauliflower and sausage mixture into the pan.
4. Select Bake, set temperature to 365°F (185°C) and set time to 27 minutes. Press Start to begin preheating.
5. Once preheated, place the pan into the air fryer.
6. When cooking is complete, the sausage should be lightly browned.
7. Divide the mixture among six serving dishes and serve warm.

Air Fried Pork Rib

Prep time: 1 hour 10 minutes | Cook time: 25 minutes | Serves 6

2½ pounds (1.1 kg) boneless country-style pork ribs, cut into 2-inch pieces
3 tablespoons olive brine
1 tablespoon minced fresh oregano leaves
⅓ cup orange juice
1 teaspoon ground cumin
1 tablespoon minced garlic
1 teaspoon salt
1 teaspoon ground black pepper
Cooking spray

1. Combine all the ingredients in a large bowl. Toss to coat the pork ribs well. Wrap the bowl in plastic and refrigerate for at least an hour to marinate.
2. Spritz the air fry basket with cooking spray.
3. Arrange the marinated pork ribs in the basket and spritz with cooking spray.
4. Select Air Fry. Set temperature to 400°F (205°C) and set time to 25 minutes. Press Start to begin preheating.
5. Once preheated, place the basket into the air fryer. Flip the ribs halfway through.
6. When cooking is complete, the ribs should be well browned.
7. Serve immediately.

Nuts Crusted Pork Rack

Prep time: 5 minutes | Cook time: 35 minutes | Serves 2

1 clove garlic, minced
2 tablespoons olive oil
1 pound (454 g) rack of pork
1 cup chopped macadamia nuts
1 tablespoon bread crumbs
1 tablespoon rosemary, chopped
1 egg
Salt and ground black pepper, to taste

1. Combine the garlic and olive oil in a small bowl. Stir to mix well.
2. On a clean work surface, rub the pork rack with the garlic oil and sprinkle with salt and black pepper on both sides.
3. Combine the macadamia nuts, bread crumbs, and rosemary in a shallow dish. Whisk the egg in a large bowl.
4. Dredge the pork in the egg, then roll the pork over the macadamia nut mixture to coat well. Shake the excess off.
5. Arrange the pork in the air fry basket.
6. Select Air Fry. Set temperature to 350°F (180°C) and set time to 30 minutes. Press Start to begin preheating.
7. Once preheated, place the basket into the air fryer.
8. After 30 minutes, remove the basket from the air fryer. Flip the pork rack. Return the basket to the air fryer and increase temperature to 390°F (199°C) and set time to 5 minutes. Keep cooking.
9. When cooking is complete, the pork should be browned.
10. Serve immediately.

Roasted Lamb Chops with Potatoes

Prep time: 10 minutes | Cook time: 20 minutes | Serves 4

8 (½-inch thick) lamb loin chops (about 2 pounds / 907 g)
2 teaspoons kosher salt or 1 teaspoon fine salt, divide
¾ cup plain whole milk yogurt
2 garlic cloves, minced or smashed
1 tablespoon freshly grated ginger (1- or 2-inch piece) or 1 teaspoon ground ginger
1 teaspoon curry powder
1 teaspoon smoked paprika
½ teaspoon cayenne pepper
12 ounces (340 g) small red potatoes, quartered
Cooking spray

1. Sprinkle the lamb chops on both sides with 1 teaspoon of kosher salt and set aside.
2. Meanwhile, make the marinade by stirring together the yogurt, garlic, ginger, curry powder, paprika, cayenne pepper, and remaining 1 teaspoon of kosher salt in a large bowl.
3. Transfer 2 tablespoons of the marinade to a resealable plastic bag, leaving those 2 tablespoons in the bowl. Place the lamb chops in the bag. Squeeze out as much air as possible and squish the bag around so that the chops are well coated with the marinade. Set aside.
4. Add the potatoes to the bowl and toss until well coated. Spritz the sheet pan with cooking spray. Arrange the potatoes in the pan.
5. Select Roast, set temperature to 375°F (190°C), and set time to 10 minutes. Select Start to begin preheating.
6. Once the unit has preheated, place the pan into the air fryer.
7. Once cooking is complete, remove the pan from the air fryer.
8. Remove the chops from the marinade, draining off all but a thin coat. Return them to the baking pan.
9. Select Broil, set the temperature to High, and set the time for 10 minutes. Select Start to begin preheating.
10. Once the unit has preheated, place the pan into the air fryer. After 5 minutes, remove the pan from the air fryer and turn over the chops and potatoes. Slide the pan into the air fryer and continue cooking until the lamb read 145°F (63°C) on a meat thermometer. If you want it more well done, continue cooking for another few minutes.
11. Remove the pan from the air fryer and serve.

Savory Pork Butt with Chilled Sauce

Prep time: 1 hour 15 minutes | Cook time: 30 minutes | Serves 4

1 teaspoon golden flaxseeds mea
1 egg white, well whisked
1 tablespoon soy sauce
1 teaspoon lemon juice, preferably freshly squeezed
1 tablespoon olive oil
1 pound (454 g) pork butt, cut into pieces 2-inches long
Salt and ground black pepper, to taste

Garlicky Coriander-Parsley Sauce:
3 garlic cloves, minced
1/3 cup fresh coriander leaves
1/3 cup fresh parsley leaves
1 teaspoon lemon juice
½ tablespoon salt
1/3 cup extra-virgin olive oil

1. Combine the flaxseeds meal, egg white, soy sauce, lemon juice, salt, black pepper, and olive oil in a large bowl. Dunk the pork strips in and press to submerge.
2. Wrap the bowl in plastic and refrigerate to marinate for at least an hour.
3. Arrange the marinated pork strips in the air fry basket.
4. Select Air Fry. Set temperature to 380ºF (193ºC) and set time to 30 minutes. Press Start to begin preheating.
5. Once preheated, place the basket into the air fryer.
6. After 15 minutes, remove the basket from the air fryer. Flip the pork. Return the basket to the air fryer and continue cooking.
7. When cooking is complete, the pork should be well browned.
8. Meanwhile, combine the ingredients for the sauce in a small bowl. Stir to mix well. Arrange the bowl in the refrigerator to chill until ready to serve.
9. Serve the air fried pork strips with the chilled sauce.

Pork Steak and Squash

Prep time: 1 hour 20 minutes | Cook time: 8 minutes | Serves 4

For the Pork:
1 pound (454 g) pork steak, cut in cubes
1 tablespoon white wine vinegar
3 tablespoons steak sauce
¼ cup soy sauce
1 teaspoon powdered chili
1 teaspoon red chili fla es
2 teaspoons smoked paprika
1 teaspoon garlic salt

For the Vegetable:
1 green squash, deseeded and cut in cubes
1 yellow squash, deseeded and cut in cubes
1 red pepper, cut in cubes
1 green pepper, cut in cubes
Salt and ground black pepper, to taste
Cooking spray

Special Equipment:
4 bamboo skewers, soaked in water for at least 30 minutes

1. Combine the ingredients for the pork in a large bowl. Press the pork to dunk in the marinade. Wrap the bowl in plastic and refrigerate for at least an hour.
2. Spritz the air fry basket with cooking spray.
3. Remove the pork from the marinade and run the skewers through the pork and vegetables alternatively. Sprinkle with salt and pepper to taste.
4. Arrange the skewers in the pan and spritz with cooking spray.
5. Select Air Fry. Set temperature to 380ºF (193ºC) and set time to 8 minutes. Press Start to begin preheating.
6. Once preheated, place the basket into the air fryer.
7. After 4 minutes, remove the basket from the air fryer. Flip the skewers. Return the basket to the air fryer and continue cooking.
8. When cooking is complete, the pork should be browned and the vegetables should be lightly charred and tender.
9. Serve immediately.

Cheesy Sausage and Mushroom Calzones

Prep time: 10 minutes | Cook time: 24 minutes | Serves 4

2 links Italian sausages (about ½ pound / 227 g)
1 pound (454 g) pizza dough, thawed
3 tablespoons olive oil, divided
¼ cup Marinara sauce
½ cup roasted mushrooms
1 cup shredded Mozzarella cheese

1. Place the sausages in a baking pan.
2. Select Roast, set temperature to 375°F (190°C), and set time to 12 minutes. Press Start to begin preheating.
3. Once preheated, place the pan into the air fryer.
4. After 6 minutes, remove the pan from the air fryer and turn over the sausages. Return the pan to the air fryer and continue cooking.
5. While the sausages cook, divide the pizza dough into 4 equal pieces. One at a time, place a piece of dough onto a square of parchment paper 9 inches in diameter. Brush the dough on both sides with ¾ teaspoon of olive oil, then top the dough with another piece of parchment. Press the dough into a 7-inch circle. Remove the top piece of parchment and set aside. Repeat with the remaining pieces of dough.
6. When cooking is complete, remove the pan from the air fryer. Place the sausages on a cutting board. Let them cool for several minutes, then slice into ¼-inch rounds and cut each round into 4 pieces.
7. One at a time, spread a tablespoon of marinara sauce over half of a dough circle, leaving a ½-inch border at the edges. Cover with a quarter of the sausage pieces and add a quarter of the mushrooms. Sprinkle with ¼ cup of cheese. Pull the other side of the dough over the filling and pinch the edges together to seal. Transfer from the parchment to the baking pan. Repeat with the other rounds of dough, sauce, sausage, mushrooms, and cheese.
8. Brush the tops of the calzones with 1 tablespoon of olive oil.
9. Select Roast, set temperature to 450°F (235°C), and set time to 12 minutes. Press Start to begin preheating.
10. Once preheated, place the pan into the air fryer.
11. After 6 minutes, remove the pan from the air fryer. The calzones should be golden brown. Turn over the calzones and brush the tops with the remaining olive oil. Return the pan to the air fryer and continue cooking.
12. When cooking is complete, the crust should be a deep golden brown on both sides. Remove the pan from the air fryer. The center should be molten; let cool for several minutes before serving.

Crunchy Tonkatsu

Prep time: 5 minutes | Cook time: 10 minutes | Serves 4

⅔ cup all-purpose flou
2 large egg whites
1 cup panko bread crumbs
4 (4-ounce / 113-g) center-cut boneless pork loin chops (about ½ inch thick)
Cooking spray

1. Pour the flour in a bowl. Whisk the egg whites in a separate bowl. Spread the bread crumbs on a large plate.
2. Dredge the pork loin chops in the flour first, press to coat well, then sha e the excess off and dunk the chops in the eggs whites, and then roll the chops over the bread crumbs. Shake the excess off.
3. Arrange the pork chops in the air fry basket and spritz with cooking spray.
4. Select Air Fry. Set temperature to 375°F (190°C) and set time to 10 minutes. Press Start to begin preheating.
5. Once preheated, place the basket into the air fryer.
6. After 5 minutes, remove the basket from the air fryer. Flip the pork chops. Return the basket to the air fryer and continue cooking.
7. When cooking is complete, the pork chops should be crunchy and lightly browned.
8. Serve immediately.

Teriyaki Country Pork Ribs

Prep time: 5 minutes | Cook time: 30 minutes | Serves 4

¼ cup soy sauce
¼ cup honey
1 teaspoon garlic powder
1 teaspoon ground dried ginger
4 (8-ounce / 227-g) boneless country-style pork ribs
Cooking spray

1. Spritz the air fry basket with cooking spray.
2. Make the teriyaki sauce: combine the soy sauce, honey, garlic powder, and ginger in a bowl. Stir to mix well.
3. Brush the ribs with half of the teriyaki sauce, then arrange the ribs in the basket. Spritz with cooking spray.
4. Select Air Fry. Set temperature to 350°F (180°C) and set time to 30 minutes. Press Start to begin preheating.
5. Once preheated, place the basket into the air fryer.
6. After 15 minutes, remove the basket from the air fryer. Flip the ribs and brush with remaining teriyaki sauce. Return the basket to the air fryer and continue cooking.
7. When cooking is complete, the internal temperature of the ribs should reach at least 145°F (63°C).
8. Serve immediately.

BBQ Sausage, Pineapple and Peppers

Prep time: 15 minutes | Cook time: 10 minutes | Serves 2 to 4

¾ pound (340 g) kielbasa sausage, cut into ½-inch slices
1 (8-ounce / 227-g) can pineapple chunks in juice, drained
1 cup bell pepper chunks
1 tablespoon barbecue seasoning
1 tablespoon soy sauce
Cooking spray

1. Spritz the air fry basket with cooking spray.
2. Combine all the ingredients in a large bowl. Toss to mix well.
3. Pour the sausage mixture in the air fry basket.
4. Select Air Fry. Set temperature to 390°F (199°C) and set time to 10 minutes. Press Start to begin preheating.
5. Once preheated, place the basket into the air fryer.
6. After 5 minutes, remove the basket from the air fryer. Stir the sausage mixture. Return the basket to the air fryer and continue cooking.
7. When cooking is complete, the sausage should be lightly browned and the bell pepper and pineapple should be soft.
8. Serve immediately.

Crispy Lechon Kawali

Prep time: 10 minutes | Cook time: 30 minutes | Serves 4

1 pound (454 g) pork belly, cut into three thick chunks
6 garlic cloves
2 bay leaves
2 tablespoons soy sauce
1 teaspoon kosher salt
1 teaspoon ground black pepper
3 cups water
Cooking spray

1. Put all the ingredients in a pressure cooker, then put the lid on and cook on high for 15 minutes.
2. Natural release the pressure and release any remaining pressure, transfer the tender pork belly on a clean work surface. Allow to cool under room temperature until you can handle.
3. Generously Spritz the air fry basket with cooking spray.
4. Cut each chunk into two slices, then put the pork slices in the basket.
5. Select Air Fry. Set temperature to 400°F (205°C) and set time to 15 minutes. Press Start to begin preheating.
6. Once preheated, place the basket into the air fryer.
7. After 7 minutes, remove the basket from the air fryer. Flip the pork. Return the basket to the air fryer and continue cooking.
8. When cooking is complete, the pork fat should be crispy.
9. Serve immediately.

Chapter 5 Red Meats | 79

Baked Pork Chops and Apple

Prep time: 10 minutes | Cook time: 45 minutes | Serves 4

2 apples, peeled, cored, and sliced
1 teaspoon ground cinnamon, divided
4 boneless pork chops (½-inch thick)
Salt and freshly ground black pepper, to taste
3 tablespoons brown sugar
¾ cup water
1 tablespoon olive oil

1. Layer apples in bottom of a baking pan. Sprinkle with ½ teaspoon of cinnamon.
2. Trim fat from pork chops. Lay on top of the apple slices. Sprinkle with salt and pepper.
3. In a small bowl, combine the brown sugar, water, and remaining cinnamon. Pour the mixture over the chops. Drizzle chops with 1 tablespoon of olive oil.
4. Select Bake, set temperature to 375°F (190°C) and set time to 45 minutes. Press Start to begin preheating.
5. Once preheated, place the pan into the air fryer.
6. When cooking is complete, an instant-read thermometer inserted in the pork should register 165°F (74°C).
7. Allow to rest for 3 minutes before serving.

Air Fried Pork Tenderloin

Prep time: 25 minutes | Cook time: 15 minutes | Serves 4

1 pound (454 g) pork tenderloin, cubed
1 teaspoon smoked paprika
Salt and ground black pepper, to taste
1 green bell pepper, cut into chunks
1 zucchini, cut into chunks
1 red onion, sliced
1 tablespoon oregano
Cooking spray

Special Equipment:
Small bamboo skewers, soaked in water for 20 minutes to keep them from burning while cooking

1. Spritz the air fry basket with cooking spray.
2. Add the pork to a bowl and season with the smoked paprika, salt and black pepper. Thread the seasoned pork cubes and vegetables alternately onto the soaked skewers. Arrange the skewers in the basket.
3. Select Air Fry. Set temperature to 350°F (180°C) and set time to 15 minutes. Press Start to begin preheating.
4. Once preheated, place the basket into the air fryer.
5. After 7 minutes, remove the basket from the air fryer. Flip the pork skewers. Return the basket to the air fryer and continue cooking.
6. When cooking is complete, the pork should be browned and vegetables are tender.
7. Transfer the skewers to the serving dishes and sprinkle with oregano. Serve hot.

Roasted Ribeye Steaks

Prep time: 35 minutes | Cook time: 10 to 12 minutes | Serves 2 to 4

2 (8-ounce / 227-g) boneless ribeye steaks
4 teaspoons Worcestershire sauce
½ teaspoon garlic powder
Salt and ground black pepper, to taste
4 teaspoons olive oil

1. Brush the steaks with Worcestershire sauce on both sides. Sprinkle with garlic powder and coarsely ground black pepper. Drizzle the steaks with olive oil. Allow steaks to marinate for 30 minutes.
2. Transfer the steaks in the air fry basket.
3. Select Roast. Set the temperature to 400°F (205°C) and set time to 4 minutes. Press Start to begin preheating.
4. Once preheated, place the basket into the air fryer.
5. After 2 minutes, remove the basket from the air fryer. Flip the steaks. Return the basket to the air fryer and continue cooking.
6. When cooking is complete, the steaks should be well browned.
7. Remove the steaks from the air fry basket and let sit for 5 minutes. Salt and serve.

Bo Luc Lac

Prep time: 50 minutes | Cook time: 4 minutes | Serves 4

For the Meat:
2 teaspoons soy sauce
4 garlic cloves, minced
1 teaspoon kosher salt
2 teaspoons sugar
¼ teaspoon ground black pepper
1 teaspoon toasted sesame oil
1½ pounds (680 g) top sirloin steak, cut into 1-inch cubes
Cooking spray

For the Salad:
1 head Bibb lettuce, leaves separated and torn into large pieces
¼ cup fresh mint leaves
½ cup halved grape tomatoes
½ red onion, halved and thinly sliced
2 tablespoons apple cider vinegar
1 garlic clove, minced
2 teaspoons sugar
¼ teaspoon kosher salt
¼ teaspoon ground black pepper
2 tablespoons vegetable oil

For Serving:
Lime wedges, for garnish
Coarse salt and freshly cracked black pepper, to taste

1. Combine the ingredients for the meat, except for the steak, in a large bowl. Stir to mix well.
2. Dunk the steak cubes in the bowl and press to coat. Wrap the bowl in plastic and marinate under room temperature for at least 30 minutes.
3. Spritz the air fry basket with cooking spray.
4. Discard the marinade and transfer the steak cubes in the prepared basket.
5. Select Air Fry. Set temperature to 450°F (235°C) and set time to 4 minutes. Press Start to begin preheating.
6. Once preheated, place the basket into the air fryer. Flip the steak cubes halfway through.
7. When cooking is complete, the steak cubes should be lightly browned but still have a little pink.
8. Meanwhile, combine the ingredients for the salad in a separate large bowl. Toss to mix well.
9. Pour the salad in a large serving bowl and top with the steak cubes. Squeeze the lime wedges over and sprinkle with salt and black pepper before serving.

Chessy Asparagus and Prosciutto Tart

Prep time: 10 minutes | Cook time: 25 minutes | Serves 4

All-purpose flou , for dusting
1 sheet (½ package) frozen puff pastry, thawed
½ cup grated Parmesan cheese
1 pound (454 g) (or more) asparagus, trimmed
8 ounces (227 g) thinly sliced prosciutto, sliced into ribbons about ½-inch wide
2 teaspoons aged balsamic vinegar

1. On a lightly floured cutting board, unwrap and unfold the puff pastry and roll it lightly with a rolling pin so as to press the folds together. Place it on the sheet pan.
2. Roll about ½ inch of the pastry edges up to form a ridge around the perimeter. Crimp the corners together to create a solid rim around the pastry. Using a fork, pierce the bottom of the pastry all over. Scatter the cheese over the bottom of the pastry.
3. Arrange the asparagus spears on top of the cheese in a single layer with 4 or 5 spears pointing one way, the next few pointing the opposite direction. You may need to trim them so they fit within the border of the pastry shell. Lay the prosciutto on top more or less evenly.
4. Select Bake, set temperature to 375°F (190°C), and set time to 25 minutes. Select Start to begin preheating.
5. Once the unit has preheated, place the pan into the air fryer.
6. After about 15 minutes, check the tart, rotating the pan if the crust is not browning evenly and continue cooking until the pastry is golden brown and the edges of the prosciutto pieces are browned.
7. Remove the pan from the air fryer. Allow to cool for 5 minutes before slicing.
8. Drizzle with the balsamic vinegar just before serving.

Roasted Pork Chop

Prep time: 5 minutes | Cook time: 20 minutes | Serves 2

2 (10-ounce / 284-g) bone-in, center cut pork chops, 1-inch thick
2 teaspoons Worcestershire sauce
Salt and ground black pepper, to taste
Cooking spray

1. Rub the Worcestershire sauce on both sides of pork chops.
2. Season with salt and pepper to taste.
3. Spritz the air fry basket with cooking spray and place the chops in the air fry basket side by side.
4. Select Roast. Set the temperature to 350°F (180°C) and set the time to 20 minutes. Press Start to begin preheating.
5. Once preheated, place the basket into the air fryer.
6. After 10 minutes, remove the basket from the air fryer. Flip the pork chops with tongs. Return the basket to the air fryer and continue cooking.
7. When cooking is complete, the pork should be well browned on both sides.
8. Let rest for 5 minutes before serving.

Balsamic Sausages and Red Grapes

Prep time: 10 minutes | Cook time: 20 minutes | Serves 6

2 pounds (905 g) seedless red grapes
3 shallots, sliced
2 teaspoons fresh thyme
2 tablespoons olive oil
½ teaspoon kosher salt
Freshly ground black pepper, to taste
6 links (about 1½ pounds / 680 g) hot Italian sausage
3 tablespoons balsamic vinegar

1. Place the grapes in a large bowl. Add the shallots, thyme, olive oil, salt, and pepper. Gently toss. Place the grapes in a baking pan. Arrange the sausage links evenly in the pan.
2. Select Roast, set temperature to 375°F (190°C), and set time to 20 minutes. Press Start to begin preheating.
3. Once preheated, place the pan into the air fryer.
4. After 10 minutes, remove the pan. Turn over the sausages and sprinkle the vinegar over the sausages and grapes. Gently toss the grapes and move them to one side of the pan. Return the pan to the air fryer and continue cooking.
5. When cooking is complete, the grapes should be very soft and the sausages browned. Serve immediately.

Baked Beef and Spinach Meatloaves

Prep time: 15 minutes | Cook time: 45 minutes | Serves 2

1 large egg, beaten
1 cup frozen spinach
⅓ cup almond meal
¼ cup chopped onion
¼ cup plain Greek milk
¼ teaspoon salt
¼ teaspoon dried sage
2 teaspoons olive oil, divided
Freshly ground black pepper, to taste
½ pound (227 g) extra-lean ground beef
¼ cup tomato paste
1 tablespoon granulated stevia
¼ teaspoon Worcestershire sauce
Cooking spray

1. Coat a shallow baking pan with cooking spray.
2. In a large bowl, combine the beaten egg, spinach, almond meal, onion, milk, salt, sage, 1 teaspoon of olive oil, and pepper.
3. Crumble the beef over the spinach mixture. Mix well to combine. Divide the meat mixture in half. Shape each half into a loaf. Place the loaves in the prepared pan.
4. In a small bowl, whisk together the tomato paste, stevia, Worcestershire sauce, and remaining 1 teaspoon of olive oil. Spoon half of the sauce over each meatloaf.
5. Select Bake. Set the temperature to 350°F (180°C) and set the time to 40 minutes. Press Start to begin preheating.
6. Once preheated, place the pan into the air fryer.
7. When cooking is complete, an instant-read thermometer inserted in the center of the meatloaves should read at least 165°F (74°C).
8. Serve immediately.

Spicy Pork with Lettuce

Prep time: 10 minutes | Cook time: 12 minutes | Serves 4

1 (1-pound / 454-g) medium pork tenderloin, silver skin and external fat trimmed
2/3 cup soy sauce, divided
1 teaspoon cornstarch
1 medium jalapeño, deseeded and minced
1 can diced water chestnuts
½ large red bell pepper, deseeded and chopped
2 scallions, chopped, white and green parts separated
1 head butter lettuce
½ cup roasted, chopped almonds
¼ cup coarsely chopped cilantro

1. Cut the tenderloin into ¼-inch slices and place them on a baking pan. Baste with about 3 tablespoons of soy sauce. Stir the cornstarch into the remaining sauce and set aside.
2. Select Roast, set temperature to 375°F (190°C), and set time to 12 minutes. Press Start to begin preheating.
3. Once preheated, place the pan into the air fryer.
4. After 5 minutes, remove the pan from the air fryer. Place the pork slices on a cutting board. Place the jalapeño, water chestnuts, red pepper, and the white parts of the scallions on the baking pan and pour the remaining sauce over. Stir to coat the vegetables with the sauce. Return the pan to the air fryer and continue cooking.
5. While the vegetables cook, chop the pork into small pieces. Separate the lettuce leaves, discarding any tough outer leaves and setting aside the small inner leaves for another use. You'll want 12 to 18 leaves, depending on size and your appetites.
6. After 5 minutes, remove the pan from the air fryer. Add the pork to the vegetables, stirring to combine. Return the pan to the air fryer and continue cooking for the remaining 2 minutes until the pork is warmed back up and the sauce has reduced slightly.
7. When cooking is complete, remove the pan from the air fryer. Place the pork and vegetables in a medium serving bowl and stir in half the green parts of the scallions. To serve, spoon some pork and vegetables into each of the lettuce leaves. Top with the remaining scallion greens and garnish with the nuts and cilantro.

Authentic Char Siu

Prep time: 8 hours 10 minutes | Cook time: 15 minutes | Serves 4

¼ cup honey
1 teaspoon Chinese five-spice powder
1 tablespoon Shaoxing wine (rice cooking wine)
1 tablespoon hoisin sauce
2 teaspoons minced garlic
2 teaspoons minced fresh ginger
2 tablespoons soy sauce
1 tablespoon sugar
1 pound (454 g) fatty pork shoulder, cut into long, 1-inch-thick pieces
Cooking spray

1. Combine all the ingredients, except for the pork should, in a microwave-safe bowl. Stir to mix well. Microwave until the honey has dissolved. Stir periodically.
2. Pierce the pork pieces generously with a fork, then put the pork in a large bowl. Pour in half of the honey mixture. Set the remaining sauce aside until ready to serve.
3. Press the pork pieces into the mixture to coat and wrap the bowl in plastic and refrigerate to marinate for at least 8 hours.
4. Spritz the air fry basket with cooking spray.
5. Discard the marinade and transfer the pork pieces in the air fry basket.
6. Select Air Fry. Set temperature to 400°F (205°C) and set time to 15 minutes. Press Start to begin preheating.
7. Once preheated, place the basket into the air fryer. Flip the pork halfway through.
8. When cooking is complete, the pork should be well browned.
9. Meanwhile, microwave the remaining marinade on high for a minute or until it has a thick consistency. Stir periodically.
10. Remove the pork from the air fryer and allow to cool for 10 minutes before serving with the thickened marinade.

Paprika Pork Chops

Prep time: 5 minutes | Cook time: 4 minutes | Serves 4 to 6

½ cup flou
1½ teaspoons salt
Freshly ground black pepper, to taste
2 eggs
½ cup milk
1½ cups toasted bread crumbs
1 teaspoon paprika
6 boneless, center cut pork chops (about 1½ pounds / 680 g), fat trimmed, pound to ½-inch thick
2 tablespoons olive oil
3 tablespoons melted butter
Lemon wedges, for serving

Sour Cream and Dill Sauce:

1 cup chicken stock
1½ tablespoons cornstarch
⅓ cup sour cream
1½ tablespoons chopped fresh dill
Salt and ground black pepper, to taste

1. Combine the flour with salt and black pepper in a large bowl. Stir to mix well. Whisk the egg with milk in a second bowl. Stir the bread crumbs and paprika in a third bowl.
2. Dredge the pork chops in the flour bowl, then in the egg milk, and then into the bread crumbs bowl. Press to coat well. Shake the excess off.
3. Arrange the pork chop in the air fry basket, then brush with olive oil and butter on all sides.
4. Select Air Fry. Set temperature to 400°F (205°C) and set time to 4 minutes. Press Start to begin preheating.
5. Once preheated, place the basket into the air fryer.
6. After 2 minutes, remove the basket from the air fryer. Flip the pork. Return the basket to the air fryer and continue cooking.
7. When cooking is complete, the pork chop should be golden brown and crispy.
8. Meanwhile, combine the chicken stock and cornstarch in a small saucepan and bring to a boil over medium-high heat. Simmer for 2 more minutes.
9. Turn off the heat, then mix in the sour cream, fresh dill, salt, and black pepper.
10. Remove the schnitzels from the air fryer to a plate and baste with sour cream and dill sauce. Squeeze the lemon wedges over and slice to serve.

Dijon Pork with Squash and Apple

Prep time: 15 minutes | Cook time: 13 minutes | Serves 4

4 boneless pork loin chops, ¾- to 1-inch thick
1 teaspoon kosher salt, divided
2 tablespoons Dijon mustard
2 tablespoons brown sugar
1 pound (454 g) butternut squash, cut into 1-inch cubes
1 large apple, peeled and cut into 12 to 16 wedges
1 medium onion, thinly sliced
½ teaspoon dried thyme
¼ teaspoon freshly ground black pepper
1 tablespoon unsalted butter, melted
½ cup chicken stock

1. Sprinkle the pork chops on both sides with ½ teaspoon of kosher salt. In a small bowl, whisk together the mustard and brown sugar. Baste about half of the mixture on one side of the pork chops. Place the chops, basted-side up, on a baking pan.
2. Place the squash in a large bowl. Add the apple, onion, thyme, remaining kosher salt, pepper, and butter and toss to coat. Arrange the squash-fruit mixture around the chops on the pan. Pour the chicken stock over the mixture, avoiding the chops.
3. Select Roast, set temperature to 350°F (180°C), and set time to 13 minutes. Press Start to begin preheating.
4. Once preheated, place the pan into the air fryer.
5. After about 7 minutes, remove the pan from the air fryer. Gently toss the squash mixture and turn over the chops. Baste the chops with the remaining mustard mixture. Return the pan to the air fryer and continue cooking.
6. When cooking is complete, the pork chops should register at least 145°F (63°C) in the center on a meat thermometer, and the squash and apples should be tender. If necessary, continue cooking for up to 3 minutes more.
7. Remove the pan from the air fryer. Spoon the squash and apples onto four plates, and place a pork chop on top. Serve immediately.

Tangy Sriracha Beef and Broccoli

Prep time: 10 minutes | Cook time: 15 minutes | Serves 4

12 ounces (340 g) broccoli, cut into florets (about 4 cups)
1 pound (454 g) flat iron steak, cut into thin strips
½ teaspoon kosher salt
¾ cup soy sauce
1 teaspoon Sriracha sauce
3 tablespoons freshly squeezed orange juice
1 teaspoon cornstarch
1 medium onion, thinly sliced

1. Line a baking pan with aluminum foil. Place the broccoli on top and sprinkle with 3 tablespoons of water. Seal the broccoli in the foil in a single layer.
2. Select Roast, set temperature to 375°F (190°C), and set time to 6 minutes. Press Start to begin preheating.
3. Once preheated, place the pan into the air fryer.
4. While the broccoli steams, sprinkle the steak with the salt. In a small bowl, whisk together the soy sauce, Sriracha, orange juice, and cornstarch. Place the onion and beef in a large bowl.
5. When cooking is complete, remove the pan from the air fryer. Open the packet of broccoli and use tongs to transfer the broccoli to the bowl with the beef and onion, discarding the foil and remaining water. Pour the sauce over the beef and vegetables and toss to coat. Place the mixture in the baking pan.
6. Select Roast, set temperature to 375°F (190°C), and set time to 9 minutes. Press Start to begin preheating.
7. Once preheated, place the pan into the air fryer.
8. After about 4 minutes, remove the pan from the air fryer and gently toss the ingredients. Return the pan to air fryer and continue cooking.
9. When cooking is complete, the sauce should be thickened, the vegetables tender, and the beef barely pink in the center. Serve warm.

Pork Cutlets with Aloha Salsa

Prep time: 20 minutes | Cook time: 7 minutes | Serves 4

2 eggs
2 tablespoons milk
¼ cup all-purpose flou
¼ cup panko bread crumbs
4 teaspoons sesame seeds
1 pound (454 g) boneless, thin pork cutlets (½-inch thick)
¼ cup cornstarch
Salt and ground lemon pepper, to taste
Cooking spray

Aloha Salsa:
1 cup fresh pineapple, chopped in small pieces
¼ cup red bell pepper, chopped
½ teaspoon ground cinnamon
1 teaspoon soy sauce
¼ cup red onion, finely choppe
⅛ teaspoon crushed red pepper
⅛ teaspoon ground black pepper

1. In a medium bowl, stir together all ingredients for salsa. Cover and refrigerate while cooking the pork.
2. Beat together eggs and milk in a large bowl. In another bowl, mix the flou , panko, and sesame seeds. Pour the cornstarch in a shallow dish.
3. Sprinkle pork cutlets with lemon pepper and salt. Dip pork cutlets in cornstarch, egg mixture, and then panko coating. Spritz both sides with cooking spray.
4. Select Air Fry. Set the temperature to 400°F (205°C) and set the time to 7 minutes. Press Start to begin preheating.
5. Once preheated, place the pan into the air fryer.
6. After 3 minutes, remove the pan from the air fryer. Flip the cutlets with tongs. Return the pan to the air fryer and continue cooking.
7. When cooking is complete, the pork should be crispy and golden brown on both sides.
8. Serve the fried cutlets with the Aloha salsa on the side.

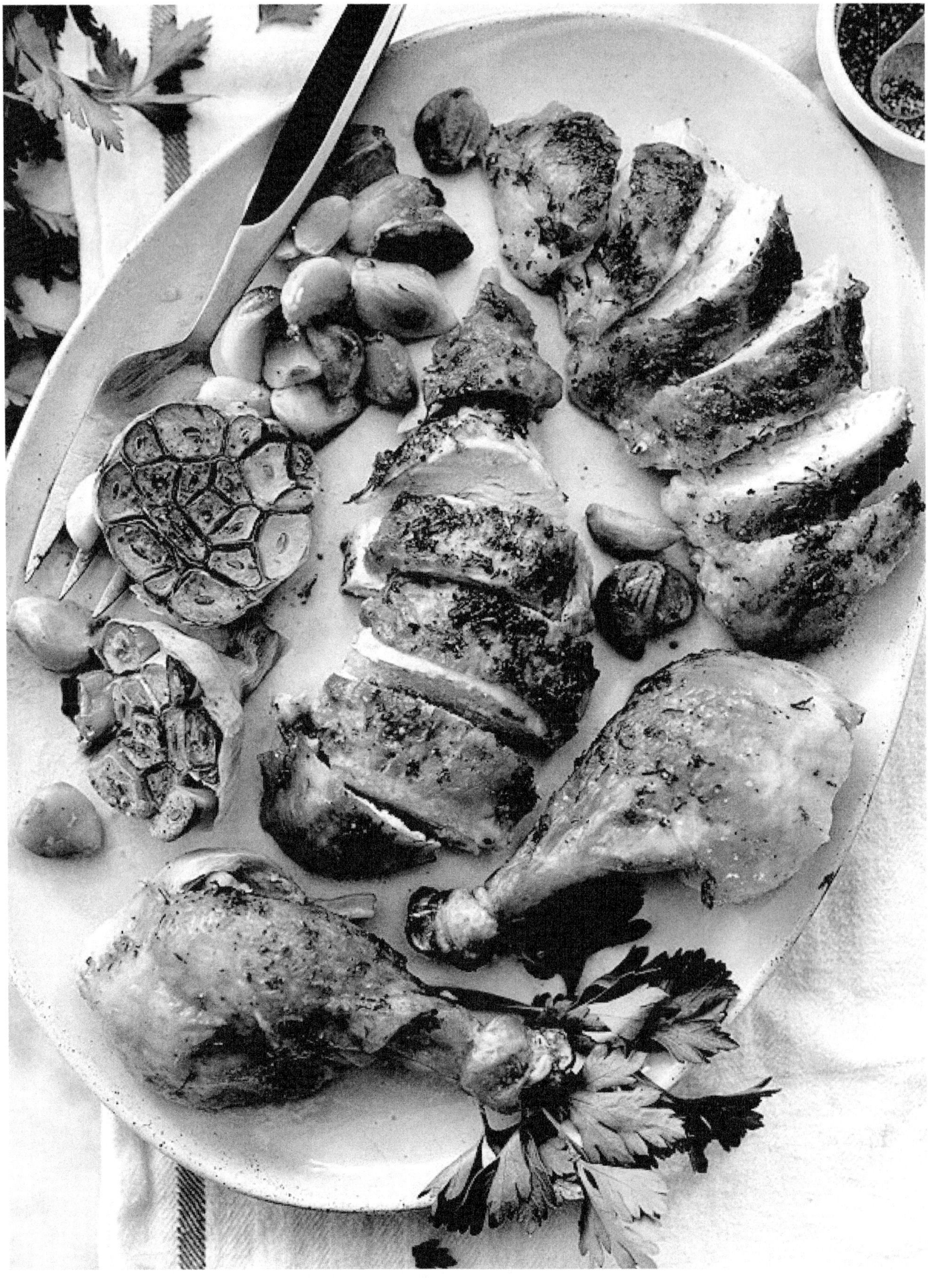

CHAPTER 6 *Poultry*

Chicken Tacos with Peanut Sauce

Prep time: 10 minutes | Cook time: 6 minutes | Serves 4

1 pound (454 g) ground chicken
2 cloves garlic, minced

Peanut Sauce:
¼ cup creamy peanut butter, at room temperature
2 tablespoons tamari
1½ teaspoons hot sauce
2 tablespoons lime juice
2 tablespoons grated fresh ginger
2 tablespoons chicken broth
2 teaspoons sugar

¼ cup diced onions
¼ teaspoon sea salt
Cooking spray

For Serving:
2 small heads butter lettuce, leaves separated
Lime slices (optional)

1. Spritz a baking pan with cooking spray.
2. Combine the ground chicken, garlic, and onions in the baking pan, then sprinkle with salt. Use a fork to break the ground chicken and combine them well.
3. Select Bake, set temperature to 350ºF (180ºC) and set time to 5 minutes. Press Start to begin preheating.
4. Once preheated, place the pan into the air fryer. Stir them halfway through the cooking time.
5. When cooking is complete, the chicken should be lightly browned.
6. Meanwhile, combine the ingredients for the sauce in a small bowl. Stir to mix well.
7. Pour the sauce in the pan of chicken, then bake for 1 more minute or until heated through.
8. Unfold the lettuce leaves on a large serving plate, then divide the chicken mixture on the lettuce leaves. Drizzle with lime juice and serve immediately.

Maple-Rosemary Turkey Breast

Prep time: 2 hours 20 minutes | Cook time: 30 minutes | Serves 6

½ teaspoon dried rosemary
2 minced garlic cloves
2 teaspoons salt
1 teaspoon ground black pepper
¼ cup olive oil
2½ pounds (1.1 kg) turkey breast
¼ cup pure maple syrup
1 tablespoon stone-ground brown mustard
1 tablespoon melted vegan butter

1. Combine the rosemary, garlic, salt, ground black pepper, and olive oil in a large bowl. Stir to mix well.
2. Dunk the turkey breast in the mixture and wrap the bowl in plastic. Refrigerate for 2 hours to marinate.
3. Remove the bowl from the refrigerator and let sit for half an hour before cooking.
4. Spritz the air fry basket with cooking spray.
5. Remove the turkey from the marinade and place in the air fry basket.
6. Select Air Fry. Set temperature to 400ºF (205ºC) and set time to 20 minutes. Press Start to begin preheating.
7. Once preheated, place the basket into the air fryer. Flip the breast halfway through.
8. When cooking is complete, the breast should be well browned.
9. Meanwhile, combine the remaining ingredients in a small bowl. Stir to mix well.
10. Pour half of the butter mixture over the turkey breast in the air fryer and air fry for 10 more minutes. Flip the breast and pour the remaining half of butter mixture over halfway through.
11. Transfer the turkey on a plate and slice to serve.

Homemade Air-Fried Chicken Wings

Prep time: 10 minutes | Cook time: 15 minutes | Serves 4

1 tablespoon olive oil
8 whole chicken wings
Chicken seasoning or rub, to taste
1 teaspoon garlic powder
Freshly ground black pepper, to taste

1. Grease the air fry basket with olive oil.
2. On a clean work surface, rub the chicken wings with chicken seasoning and rub, garlic powder, and ground black pepper.
3. Arrange the well-coated chicken wings in the air fry basket.
4. Select Air Fry. Set temperature to 400°F (205°C) and set time to 15 minutes. Press Start to begin preheating.
5. Once preheated, place the basket into the air fryer. Flip the chicken wings halfway through.
6. When cooking is complete, the internal temperature of the chicken wings should reach at least 165°F (74°C).
7. Remove the chicken wings from the air fryer. Serve immediately.

Stuffed Chicken with Bruschetta

Prep time: 10 minutes | Cook time: 10 minutes | Serves 4

Bruschetta Stuffing:
1 tomato, diced
3 tablespoons balsamic vinegar
1 teaspoon Italian seasoning
2 tablespoons chopped fresh basil
3 garlic cloves, minced
2 tablespoons extra-virgin olive oil

Chicken:
4 (4-ounce / 113-g) boneless, skinless chicken breasts, cut 4 slits each
1 teaspoon Italian seasoning
Chicken seasoning or rub, to taste
Cooking spray

1. Spritz the air fry basket with cooking spray.
2. Combine the ingredients for the bruschetta stuffing in a bowl. Stir to mix well. Set aside.
3. Rub the chicken breasts with Italian seasoning and chicken seasoning on a clean work surface.
4. Arrange the chicken breasts, slits side up, in the air fry basket and spritz with cooking spray.
5. Select Air Fry. Set temperature to 370°F (188°C) and set time to 10 minutes. Press Start to begin preheating.
6. Once preheated, place the basket into the air fryer. Flip the breast and fill the slits with the bruschetta stuffing half ay through.
7. When cooking is complete, the chicken should be well browned.
8. Serve immediately.

Panko-Ctusted Chicken Fingers

Prep time: 20 minutes | Cook time: 10 minutes | Makes 12 chicken fingers

½ cup all-purpose flou
2 cups panko bread crumbs
2 tablespoons canola oil
1 large egg
3 boneless and skinless chicken breasts, each cut into 4 strips
Kosher salt and freshly ground black pepper, to taste
Cooking spray

1. Spritz the air fry basket with cooking spray.
2. Pour the flour in a large bowl. Combine the panko and canola oil on a shallow dish. Whisk the egg in a separate bowl.
3. Rub the chicken strips with salt and ground black pepper on a clean work surface, then dip the chicken in the bowl of flou . Shake the excess off and dunk the chicken strips in the bowl of whisked egg, then roll the strips over the panko to coat well.
4. Arrange the strips in the air fry basket.
5. Select Air Fry. Set temperature to 360°F (182°C) and set time to 10 minutes. Press Start to begin preheating.
6. Once preheated, place the basket into the air fryer. Flip the strips halfway through.
7. When cooking is complete, the strips should be crunchy and lightly browned.
8. Serve immediately.

BBQ-Honey Basted Drumsticks

Prep time: 5 minutes | Cook time: 18 minutes | Serves 5

1 tablespoon olive oil	Salt and ground black pepper, to taste
10 chicken drumsticks	1 cup barbecue sauce
Chicken seasoning or rub, to taste	¼ cup honey

1. Grease the air fry basket with olive oil.
2. Rub the chicken drumsticks with chicken seasoning or rub, salt and ground black pepper on a clean work surface.
3. Arrange the chicken drumsticks in the air fry basket.
4. Select Air Fry. Set temperature to 390°F (199°C) and set time to 18 minutes. Press Start to begin preheating.
5. Once preheated, place the basket into the air fryer. Flip the drumsticks halfway through.
6. When cooking is complete, the drumsticks should be lightly browned.
7. Meanwhile, combine the barbecue sauce and honey in a small bowl. Stir to mix well.
8. Remove the drumsticks from the air fryer and baste with the sauce mixture to serve.

Apricot-Glazed Drumsticks

Prep time: 15 minutes | Cook time: 30 minutes | Makes 6 drumsticks

For the Glaze:

½ cup apricot preserves	powder
½ teaspoon tamari	2 teaspoons Dijon mustard
¼ teaspoon chili	

For the Chicken:

6 chicken drumsticks	½ teaspoon ground black pepper
½ teaspoon seasoning salt	Cooking spray
1 teaspoon salt	

Make the glaze:

1. Combine the ingredients for the glaze in a saucepan, then heat over low heat for 10 minutes or until thickened.
2. Turn off the heat and sit until ready to use.

Make the Chicken:

1. Spritz the air fry basket with cooking spray.
2. Combine the seasoning salt, salt, and pepper in a small bowl. Stir to mix well.
3. Place the chicken drumsticks in the air fry basket. Spritz with cooking spray and sprinkle with the salt mixture on both sides.
4. Select Air Fry. Set temperature to 370°F (188°C) and set time to 20 minutes. Press Start to begin preheating.
5. Once preheated, place the basket into the air fryer. Flip the chicken halfway through.
6. When cooking is complete, the chicken should be well browned.
7. Baste the chicken with the glaze and air fry for 2 more minutes or until the chicken tenderloin is glossy.
8. Serve immediately.

Baked Garlicky Whole Chicken

Prep time: 10 minutes | Cook time: 1 hour | Serves 2 to 4

½ cup melted butter	1 teaspoon ground black pepper
3 tablespoons garlic, minced	1 (1-pound / 454-g) whole chicken
Salt, to taste	

1. Combine the butter with garlic, salt, and ground black pepper in a small bowl.
2. Brush the butter mixture over the whole chicken, then place the chicken in the air fry basket, skin side down.
3. Select Bake, set temperature to 350°F (180°C) and set time to 60 minutes. Press Start to begin preheating.
4. Once preheated, place the basket into the air fryer. Flip the chicken halfway through.
5. When cooking is complete, an instant-read thermometer inserted in the thickest part of the chicken should register at least 165°F (74°C).
6. Remove the chicken from the air fryer and allow to cool for 15 minutes before serving.

Classic Hawaiian Chicken Bites

Prep time: 1 hour 15 minutes | Cook time: 15 minutes | Serves 4

½ cup pineapple juice
2 tablespoons apple cider vinegar
½ tablespoon minced ginger
½ cup ketchup
2 garlic cloves, minced
½ cup brown sugar
2 tablespoons sherry
½ cup soy sauce
4 chicken breasts, cubed
Cooking spray

1. Combine the pineapple juice, cider vinegar, ginger, ketchup, garlic, and sugar in a saucepan. Stir to mix well. Heat over low heat for 5 minutes or until thickened. Fold in the sherry and soy sauce.
2. Dunk the chicken cubes in the mixture. Press to submerge. Wrap the bowl in plastic and refrigerate to marinate for at least an hour.
3. Spritz the air fry basket with cooking spray.
4. Remove the chicken cubes from the marinade. Shake the excess off and put in the air fry basket. Spritz with cooking spray.
5. Select Air Fry. Set temperature to 360ºF (182ºC) and set time to 15 minutes. Press Start to begin preheating.
6. Once preheated, place the basket into the air fryer. Flip the chicken cubes at least three times during the air frying.
7. When cooking is complete, the chicken cubes should be glazed and well browned.
8. Serve immediately.

Bacon-Wrapped Cheesy Chicken

Prep time: 10 minutes | Cook time: 20 minutes | Serves 4

4 (5-ounce / 142-g) boneless, skinless chicken breasts, pounded to ¼ inch thick
1 cup cream cheese
2 tablespoons chopped fresh chives
8 slices thin-cut bacon
Sprig of fresh cilantro, for garnish
Cooking spray

1. Spritz the air fry basket with cooking spray.
2. On a clean work surface, slice the chicken horizontally to make a 1-inch incision on top of each chicken breast with a knife, then cut into the chicken to make a pocket. Leave a ½-inch border along the sides and bottom.
3. Combine the cream cheese and chives in a bowl. Stir to mix well, then gently pour the mixture into the chicken pockets.
4. Wrap each stuffed chicken breast with 2 bacon slices, then secure the ends with toothpicks.
5. Arrange them in the air fry basket.
6. Select Air Fry. Set temperature to 400ºF (205ºC) and set time to 20 minutes. Press Start to begin preheating.
7. Once preheated, place the basket into the air fryer. Flip the bacon-wrapped chicken halfway through the cooking time.
8. When cooking is complete, the bacon should be browned and crispy.
9. Transfer them on a large plate and serve with cilantro on top.

Cheesy Chicken and Pepperoni Pizza

Prep time: 15 minutes | Cook time: 15 minutes | Serves 6

2 cups cooked chicken, cubed
1 cup pizza sauce
20 slices pepperoni
¼ cup grated Parmesan cheese
1 cup shredded Mozzarella cheese
Cooking spray

1. Spritz a baking pan with cooking spray.
2. Arrange the chicken cubes in the prepared baking pan, then top the cubes with pizza sauce and pepperoni. Stir to coat the cubes and pepperoni with sauce. Scatter the cheeses on top.
3. Select Air Fry. Set temperature to 375ºF (190ºC) and set time to 15 minutes. Press Start to begin preheating.
4. Once preheated, place the pan into the air fryer.
5. When cooking is complete, the pizza should be frothy and the cheeses should be melted.
6. Serve immediately.

Broiled Goulash

Prep time: 5 minutes | Cook time: 17 minutes | Serves 2

2 red bell peppers, chopped
1 pound (454 g) ground chicken
2 medium tomatoes, diced
½ cup chicken broth
Salt and ground black pepper, to taste
Cooking spray

1. Spritz a baking pan with cooking spray.
2. Set the bell pepper in the baking pan.
3. Select Broil, set temperature to 365°F (185°C) and set time to 5 minutes. Press Start to begin preheating.
4. Once preheated, place the pan into the air fryer. Stir the bell pepper halfway through.
5. When broiling is complete, the bell pepper should be tender.
6. Add the ground chicken and diced tomatoes in the baking pan and stir to mix well.
7. Set the time of air fryer to 12 minutes. Press Start. Stir the mixture and mix in the chicken broth, salt and ground black pepper halfway through.
8. When cooking is complete, the chicken should be well browned.
9. Serve immediately.

Buffalo Chicken Drumettes

Prep time: 10 minutes | Cook time: 20 minutes | Serves 6

16 chicken drumettes (party wings)
Chicken seasoning or rub, to taste
1 teaspoon garlic powder
Ground black pepper, to taste
¼ cup buffalo wings sauce
Cooking spray

1. Spritz the air fry basket with cooking spray.
2. Rub the chicken wings with chicken seasoning, garlic powder, and ground black pepper on a clean work surface.
3. Arrange the chicken wings in the air fry basket. Spritz with cooking spray.
4. Select Air Fry. Set temperature to 400°F (205°C) and set time to 10 minutes. Press Start to begin preheating.
5. Once preheated, place the basket into the air fryer. Flip the chicken wings halfway through.
6. When cooking is complete, the chicken wings should be lightly browned.
7. Transfer the chicken wings in a large bowl, then pour in the buffalo wings sauce and toss to coat well.
8. Put the wings back to the air fryer and set time to 7 minutes. Flip the wings halfway through.
9. When cooking is complete, the wings should be heated through. Serve immediately.

Breaded Chicken Nuggets

Prep time: 10 minutes | Cook time: 8 minutes | Serves 4

1 pound (454 g) boneless, skinless chicken breasts, cut into 1-inch pieces
2 tablespoons panko bread crumbs
6 tablespoons bread crumbs
Chicken seasoning or rub, to taste
Salt and ground black pepper, to taste
2 eggs
Cooking spray

1. Spritz the air fry basket with cooking spray.
2. Combine the bread crumbs, chicken seasoning, salt, and black pepper in a large bowl. Stir to mix well. Whisk the eggs in a separate bowl.
3. Dunk the chicken pieces in the egg mixture, then in the bread crumb mixture. Shake the excess off.
4. Arrange the well-coated chicken pieces in the air fry basket. Spritz with cooking spray.
5. Select Air Fry. Set temperature to 400°F (205°C) and set time to 8 minutes. Press Start to begin preheating.
6. Once preheated, place the basket into the air fryer. Flip the chicken halfway through.
7. When cooking is complete, the chicken should be crispy and golden brown.
8. Serve immediately.

Chicken, Bell Pepper and Onion Rolls

Prep time: 10 minutes | Cook time: 12 minutes | Serves 4

2 (4-ounce / 113-g) boneless, skinless chicken breasts, slice in half horizontally
1 tablespoon olive oil
Juice of ½ lime
2 tablespoons taco seasoning
½ green bell pepper, cut into strips
½ red bell pepper, cut into strips
¼ onion, sliced

1. Unfold the chicken breast slices on a clean work surface. Rub with olive oil, then drizzle with lime juice and sprinkle with taco seasoning.
2. Top the chicken slices with equal amount of bell peppers and onion. Roll them up and secure with toothpicks.
3. Arrange the chicken roll-ups in the air fry basket.
4. Select Air Fry. Set temperature to 400°F (205°C) and set time to 12 minutes. Press Start to begin preheating.
5. Once preheated, place the basket into the air fryer. Flip the chicken roll-ups halfway through.
6. When cooking is complete, the internal temperature of the chicken should reach at least 165°F (74°C).
7. Remove the chicken from the air fryer. Discard the toothpicks and serve immediately.

Barbecue Chicken Tostadas with Coleslaw

Prep time: 15 minutes | Cook time: 10 minutes | Makes 4 tostadas

Coleslaw:
¼ cup sour cream
¼ small green cabbage, finely chopped
½ tablespoon white vinegar
½ teaspoon garlic powder
½ teaspoon salt
¼ teaspoon ground black pepper

Tostadas:
2 cups pulled rotisserie chicken
½ cup barbecue sauce
4 corn tortillas
½ cup shredded Mozzarella cheese
Cooking spray

Make the Coleslaw:
1. Combine the ingredients for the coleslaw in a large bowl. Toss to mix well.
2. Refrigerate until ready to serve.

Make the Tostadas:
1. Spritz the air fry basket with cooking spray.
2. Toss the chicken with barbecue sauce in a separate large bowl to combine well. Set aside.
3. Place one tortilla in the air fry basket and spritz with cooking spray.
4. Select Air Fry. Set temperature to 370°F (188°C) and set time to 10 minutes. Press Start to begin preheating.
5. Once preheated, place the basket into the air fryer. Flip the tortilla and spread the barbecue chicken and cheese over halfway through.
6. When cooking is complete, the tortilla should be browned and the cheese should be melted.
7. Serve the tostadas with coleslaw on top.

Cajun Chicken Drumsticks

Prep time: 5 minutes | Cook time: 18 minutes | Serves 5

1 tablespoon olive oil
10 chicken drumsticks
1½ tablespoons Cajun seasoning
Salt and ground black pepper, to taste

1. Grease the air fry basket with olive oil.
2. On a clean work surface, rub the chicken drumsticks with Cajun seasoning, salt, and ground black pepper.
3. Arrange the seasoned chicken drumsticks in the air fry basket.
4. Select Air Fry. Set temperature to 390°F (199°C) and set time to 18 minutes. Press Start to begin preheating.
5. Once preheated, place the basket into the air fryer. Flip the drumsticks halfway through.
6. When cooking is complete, the drumsticks should be lightly browned.
7. Remove the chicken drumsticks from the air fryer. Serve immediately.

Balsamic Marmalade Duck Breasts

Prep time: 5 minutes | Cook time: 13 minutes | Serves 4

4 (6-ounce / 170-g) skin-on duck breasts
1 teaspoon salt
¼ cup orange marmalade
1 tablespoon white balsamic vinegar
¾ teaspoon ground black pepper

1. Cut 10 slits into the skin of the duck breasts, then sprinkle with salt on both sides.
2. Place the breasts in the air fry basket, skin side up.
3. Select Air Fry. Set temperature to 400°F (205°C) and set time to 10 minutes. Press Start to begin preheating.
4. Once preheated, place the basket into the air fryer.
5. Meanwhile, combine the remaining ingredients in a small bowl. Stir to mix well.
6. When cooking is complete, brush the duck skin with the marmalade mixture. Flip the breast and air fry for 3 more minutes or until the skin is crispy and the breast is well browned.
7. Serve immediately.

Strawberry-Glazed Turkey Breast

Prep time: 15 minutes | Cook time: 37 minutes | Serves 2

2 pounds (907 g) turkey breast
1 tablespoon olive oil
Salt and ground black pepper, to taste
1 cup fresh strawberries

1. Rub the turkey bread with olive oil on a clean work surface, then sprinkle with salt and ground black pepper.
2. Transfer the turkey in the air fry basket and spritz with cooking spray.
3. Select Air Fry. Set temperature to 375°F (190°C) and set time to 30 minutes. Press Start to begin preheating.
4. Once preheated, place the basket into the air fryer. Flip the turkey breast halfway through.
5. Meanwhile, put the strawberries in a food processor and pulse until smooth.
6. When cooking is complete, spread the puréed strawberries over the turkey and fry for 7 more minutes.
7. Serve immediately.

Fried Chicken and Roma Tomato

Prep time: 10 minutes | Cook time: 35 minutes | Serves 8

3 pounds (1.4 kg) chicken breasts, bone-in
1 teaspoon minced fresh basil
1 teaspoon minced fresh rosemary
2 tablespoons minced fresh parsley
1 teaspoon cayenne pepper
½ teaspoon salt
½ teaspoon freshly ground black pepper
4 medium Roma tomatoes, halved
Cooking spray

1. Spritz the air fry basket with cooking spray.
2. Combine all the ingredients, except for the chicken breasts and tomatoes, in a large bowl. Stir to mix well.
3. Dunk the chicken breasts in the mixture and press to coat well.
4. Transfer the chicken breasts to the air fry basket.
5. Select Air Fry. Set temperature to 370°F (188°C) and set time to 20 minutes. Press Start to begin preheating.
6. Once preheated, place the basket into the air fryer. Flip the breasts halfway through the cooking time.
7. When cooking is complete, the internal temperature of the thickest part of the breasts should reach at least 165°F (74°C).
8. Remove the cooked chicken breasts from the air fryer and adjust the temperature to 350°F (180°C).
9. Place the tomatoes in the air fry basket and spritz with cooking spray. Sprinkle with a touch of salt.
10. Set time to 10 minutes. Stir the tomatoes halfway through the cooking time.
11. When cooking is complete, the tomatoes should be tender.
12. Serve the tomatoes with chicken breasts on a large serving plate.

Chicken Thighs on Waffles with Honey

Prep time: 1 hour 20 minutes | Cook time: 20 minutes | Serves 4

For the chicken:
4 chicken thighs, skin on
1 cup low-fat buttermilk
½ cup all-purpose flou
½ teaspoon garlic powder
½ teaspoon mustard powder
1 teaspoon kosher salt
½ teaspoon freshly ground black pepper
¼ cup honey, for serving
Cooking spray

For the waffles:
½ cup all-purpose flou
½ cup whole wheat pastry flou
1 large egg, beaten
1 cup low-fat buttermilk
1 teaspoon baking powder
2 tablespoons canola oil
½ teaspoon kosher salt
1 tablespoon granulated sugar

1. Combine the chicken thighs with buttermilk in a large bowl. Wrap the bowl in plastic and refrigerate to marinate for at least an hour.
2. Spritz the air fry basket with cooking spray.
3. Combine the flou , mustard powder, garlic powder, salt, and black pepper in a shallow dish. Stir to mix well.
4. Remove the thighs from the buttermilk and pat dry with paper towels. Sit the bowl of buttermilk aside.
5. Dip the thighs in the flour mixture first then into the buttermilk, and then into the flour mixture. Sha e the excess off.
6. Arrange the thighs in the air fry basket and spritz with cooking spray.
7. Select Air Fry. Set temperature to 360°F (182°C) and set time to 20 minutes. Press Start to begin preheating.
8. Once preheated, place the basket into the air fryer. Flip the thighs halfway through.
9. When cooking is complete, an instant-read thermometer inserted in the thickest part of the chicken thighs should register at least 165°F (74°C).
10. Meanwhile, make the waffles: combine the ingredients for the waffles in a large bowl. Stir to mix well, then arrange the mixture in a waffle iron and cook until a golden and fragrant waffle forms
11. Remove the waffles from the affle iron and slice into 4 pieces. Remove the chicken thighs from the air fryer and allow to cool for 5 minutes.
12. Arrange each chicken thigh on each waffle p ece and drizzle with 1 tablespoon of honey. Serve warm.

Golden Chicken Schnitzel

Prep time: 15 minutes | Cook time: 5 minutes | Serves 4

½ cup all-purpose flou
1 teaspoon marjoram
½ teaspoon thyme
1 teaspoon dried parsley fla es
½ teaspoon salt
1 egg
1 teaspoon lemon juice
1 teaspoon water
1 cup bread crumbs
4 chicken tenders, pounded thin, cut in half lengthwise
Cooking spray

1. Spritz the air fry basket with cooking spray.
2. Combine the flou , marjoram, thyme, parsley, and salt in a shallow dish. Stir to mix well.
3. Whisk the egg with lemon juice and water in a large bowl. Pour the bread crumbs in a separate shallow dish.
4. Roll the chicken halves in the flour mixture first, then in the egg mixture, and then roll over the bread crumbs to coat well. Shake the excess off.
5. Arrange the chicken halves in the air fry basket and spritz with cooking spray on both sides.
6. Select Air Fry. Set temperature to 390°F (199°C) and set time to 5 minutes. Press Start to begin preheating.
7. Once preheated, place the basket into the air fryer. Flip the halves halfway through.
8. When cooking is complete, the chicken halves should be golden brown and crispy.
9. Serve immediately.

Air-Fried Korean Chicken Wings

Prep time: 10 minutes | Cook time: 25 minutes | Serves 4

Wings:
2 pounds (907 g) chicken wings
1 teaspoon salt
1 teaspoon ground black pepper

Sauce:
2 tablespoons gochujang
1 tablespoon mayonnaise
1 tablespoon minced ginger
1 tablespoon minced garlic
1 teaspoon agave nectar
2 packets Splenda
1 tablespoon sesame oil

For Garnish:
2 teaspoons sesame seeds
¼ cup chopped green onions

1. Line a baking pan with aluminum foil, then arrange the rack on the pan.
2. On a clean work surface, rub the chicken wings with salt and ground black pepper, then arrange the seasoned wings on the rack.
3. Select Air Fry. Set temperature to 400°F (205°C) and set time to 20 minutes. Press Start to begin preheating.
4. Once preheated, place the pan into the air fryer. Flip the wings halfway through.
5. When cooking is complete, the wings should be well browned.
6. Meanwhile, combine the ingredients for the sauce in a small bowl. Stir to mix well. Reserve half of the sauce in a separate bowl until ready to serve.
7. Remove the air fried chicken wings from the air fryer and toss with remaining half of the sauce to coat well.
8. Place the wings back to the air fryer. Select Air Fry. Set time to 5 minutes.
9. When cooking is complete, the internal temperature of the wings should reach at least 165°F (74°C).
10. Remove the wings from the air fryer and place on a large plate. Sprinkle with sesame seeds and green onions. Serve with reserved sauce.

Cherry-Glazed Whole Duck

Prep time: 20 minutes | Cook time: 32 minutes | Serves 12

1 whole duck (about 5 pounds / 2.3 kg in total), split in half, back and rib bones removed, fat trimmed
1 teaspoon olive oil
Salt and freshly ground black pepper, to taste

Cherry Sauce:
1 tablespoon butter
1 shallot, minced
½ cup sherry
1 cup chicken stock
1 teaspoon white wine vinegar
¾ cup cherry preserves
1 teaspoon fresh thyme leaves
Salt and freshly ground black pepper, to taste

1. On a clean work surface, rub the duck with olive oil, then sprinkle with salt and ground black pepper to season.
2. Place the duck in the air fry basket, breast side up.
3. Select Air Fry. Set temperature to 400°F (205°C) and set time to 25 minutes. Press Start to begin preheating.
4. Once preheated, place the basket into the air fryer. Flip the ducks halfway through the cooking time.
5. Meanwhile, make the cherry sauce: Heat the butter in a skillet over medium-high heat or until melted.
6. Add the shallot and sauté for 5 minutes or until lightly browned.
7. Add the sherry and simmer for 6 minutes or until it reduces in half.
8. Add the chicken stick, white wine vinegar, and cherry preserves. Stir to combine well. Simmer for 6 more minutes or until thickened.
9. Fold in the thyme leaves and sprinkle with salt and ground black pepper. Stir to mix well.
10. When the cooking of the duck is complete, glaze the duck with a quarter of the cherry sauce, then air fry for another 4 minutes.
11. Flip the duck and glaze with another quarter of the cherry sauce. Air fry for an additional 3 minutes.
12. Transfer the duck on a large plate and serve with remaining cherry sauce.

Panko-Crusted Chicken Livers

Prep time: 10 minutes | Cook time: 10 minutes | Serves 4

2 eggs
2 tablespoons water
¾ cup flou
2 cups panko bread crumbs
1 teaspoon salt
½ teaspoon ground black pepper
20 ounces (567 g) chicken livers
Cooking spray

1. Spritz the air fry basket with cooking spray.
2. Whisk the eggs with water in a large bowl. Pour the flour in a sepa ate bowl. Pour the panko on a shallow dish and sprinkle with salt and pepper.
3. Dredge the chicken livers in the flou . Shake the excess off, then dunk the livers in the whisked eggs, and then roll the livers over the panko to coat well.
4. Arrange the livers in the air fry basket and spritz with cooking spray.
5. Select Air Fry. Set temperature to 390°F (199°C) and set time to 10 minutes. Press Start to begin preheating.
6. Once preheated, place the basket into the air fryer. Flip the livers halfway through.
7. When cooking is complete, the livers should be golden and crispy.
8. Serve immediately.

Honey-Glazed Chicken Breasts

Prep time: 5 minutes | Cook time: 10 minutes | Serves 4

4 (4-ounce / 113-g) boneless, skinless chicken breasts
Chicken seasoning or rub, to taste
Salt and ground black pepper, to taste
¼ cup honey
2 tablespoons soy sauce
2 teaspoons grated fresh ginger
2 garlic cloves, minced
Cooking spray

1. Spritz the air fry basket with cooking spray.
2. Rub the chicken breasts with chicken seasoning, salt, and black pepper on a clean work surface.
3. Arrange the chicken breasts in the air fry basket and spritz with cooking spray.
4. Select Air Fry. Set temperature to 400°F (205°C) and set time to 10 minutes. Press Start to begin preheating.
5. Once preheated, place the basket into the air fryer. Flip the chicken breasts halfway through.
6. When cooking is complete, the internal temperature of the thickest part of the chicken should reach at least 165°F (74°C).
7. Meanwhile, combine the honey, soy sauce, ginger, and garlic in a saucepan and heat over medium-high heat for 3 minutes or until thickened. Stir constantly.
8. Remove the chicken from the air fryer and serve with the honey glaze.

Air-Fried Duck Leg Quarters

Prep time: 5 minutes | Cook time: 45 minutes | Serves 4

4 (½-pound / 227-g) skin-on duck leg quarters
2 medium garlic cloves, minced
½ teaspoon salt
½ teaspoon ground black pepper

1. Spritz the air fry basket with cooking spray.
2. On a clean work surface, rub the duck leg quarters with garlic, salt, and black pepper.
3. Arrange the leg quarters in the air fry basket and spritz with cooking spray.
4. Select Air Fry. Set temperature to 300°F (150°C) and set time to 30 minutes. Press Start to begin preheating.
5. Once preheated, place the basket into the air fryer.
6. After 30 minutes, remove the basket from the air fryer. Flip the leg quarters. Increase temperature to 375°F (190°C) and set time to 15 minutes. Return the basket to the air fryer and continue cooking.
7. When cooking is complete, the leg quarters should be well browned and crispy.
8. Remove the duck leg quarters from the air fryer and allow to cool for 10 minutes before serving.

Air-Fried Crispy Chicken Skin

Prep time: 5 minutes | Cook time: 6 minutes | Serves 4

1 pound (454 g) chicken skin, cut into slices
1 teaspoon melted butter
½ teaspoon crushed chili flakes
1 teaspoon dried dill
Salt and ground black pepper, to taste

1. Combine all the ingredients in a large bowl. Toss to coat the chicken skin well.
2. Transfer the skin in the air fry basket.
3. Select Air Fry. Set temperature to 360°F (182°C) and set time to 6 minutes. Press Start to begin preheating.
4. Once preheated, place the basket into the air fryer. Stir the skin halfway through.
5. When cooking is complete, the skin should be crispy.
6. Serve immediately.

Paprika Chicken Skewers

Prep time: 5 minutes | Cook time: 10 minutes | Serves 4

4 (6-ounce / 170-g) boneless, skinless chicken breasts, sliced into strips

Satay Sauce:
¼ cup creamy almond butter
½ teaspoon hot sauce
1½ tablespoons coconut vinegar
2 tablespoons chicken broth
1 teaspoon peeled and minced fresh ginger
1 clove garlic, minced
1 teaspoon sugar
1 teaspoon sea salt
1 teaspoon paprika
Cooking spray

For Serving:
¼ cup chopped cilantro leaves
Red pepper flakes, to taste
Thinly sliced red, orange, or / and yellow bell peppers

Special Equipment:
16 wooden or bamboo skewers, soaked in water for 15 minutes

1. Spritz the air fry basket with cooking spray.
2. Run the bamboo skewers through the chicken strips, then arrange the chicken skewers in the air fry basket and sprinkle with salt and paprika.
3. Select Air Fry. Set temperature to 400°F (205°C) and set time to 10 minutes. Press Start to begin preheating.
4. Once preheated, place the basket into the air fryer. Flip the chicken skewers halfway during the cooking.
5. When cooking is complete, the chicken should be lightly browned.
6. Meanwhile, combine the ingredients for the sauce in a small bowl. Stir to mix well.
7. Transfer the cooked chicken skewers on a large plate, then top with cilantro, sliced bell peppers, red pepper flakes. Serve with the sauce or just baste the sauce over before serving.

Baked Turkey and Carrot Meatloaves

Prep time: 6 minutes | Cook time: 24 minutes | Serves 4

¼ cup grated carrot
2 garlic cloves, minced
2 tablespoons ground almonds
⅓ cup minced onion
2 teaspoons olive oil
1 teaspoon dried marjoram
1 egg white
¾ pound (340 g) ground turkey breast

1. In a medium bowl, stir together the carrot, garlic, almonds, onion, olive oil, marjoram, and egg white.
2. Add the ground turkey. Mix until combined.
3. Double 16 foil muffin cup liners to make 8 cups. Divide the turkey mixture evenly among the liners.
4. Select Bake, set temperature to 400°F (205°C) and set time to 24 minutes. Press Start to begin preheating.
5. Once preheated, place the muffin cups into the air fryer.
6. When cooking is complete, the meatloaves should reach an internal temperature of 165°F (74°C) on a meat thermometer.
7. Serve immediately.

Panko-Crusted Chicken Cutlets

Prep time: 15 minutes | Cook time: 15 minutes | Serves 4

2 tablespoons panko bread crumbs
¼ cup grated Parmesan cheese
⅛ tablespoon paprika
½ tablespoon garlic powder
2 large eggs
4 chicken cutlets
1 tablespoon parsley
Salt and ground black pepper, to taste
Cooking spray

1. Spritz the air fry basket with cooking spray.
2. Combine the bread crumbs, Parmesan, paprika, garlic powder, salt, and ground black pepper in a large bowl. Stir to mix well. Beat the eggs in a separate bowl.
3. Dredge the chicken cutlets in the beaten eggs, then roll over the bread crumbs mixture to coat well. Shake the excess off.
4. Transfer the chicken cutlets in the air fry basket and spritz with cooking spray.
5. Select Air Fry. Set temperature to 400ºF (205ºC) and set time to 15 minutes. Press Start to begin preheating.
6. Once preheated, place the basket into the air fryer. Flip the cutlets halfway through.
7. When cooking is complete, the cutlets should be crispy and golden brown.
8. Serve with parsley on top.

Golden Sweet-Sour Chicken Nuggets

Prep time: 15 minutes | Cook time: 15 minutes | Serves 4

1 cup cornstarch
Chicken seasoning or rub, to taste
Salt and ground black pepper, to taste
2 eggs
2 (4-ounce/ 113-g) boneless, skinless chicken breasts, cut into 1-inch pieces
1½ cups sweet-and-sour sauce
Cooking spray

1. Spritz the air fry basket with cooking spray.
2. Combine the cornstarch, chicken seasoning, salt, and pepper in a large bowl. Stir to mix well. Whisk the eggs in a separate bowl.
3. Dredge the chicken pieces in the bowl of cornstarch mixture first, then in the bowl of whisked eggs, and then in the cornstarch mixture again.
4. Arrange the well-coated chicken pieces in the air fry basket. Spritz with cooking spray.
5. Select Air Fry. Set temperature to 360ºF (182ºC) and set time to 15 minutes. Press Start to begin preheating.
6. Once preheated, place the basket into the air fryer. Flip the chicken halfway through.
7. When cooking is complete, the chicken should be golden brown and crispy.
8. Transfer the chicken pieces on a large serving plate, then baste with sweet-and-sour sauce before serving.

Tangy Cilantro Chicken Breast

Prep time: 35 minutes | Cook time: 10 minutes | Serves 4

4 (4-ounce / 113-g) boneless, skinless chicken breasts
½ cup chopped fresh cilantro
Juice of 1 lime
Chicken seasoning or rub, to taste
Salt and ground black pepper, to taste
Cooking spray

1. Put the chicken breasts in the large bowl, then add the cilantro, lime juice, chicken seasoning, salt, and black pepper. Toss to coat well.
2. Wrap the bowl in plastic and refrigerate to marinate for at least 30 minutes.
3. Spritz the air fry basket with cooking spray.
4. Remove the marinated chicken breasts from the bowl and place in the air fry basket. Spritz with cooking spray.
5. Select Air Fry. Set temperature to 400ºF (205ºC) and set time to 10 minutes. Press Start to begin preheating.
6. Once preheated, place the basket into the air fryer. Flip the breasts halfway through.
7. When cooking is complete, the internal temperature of the chicken should reach at least 165ºF (74ºC).
8. Serve immediately.

Peach-Glazed Chicken with Cherry

Prep time: 8 minutes | Cook time: 15 minutes | Serves 4

- ⅓ cup peach preserves
- 1 teaspoon ground rosemary
- ½ teaspoon black pepper
- ½ teaspoon salt
- ½ teaspoon marjoram
- 1 teaspoon light olive oil
- 1 pound (454 g) boneless chicken breasts, cut in 1½-inch chunks
- 1 (10-ounce / 284-g) package frozen dark cherries, thawed and drained
- Cooking spray

1. In a medium bowl, mix peach preserves, rosemary, pepper, salt, marjoram, and olive oil.
2. Stir in chicken chunks and toss to coat well with the preserve mixture.
3. Spritz the air fry basket with cooking spray and lay chicken chunks in the air fry basket.
4. Select Bake. Set the temperature to 400°F (205°C) and set the time to 15 minutes. Press Start to begin preheating.
5. Once preheated, place the basket into the air fryer.
6. After 7 minutes, remove the basket from the air fryer. Flip the chicken chunks. Return the basket to the air fryer and continue cooking.
7. When cooking is complete, the chicken should no longer pink and the juices should run clear.
8. Scatter the cherries over and cook for an additional minute to heat cherries.
9. Serve immediately.

Cheesy Dijon Turkey Burgers

Prep time: 10 minutes | Cook time: 25 minutes | Serves 4

- 2 medium yellow onions
- 1 tablespoon olive oil
- 1½ teaspoons kosher salt, divided
- 1¼ pound (567 g) ground turkey
- ⅓ cup mayonnaise
- 1 tablespoon Dijon mustard
- 2 teaspoons Worcestershire sauce
- 4 slices sharp Cheddar cheese (about 4 ounces / 113 g in total)
- 4 hamburger buns, sliced

1. Trim the onions and cut them in half through the root. Cut one of the halves in half. Grate one quarter. Place the grated onion in a large bowl. Thinly slice the remaining onions and place in a medium bowl with the oil and ½ teaspoon of kosher salt. Toss to coat. Place the onions in a single layer on a baking pan.
2. Select Roast, set temperature to 350°F (180°C), and set time to 10 minutes. Press Start to begin preheating.
3. Once preheated, place the pan into the air fryer.
4. While the onions are cooking, add the turkey to the grated onion. Add the remaining kosher salt, mayonnaise, mustard, and Worcestershire sauce. Mix just until combined, being careful not to overwork the turkey. Divide the mixture into 4 patties, each about ¾-inch thick.
5. When cooking is complete, remove the pan from the air fryer. Move the onions to one side of the pan and place the burgers on the pan. Poke your finger into the center of each burger to make a deep indentation.
6. Select Broil, set temperature to High, and set time to 12 minutes. Press Start to begin preheating.
7. Once preheated, place the pan into the air fryer. After 6 minutes, remove the pan. Turn the burgers and stir the onions. Return the pan to the air fryer and continue cooking. After about 4 minutes, remove the pan and place the cheese slices on the burgers. Return the pan to the air fryer and continue cooking for about 1 minute, or until the cheese is melted and the center of the burgers has reached at least 165°F (74°C) on a meat thermometer.
8. When cooking is complete, remove the pan from the air fryer. Loosely cover the burgers with foil.
9. Lay out the buns, cut-side up, on the air fryer rack. Select Broil, set temperature to High, and set time to 3 minutes. Place the pan into the air fryer. Check the buns after 2 minutes; they should be lightly browned.
10. Remove the buns from the air fryer. Assemble the burgers and serve.

Baked Cheesy Marinara Chicken

Prep time: 30 minutes | Cook time: 1 hour | Serves 2

1 large egg
¼ cup almond meal
2 (6-ounce / 170-g) boneless, skinless chicken breast halves
1 (8-ounce / 227-g) jar marinara sauce, divided
4 tablespoons shredded Mozzarella cheese, divided
4 tablespoons grated Parmesan cheese, divided
4 tablespoons chopped fresh basil, divided
Salt and freshly ground black pepper, to taste
Cooking spray

1. Spritz the air fry basket with cooking spray.
2. In a shallow bowl, beat the egg.
3. In a separate shallow bowl, place the almond meal.
4. Dip 1 chicken breast half into the egg, then into the almond meal to coat. Place the coated chicken in the air fry basket. Repeat with the remaining 1 chicken breast half.
5. Select Bake, set temperature to 350ºF (180ºC) and set time to 40 minutes. Press Start to begin preheating.
6. Once preheated, place the basket into the air fryer.
7. After 20 minutes, remove the basket from the air fryer and flip the chic en. Return the basket to air fryer and continue cooking.
8. When cooking is complete, the chicken should no longer pink and the juices run clear.
9. In a baking pan, pour half of marinara sauce.
10. Place the cooked chicken in the sauce. Cover with the remaining marinara.
11. Sprinkle 2 tablespoons of Mozzarella cheese and 2 tablespoons of soy Parmesan cheese on each chicken breast. Top each with 2 tablespoons of basil.
12. Place the baking pan back in the air fryer and set the baking time to 20 minutes. Flip the chicken halfway through the cooking time.
13. When cooking is complete, an instant-read thermometer inserted into the center of the chicken should read at least 165ºF (74ºC).
14. Remove the pan from air fryer and divide between 2 plates. Season with salt and pepper and serve.

Herbed Dijon Turkey Breast

Prep time: 5 minutes | Cook time: 30 minutes | Serves 4

1 teaspoon chopped fresh sage
1 teaspoon chopped fresh tarragon
1 teaspoon chopped fresh thyme leaves
1 teaspoon chopped fresh rosemary leaves
1½ teaspoons sea salt
1 teaspoon ground black pepper
1 (2-pound / 907-g) turkey breast
3 tablespoons Dijon mustard
3 tablespoons butter, melted
Cooking spray

1. Spritz the air fry basket with cooking spray.
2. Combine the herbs, salt, and black pepper in a small bowl. Stir to mix well. Set aside.
3. Combine the Dijon mustard and butter in a separate bowl. Stir to mix well.
4. Rub the turkey with the herb mixture on a clean work surface, then brush the turkey with Dijon mixture.
5. Arrange the turkey in the air fry basket.
6. Select Air Fry. Set temperature to 390ºF (199ºC) and set time to 30 minutes. Press Start to begin preheating.
7. Once preheated, place the basket into the air fryer. Flip the turkey breast halfway through.
8. When cooking is complete, an instant-read thermometer inserted in the thickest part of the turkey breast should reach at least 165ºF (74ºC).
9. Transfer the cooked turkey breast on a large plate and slice to serve.

Spicy Chicken, Sausage and Pepper

Prep time: 10 minutes | Cook time: 27 minutes | Serves 4

4 bone-in, skin-on chicken thighs (about 1½ pounds / 680 g)
1½ teaspoon kosher salt, divided
1 link sweet Italian sausage (about 4 ounces / 113 g), whole
8 ounces (227 g) miniature bell peppers, halved and deseeded
1 small onion, thinly sliced
2 garlic cloves, minced
1 tablespoon olive oil
4 hot pickled cherry peppers, deseeded and quartered, along with 2 tablespoons pickling liquid from the jar
¼ cup chicken stock
Cooking spray

1. Salt the chicken thighs on both sides with 1 teaspoon of kosher salt. Spritz a baking pan with cooking spray and place the thighs skin-side down on the pan. Add the sausage.
2. Select Roast, set temperature to 375°F (190°C), and set time to 27 minutes. Press Start to begin preheating.
3. Once preheated, place the pan into the air fryer.
4. While the chicken and sausage cook, place the bell peppers, onion, and garlic in a large bowl. Sprinkle with the remaining kosher salt and add the olive oil. Toss to coat.
5. After 10 minutes, remove the pan from the air fryer and flip the chicen thighs and sausage. Add the pepper mixture to the pan. Return the pan to the air fryer and continue cooking.
6. After another 10 minutes, remove the pan from the air fryer and add the pickled peppers, pickling liquid, and stock. Stir the pickled peppers into the peppers and onion. Return the pan to the air fryer and continue cooking.
7. When cooking is complete, the peppers and onion should be soft and the chicken should read 165°F (74°C) on a meat thermometer. Remove the pan from the air fryer. Slice the sausage into thin pieces and stir it into the pepper mixture. Spoon the peppers over four plates. Top with a chicken thigh.

Chicken with Mashed Potato and Corn

Prep time: 10 minutes | Cook time: 25 minutes | Serves 4

4 bone-in, skin-on chicken thighs
2 teaspoons kosher salt, divided
1 cup Bisquick baking mix
½ cup butter, melted, divided
1 pound (454 g) small red potatoes, quartered
3 ears corn, shucked and cut into rounds 1- to 1½-inches thick
⅓ cup heavy whipping cream
½ teaspoon freshly ground black pepper

1. Sprinkle the chicken on all sides with 1 teaspoon of kosher salt. Place the baking mix in a shallow dish. Brush the thighs on all sides with ¼ cup of butter, then dredge them in the baking mix, coating them all on sides. Place the chicken in the center of a baking pan.
2. Place the potatoes in a large bowl with 2 tablespoons of butter and toss to coat. Place them on one side of the chicken on the pan.
3. Place the corn in a medium bowl and drizzle with the remaining butter. Sprinkle with ¼ teaspoon of kosher salt and toss to coat. Place on the pan on the other side of the chicken.
4. Select Roast, set temperature to 375°F (190°C), and set time to 25 minutes. Press Start to begin preheating.
5. Once preheated, place the pan into the air fryer.
6. After 20 minutes, remove the pan from the air fryer and transfer the potatoes back to the bowl. Return the pan to air fryer and continue cooking.
7. As the chicken continues cooking, add the cream, black pepper, and remaining kosher salt to the potatoes. Lightly mash the potatoes with a potato masher.
8. When cooking is complete, the corn should be tender and the chicken cooked through, reading 165°F (74°C) on a meat thermometer. Remove the pan from the air fryer and serve the chicken with the smashed potatoes and corn on the side.

Parmesan Chicken Skewers with Corn

Prep time: 17 minutes | Cook time: 10 minutes | Serves 4

1 pound (454 g) boneless, skinless chicken breast, cut into 1½-inch chunks	3 tablespoons vegetable oil, divided
1 green bell pepper, deseeded and cut into 1-inch pieces	2 teaspoons kosher salt, divided
	2 cups corn, drained
1 red bell pepper, deseeded and cut into 1-inch pieces	¼ teaspoon granulated garlic
	1 teaspoon freshly squeezed lime juice
1 large onion, cut into large chunks	1 tablespoon mayonnaise
2 tablespoons fajita seasoning	3 tablespoons grated Parmesan cheese

Special Equipment:
12 wooden skewers, soaked in water for at least 30 minutes

1. Place the chicken, bell peppers, and onion in a large bowl. Add the fajita seasoning, 2 tablespoons of vegetable oil, and 1½ teaspoons of kosher salt. Toss to coat evenly.
2. Alternate the chicken and vegetables on the skewers, making about 12 skewers.
3. Place the corn in a medium bowl and add the remaining vegetable oil. Add the remaining kosher salt and the garlic, and toss to coat. Place the corn in an even layer on a baking pan and place the skewers on top.
4. Select Roast, set temperature to 375ºF (190ºC), and set time to 10 minutes. Press Start to begin preheating.
5. Once preheated, place the pan into the air fryer.
6. After about 5 minutes, remove the pan from the air fryer and turn the skewers. Return the pan to the air fryer and continue cooking.
7. When cooking is complete, remove the pan from the air fryer. Place the skewers on a platter. Put the corn back to the bowl and combine with the lime juice, mayonnaise, and Parmesan cheese. Stir to mix well. Serve the skewers with the corn.

Chicken Thighs with Veggies

Prep time: 10 minutes | Cook time: 27 minutes | Serves 4

4 bone-in, skin-on chicken thighs	3 cups shredded cabbage
1½ teaspoon kosher salt, divided	½ small red onion, thinly sliced
1 tablespoon smoked paprika	4 large radishes, julienned
½ teaspoon granulated garlic	3 tablespoons red wine vinegar
½ teaspoon dried oregano	2 tablespoons olive oil
¼ teaspoon freshly ground black pepper	Cooking spray

1. Salt the chicken thighs on both sides with 1 teaspoon of kosher salt. In a small bowl, combine the paprika, garlic, oregano, and black pepper. Sprinkle half this mixture over the skin sides of the thighs. Spritz a baking pan with cooking spray and place the thighs skin-side down on the pan. Sprinkle the remaining spice mixture over the other sides of the chicken pieces.
2. Select Roast, set temperature to 375ºF (190ºC), and set time to 27 minutes. Press Start to begin preheating.
3. Once preheated, place the pan into the air fryer.
4. After 10 minutes, remove the pan from the air fryer and turn over the chicken thighs. Return the pan to the air fryer and continue cooking.
5. While the chicken cooks, place the cabbage, onion, and radishes in a large bowl. Sprinkle with the remaining kosher salt, vinegar, and olive oil. Toss to coat.
6. After another 9 to 10 minutes, remove the pan from the air fryer and place the chicken thighs on a cutting board. Place the cabbage mixture in the pan and toss with the chicken fat and spices.
7. Spread the cabbage in an even layer on the pan and place the chicken on it, skin-side up. Place the pan into the air fryer and continue cooking. Roast for another 7 to 8 minutes.
8. When cooking is complete, the cabbage is just becoming tender. Remove the pan from the air fryer. Taste and adjust the seasoning if necessary. Serve.

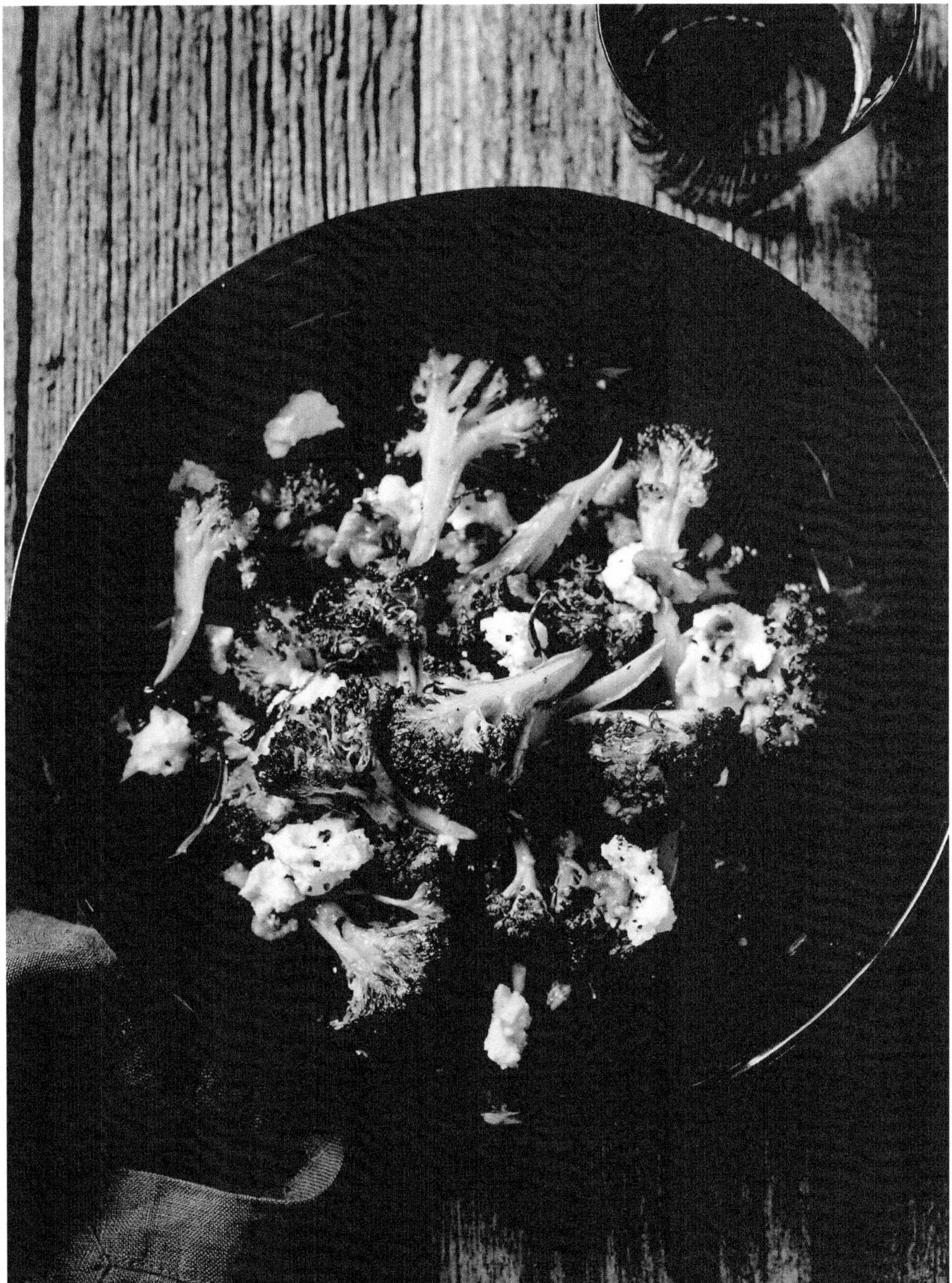

CHAPTER 7 *Vegan and Vegetarian*

Smoked Paprika Cauliflower

Prep time: 10 minutes | Cook time: 20 minutes | Serves 4

1 large head cauliflowe , broken into small floret
2 teaspoons smoked paprika
1 teaspoon garlic powder
Salt and freshly ground black pepper, to taste
Cooking spray

1. Spray the air fry basket with cooking spray.
2. In a medium bowl, toss the cauliflower florets with the smo ed paprika and garlic powder until evenly coated. Sprinkle with salt and pepper.
3. Place the cauliflower florets in the ai fry basket and lightly mist with cooking spray.
4. Select Air Fry, set temperature to 400°F (205°C), and set time to 20 minutes. Select Start to begin preheating.
5. Once preheated, place the air fry basket into the air fryer. Stir the cauliflower four times during cooking.
6. Remove the cauliflower from the air fr er and serve hot.

Air-Fried Cheesy Broccoli Tots

Prep time: 20 minutes | Cook time: 15 minutes | Serves 4

12 ounces (340 g) frozen broccoli, thawed, drained, and patted dry
1 large egg, lightly beaten
½ cup seasoned whole-wheat bread crumbs
¼ cup shredded reduced-fat sharp Cheddar cheese
¼ cup grated Parmesan cheese
1½ teaspoons minced garlic
Salt and freshly ground black pepper, to taste
Cooking spray

1. Spritz the air fry basket lightly with cooking spray.
2. Place the remaining ingredients into a food processor and process until the mixture resembles a coarse meal. Transfer the mixture to a bowl.
3. Using a tablespoon, scoop out the broccoli mixture and form into 24 oval "tater tot" shapes with your hands.
4. Put the tots in the prepared basket in a single layer, spacing them 1 inch apart. Mist the tots lightly with cooking spray.
5. Select Air Fry, set temperature to 375°F (190°C), and set time to 15 minutes. Select Start to begin preheating.
6. Once preheated, place the air fry basket into the air fryer. Flip the tots halfway through the cooking time.
7. When done, the tots will be lightly browned and crispy. Remove from the air fryer and serve on a plate.

Air-Fried Winter Veggies

Prep time: 5 minutes | Cook time: 16 minutes | Serves 2

1 parsnip, sliced
1 cup sliced butternut squash
1 small red onion, cut into wedges
½ chopped celery stalk
1 tablespoon chopped fresh thyme
2 teaspoons olive oil
Salt and black pepper, to taste

1. Toss all the ingredients in a large bowl until the vegetables are well coated.
2. Transfer the vegetables to the air fry basket.
3. Select Air Fry, set temperature to 380°F (193°C), and set time to 16 minutes. Select Start to begin preheating.
4. Once preheated, place the basket into the air fryer. Stir the vegetables halfway through the cooking time.
5. When cooking is complete, the vegetables should be golden brown and tender. Remove from the air fryer and serve warm.

Kung Pao Tofu

Prep time: 10 minutes | Cook time: 10 minutes | Serves 4

⅓ cup Asian-Style sauce
1 teaspoon cornstarch
½ teaspoon red pepper flakes, or more to taste
1 pound (454 g) firm or extra-firm tofu, cut into 1-inch cubes
1 small carrot, peeled and cut into ¼-inch-thick coins
1 small green bell pepper, cut into bite-size pieces
3 scallions, sliced, whites and green parts separated
3 tablespoons roasted unsalted peanuts

1. In a large bowl, whisk together the sauce, cornstarch, and red pepper flakes. Fold in the tofu, carrot, pepper, and the white parts of the scallions and toss to coat. Spread the mixture evenly on the sheet pan.
2. Select Roast, set temperature to 375°F (190°C), and set time to 10 minutes. Select Start to begin preheating.
3. Once preheated, place the pan into the air fryer. Stir the ingredients once halfway through the cooking time.
4. When done, remove the pan from the air fryer. Serve sprinkled with the peanuts and scallion greens.

Homemade Maple Pecan Granola

Prep time: 5 minutes | Cook time: 20 minutes | Serves 4

1½ cups rolled oats
¼ cup maple syrup
¼ cup pecan pieces
1 teaspoon vanilla extract
½ teaspoon ground cinnamon

1. Line a baking sheet with parchment paper.
2. Mix together the oats, maple syrup, pecan pieces, vanilla, and cinnamon in a large bowl and stir until the oats and pecan pieces are completely coated. Spread the mixture evenly on the baking sheet.
3. Select Bake, set temperature to 300°F (150°C), and set time to 20 minutes. Select Start to begin preheating.
4. Once preheated, place the baking sheet into the air fryer. Stir once halfway through the cooking time.
5. When done, remove from the air fryer and cool for 30 minutes before serving. The granola may still be a bit soft right after removing, but it will gradually firm up as it cools.

Spicy Honey Broccoli

Prep time: 10 minutes | Cook time: 15 to 20 minutes | Serves 4

½ teaspoon olive oil, plus more for greasing
1 pound (454 g) fresh broccoli, cut into floret
½ tablespoon minced garlic
Salt, to taste

Sauce:
1½ tablespoons soy sauce
2 teaspoons hot sauce or sriracha
1½ teaspoons honey
1 teaspoon white vinegar
Freshly ground black pepper, to taste

1. Grease the air fry basket with olive oil.
2. Add the broccoli florets, ½ teaspoon of olive oil, and garlic to a large bowl and toss well. Season with salt to taste.
3. Put the broccoli in the air fry basket in a single layer.
4. Select Air Fry, set temperature to 400°F (205°C), and set time to 15 minutes. Select Start to begin preheating.
5. Once preheated, place the air fry basket into the air fryer. Stir the broccoli florets three times during cooking.
6. Meanwhile, whisk together all the ingredients for the sauce in a small bowl until well incorporated. If the honey doesn't incorporate well, microwave the sauce for 10 to 20 seconds until the honey is melted.
7. When cooking is complete, the broccoli should be lightly browned and crispy. Continue cooking for 5 minutes, if desired. Remove from the air fryer to a serving bowl. Pour over the sauce and toss to combine. Add more salt and pepper, if needed. Serve warm.

Balck Bean Cheese Tacos

Prep time: 12 minutes | Cook time: 7 minutes | Serves 4

1 (15-ounce / 425-g) can black beans, drained and rinsed
½ cup prepared salsa
1½ teaspoons chili powder
4 ounces (113 g) grated Monterey Jack cheese
2 tablespoons minced onion
8 (6-inch) flour tortillas
2 tablespoons vegetable or extra-virgin olive oil
Shredded lettuce, for serving

1. In a medium bowl, add the beans, salsa and chili powder. Coarsely mash them with a potato masher. Fold in the cheese and onion and stir until combined.
2. Arrange the flour tortillas on a cutting board and spoon 2 to 3 tablespoons of the filling into each tortilla. old the tortillas over, pressing lightly to even out the filling. Brush the tacos on one side with half the olive oil and put them, oiled side down, on the sheet pan. Brush the top side with the remaining olive oil.
3. Select Air Fry, set temperature to 400°F (205°C), and set time to 7 minutes. Select Start to begin preheating.
4. Once preheated, place the pan into the air fryer. Flip the tacos halfway through the cooking time.
5. Remove the pan from the air fryer and allow to cool for 5 minutes. Serve with the shredded lettuce on the side.

Baked Veggies with Basil

Prep time: 15 minutes | Cook time: 20 minutes | Serves 2

1 small eggplant, halved and sliced
1 yellow bell pepper, cut into thick strips
1 red bell pepper, cut into thick strips
2 garlic cloves, quartered
1 red onion, sliced
1 tablespoon extra-virgin olive oil
Salt and freshly ground black pepper, to taste
½ cup chopped fresh basil, for garnish
Cooking spray

1. Grease a nonstick baking dish with cooking spray.
2. Place the eggplant, bell peppers, garlic, and red onion in the greased baking dish. Drizzle with the olive oil and toss to coat well. Spritz any uncoated surfaces with cooking spray.
3. Select Bake, set temperature to 350°F (180°C), and set time to 20 minutes. Select Start to begin preheating.
4. Once preheated, place the baking dish into the air fryer. Flip the vegetables halfway through the cooking time.
5. When done, remove from the air fryer and sprinkle with salt and pepper.
6. Sprinkle the basil on top for garnish and serve.

Lemony Tahini Kale

Prep time: 5 minutes | Cook time: 15 minutes | Serves 2 to 4

Dressing:
¼ cup tahini
¼ cup fresh lemon juice
2 tablespoons olive oil
1 teaspoon sesame seeds
½ teaspoon garlic powder
¼ teaspoon cayenne pepper

Kale:
4 cups packed torn kale leaves (stems and ribs removed and leaves torn into palm-size pieces)
Kosher salt and freshly ground black pepper, to taste

1. Make the dressing: Whisk together the tahini, lemon juice, olive oil, sesame seeds, garlic powder, and cayenne pepper in a large bowl until well mixed.
2. Add the kale and massage the dressing thoroughly all over the leaves. Sprinkle the salt and pepper to season.
3. Place the kale in the air fry basket in a single layer.
4. Select Air Fry, set temperature to 350°F (180°C), and set time to 15 minutes. Select Start to begin preheating.
5. Once preheated, place the air fry basket into the air fryer.
6. When cooking is complete, the leaves should be slightly wilted and crispy. Remove from the air fryer and serve on a plate.

Tortellini and Vegetable

Prep time: 10 minutes | Cook time: 16 minutes | Serves 4

8 ounces (227 g) sugar snap peas, trimmed
½ pound (227 g) asparagus, trimmed and cut into 1-inch pieces
2 teaspoons kosher salt or 1 teaspoon fine salt, divide
1 tablespoon extra-virgin olive oil
1½ cups water
1 (20-ounce / 340-g) package frozen cheese tortellini
2 garlic cloves, minced
1 cup heavy (whipping) cream
1 cup cherry tomatoes, halved
½ cup grated Parmesan cheese
¼ cup chopped fresh parsley or basil

1. Add the peas and asparagus to a large bowl. Add ½ teaspoon of kosher salt and the olive oil and toss until well coated. Place the veggies in the sheet pan.
2. Select Bake, set the temperature to 450°F (235°C), and set the time for 4 minutes. Select Start to begin preheating.
3. Once the unit has preheated, place the pan into the air fryer.
4. Meanwhile, dissolve 1 teaspoon of kosher salt in the water.
5. Once cooking is complete, remove the pan from the air fryer and arrange the tortellini on the pan. Pour the salted water over the tortellini. Transfer the pan back to the air fryer.
6. Select Bake, set temperature to 450°F (235°C), and set time for 7 minutes. Place the pan into the air fryer.
7. Meantime, stir together the garlic, heavy cream, and remaining ½ teaspoon of kosher salt in a small bowl.
8. Once cooking is complete, remove the pan from the air fryer. Blot off any remaining water with a paper towel. Gently stir the ingredients. Drizzle the cream over and top with the tomatoes.
9. Select Roast, set the temperature to 375°F (190°C), and set the time for 5 minutes. Place the pan into the air fryer.
10. Once the unit has preheated, place the pan in the air fryer.
11. After 4 minutes, remove the pan from the air fryer.
12. Add the Parmesan cheese and stir until the cheese is melted
13. Serve topped with the parsley.

Roasted Veggies Balls

Prep time: 15 minutes | Cook time: 18 minutes | Serves 3

½ cup grated carrots
½ cup sweet onions
2 tablespoons olive oil
1 cup rolled oats
½ cup roasted cashews
2 cups cooked chickpeas
Juice of 1 lemon
2 tablespoons soy sauce
1 tablespoon flax meal
1 teaspoon garlic powder
1 teaspoon cumin
½ teaspoon turmeric

1. Mix the carrots, onions, and olive oil in a baking dish and stir to combine.
2. Select Roast, set temperature to 350°F (180°C) and set time to 6 minutes. Select Start to begin preheating.
3. Once preheated, place the baking dish into the air fryer. Stir the vegetables halfway through.
4. When cooking is complete, the vegetables should be tender.
5. Meanwhile, put the oats and cashews in a food processor or blender and pulse until coarsely ground. Transfer the mixture to a large bowl. Add the chickpeas, lemon juice, and soy sauce to the food processor and pulse until smooth. Transfer the chickpea mixture to the bowl of oat and cashew mixture.
6. Remove the carrots and onions from the air fryer to the bowl of chickpea mixture. Add the flax meal, garlic powde , cumin, and turmeric and stir to incorporate.
7. Scoop tablespoon-sized portions of the veggie mixture and roll them into balls with your hands. Transfer the balls to the air fry basket.
8. Increase the temperature to 370°F (188°C) and set time to 12 minutes on Bake. Place the basket into the air fryer. Flip the balls halfway through the cooking time.
9. When cooking is complete, the balls should be golden brown.
10. Serve warm.

Caramelized Eggplant with Yogurt

Prep time: 5 minutes | Cook time: 15 minutes | Serves 2

1 medium eggplant, quartered and cut crosswise into ½-inch-thick slices
2 tablespoons vegetable oil
Kosher salt and freshly ground black pepper, to taste
½ cup plain yogurt (not Greek)
2 tablespoons harissa paste
1 garlic clove, grated
2 teaspoons honey

1. Toss the eggplant slices with the vegetable oil, salt, and pepper in a large bowl until well coated.
2. Lay the eggplant slices in the air fry basket.
3. Select Air Fry, set temperature to 400°F (205°C), and set time to 15 minutes. Select Start to begin preheating.
4. Once preheated, place the air fry basket into the air fryer. Stir the slices two to three times during cooking.
5. Meanwhile, make the yogurt sauce by whisking together the yogurt, harissa paste, and garlic in a small bowl.
6. When cooking is complete, the eggplant slices should be golden brown. Spread the yogurt sauce on a platter, and pile the eggplant slices over the top. Serve drizzled with the honey.

Caramelized Wax Beans

Prep time: 5 minutes | Cook time: 12 minutes | Serves 4

2 pounds (907 g) wax beans
2 tablespoons extra-virgin olive oil
Salt and freshly ground black pepper, to taste
Juice of ½ lemon, for serving

1. Line a baking sheet with aluminum foil.
2. Toss the wax beans with the olive oil in a large bowl. Lightly season with salt and pepper.
3. Spread out the wax beans on the sheet pan.
4. Select Roast, set temperature to 400°F (205°C), and set time to 12 minutes. Select Start to begin preheating.
5. Once preheated, place the baking sheet into the air fryer.
6. When done, the beans will be caramelized and tender. Remove from the air fryer to a plate and serve sprinkled with the lemon juice.

Bell Peppers with Garlic

Prep time: 10 minutes | Cook time: 22 minutes | Serves 4

1 green bell pepper, sliced into 1-inch strips
1 red bell pepper, sliced into 1-inch strips
1 orange bell pepper, sliced into 1-inch strips
1 yellow bell pepper, sliced into 1-inch strips
2 tablespoons olive oil, divided
½ teaspoon dried marjoram
Pinch salt
Freshly ground black pepper, to taste
1 head garlic

1. Toss the bell peppers with 1 tablespoon of olive oil in a large bowl until well coated. Season with the marjoram, salt, and pepper. Toss again and set aside.
2. Cut off the top of a head of garlic. Place the garlic cloves on a large square of aluminum foil. Drizzle the top with the remaining 1 tablespoon of olive oil and wrap the garlic cloves in foil.
3. Transfer the garlic to the air fry basket.
4. Select Roast, set temperature to 330°F (166°C) and set time to 15 minutes. Select Start to begin preheating.
5. Once preheated, place the basket into the air fryer.
6. After 15 minutes, remove the air fry basket from the air fryer and add the bell peppers. Return to the air fryer and set time to 7 minutes.
7. When cooking is complete or until the garlic is soft and the bell peppers are tender.
8. Transfer the cooked bell peppers to a plate. Remove the garlic and unwrap the foil. Let the garlic rest for a few minutes. Once cooled, squeeze the roasted garlic cloves out of their skins and add them to the plate of bell peppers. Stir well and serve immediately.

Thai Spicy Veggies with Nuts

Prep time: 10 minutes | Cook time: 8 minutes | Serves 4

1 small head Napa cabbage, shredded, divided
1 medium carrot, cut into thin coins
8 ounces (227 g) snow peas
1 red or green bell pepper, sliced into thin strips
1 tablespoon vegetable oil
2 tablespoons soy sauce
1 tablespoon sesame oil
2 tablespoons brown sugar
2 tablespoons freshly squeezed lime juice
2 teaspoons red or green Thai curry paste
1 serrano chile, deseeded and minced
1 cup frozen mango slices, thawed
½ cup chopped roasted peanuts or cashews

1. Put half the Napa cabbage in a large bowl, along with the carrot, snow peas, and bell pepper. Drizzle with the vegetable oil and toss to coat. Spread them evenly on the sheet pan.
2. Select Roast, set temperature to 375°F (190°C), and set time to 8 minutes. Select Start to begin preheating.
3. Once preheated, place the pan into the air fryer.
4. Meanwhile, whisk together the soy sauce, sesame oil, brown sugar, lime juice, and curry paste in a small bowl.
5. When done, the vegetables should be tender and crisp. Remove the pan and put the vegetables back into the bowl. Add the chile, mango slices, and the remaining cabbage. Pour over the dressing and toss to coat. Top with the roasted nuts and serve.

Roasted Cinnamon Celery Roots

Prep time: 10 minutes | Cook time: 20 minutes | Serves 4

2 celery roots, peeled and diced
1 teaspoon extra-virgin olive oil
1 teaspoon butter, melted
½ teaspoon ground cinnamon
Sea salt and freshly ground black pepper, to taste

1. Line a baking sheet with aluminum foil.
2. Toss the celery roots with the olive oil in a large bowl until well coated. Transfer them to the prepared baking sheet.
3. Select Roast, set temperature to 350°F (180°C), and set time to 20 minutes. Select Start to begin preheating.
4. Once preheated, place the baking sheet into the air fryer.
5. When done, the celery roots should be very tender. Remove from the air fryer to a serving bowl. Stir in the butter and cinnamon and mash them with a potato masher until fluf y.
6. Season with salt and pepper to taste. Serve immediately.

Balsamic Asparagus Spears

Prep time: 15 minutes | Cook time: 10 minutes | Serves 4

4 tablespoons olive oil, plus more for greasing
4 tablespoons balsamic vinegar
1½ pounds (680 g) asparagus spears, trimmed
Salt and freshly ground black pepper, to taste

1. Grease the air fry basket with olive oil.
2. In a shallow bowl, stir together the 4 tablespoons of olive oil and balsamic vinegar to make a marinade.
3. Put the asparagus spears in the bowl so they are thoroughly covered by the marinade and allow to marinate for 5 minutes.
4. Put the asparagus in the greased basket in a single layer and season with salt and pepper.
5. Select Air Fry, set temperature to 350°F (180°C), and set time to 10 minutes. Select Start to begin preheating.
6. Once preheated, place the air fry basket into the air fryer. Flip the asparagus halfway through the cooking time.
7. When done, the asparagus should be tender and lightly browned. Cool for 5 minutes before serving.

Roasted Honey-Glazed Carrot

Prep time: 5 minutes | Cook time: 12 minutes | Serves 4

1 pound (454 g) baby carrots
2 tablespoons olive oil
1 tablespoon honey
1 teaspoon dried dill
Salt and black pepper, to taste

1. Place the carrots in a large bowl. Add the olive oil, honey, dill, salt, and pepper and toss to coat well.
2. Transfer the carrots to the air fry basket.
3. Select Roast, set temperature to 350ºF (180ºC), and set time to 12 minutes. Select Start to begin preheating.
4. Once preheated, place the basket into the air fryer. Stir the carrots once during cooking.
5. When cooking is complete, the carrots should be crisp-tender. Remove from the air fryer and serve warm.

Asian Spicy Broccoli

Prep time: 5 minutes | Cook time: 10 minutes | Serves 2

12 ounces (340 g) broccoli floret
2 tablespoons Asian hot chili oil
1 teaspoon ground Sichuan peppercorns (or black pepper)
2 garlic cloves, finely chopped
1 (2-inch) piece fresh ginger, peeled and finely choppe
Kosher salt and freshly ground black pepper

1. Toss the broccoli florets with the chili oil, Sichuan peppercorns, garlic, ginger, salt, and pepper in a mixing bowl until thoroughly coated.
2. Transfer the broccoli florets to the air fry basket.
3. Select Air Fry, set temperature to 375ºF (190ºC), and set time to 10 minutes. Select Start to begin preheating.
4. Once preheated, place the air fry basket into the air fryer. Stir the broccoli florets halfway through the cooking time.
5. When cooking is complete, the broccoli florets should be lightly browned and tender. Remove the broccoli from the air fryer and serve on a plate.

Garlicky Stuffed WhiteMushroom

Prep time: 5 minutes | Cook time: 12 minutes | Serves 2

18 medium-sized white mushrooms
1 small onion, peeled and chopped
4 garlic cloves, peeled and minced
2 tablespoons olive oil
2 teaspoons cumin powder
A pinch ground allspice
Fine sea salt and freshly ground black pepper, to taste

1. On a clean work surface, remove the mushroom stems. Using a spoon, scoop out the mushroom gills and discard.
2. Thoroughly combine the onion, garlic, olive oil, cumin powder, allspice, salt, and pepper in a mixing bowl. Stuff the mushrooms evenly with the mixture.
3. Place the stuffed mushrooms in the air fry basket.
4. Select Roast, set temperature to 345ºF (174ºC) and set time to 12 minutes. Select Start to begin preheating.
5. Once preheated, place the basket into the air fryer.
6. When cooking is complete, the mushroom should be browned.
7. Cool for 5 minutes before serving.

Baked Turnip, Zucchini, Onion

Prep time: 5 minutes | Cook time: 18 minutes | Serves 4

3 turnips, sliced
1 large zucchini, sliced
1 large red onion, cut into rings
2 cloves garlic, crushed
1 tablespoon olive oil
Salt and black pepper, to taste

1. Put the turnips, zucchini, red onion, and garlic in a baking pan. Drizzle the olive oil over the top and sprinkle with the salt and pepper.
2. Select Bake, set temperature to 330ºF (166ºC), and set time to 18 minutes. Select Start to begin preheating.
3. Once preheated, place the pan into the air fryer.
4. When cooking is complete, the vegetables should be tender. Remove from the air fryer and serve on a plate.

Teriyaki Cauliflower Florets

Prep time: 5 minutes | Cook time: 14 minutes | Serves 4

½ cup soy sauce
⅓ cup water
1 tablespoon brown sugar
1 teaspoon sesame oil
1 teaspoon cornstarch
2 cloves garlic, chopped
½ teaspoon chili powder
1 big cauliflower head, cut into floret

1. Make the teriyaki sauce: In a small bowl, whisk together the soy sauce, water, brown sugar, sesame oil, cornstarch, garlic, and chili powder until well combined.
2. Place the cauliflower florets in a larg bowl and drizzle the top with the prepared teriyaki sauce and toss to coat well.
3. Put the cauliflower florets in the air fr basket.
4. Select Air Fry, set temperature to 340ºF (171ºC) and set time to 14 minutes. Select Start to begin preheating.
5. Once preheated, place the basket into the air fryer. Stir the cauliflower half ay through.
6. When cooking is complete, the cauliflower should be crisp-tende .
7. Let the cauliflower cool for 5 minutes before serving.

Cornflakes-Crusted Tofu Sticks

Prep time: 5 minutes | Cook time: 14 minutes | Serves 4

2 tablespoons olive oil, divided
½ cup flou
½ cup crushed cornfla es
Salt and black pepper, to taste
14 ounces (397 g) firm tofu, cut into ½-inch-thick strips

1. Grease the air fry basket with 1 tablespoon of olive oil.
2. Combine the flou , cornfla es, salt, and pepper on a plate.
3. Dredge the tofu strips in the flour mixture until they are completely coated. Transfer the tofu strips to the greased basket.
4. Drizzle the remaining 1 tablespoon of olive oil over the top of tofu strips.
5. Select Air Fry, set temperature to 360ºF (182ºC), and set time to 14 minutes. Select Start to begin preheating.
6. Once preheated, place the basket into the air fryer. Flip the tofu strips halfway through the cooking time.
7. When cooking is complete, the tofu strips should be crispy. Remove from the air fryer and serve warm.

Breaded Eggplant Slices

Prep time: 5 minutes | Cook time: 12 minutes | Serves 4

1 cup flou
4 eggs
Salt, to taste
2 cups bread crumbs
1 teaspoon Italian seasoning
2 eggplants, sliced
2 garlic cloves, sliced
2 tablespoons chopped parsley
Cooking spray

1. Spritz the air fry basket with cooking spray. Set aside.
2. On a plate, place the flou . In a shallow bowl, whisk the eggs with salt. In another shallow bowl, combine the bread crumbs and Italian seasoning.
3. Dredge the eggplant slices, one at a time, in the flou , then in the whisked eggs, finally in the bread crumb mixture to coat well.
4. Lay the coated eggplant slices in the air fry basket.
5. Select Air Fry, set temperature to 390ºF (199ºC), and set time to 12 minutes. Select Start to begin preheating.
6. Once preheated, place the basket into the air fryer. Flip the eggplant slices halfway through the cooking time.
7. When cooking is complete, the eggplant slices should be golden brown and crispy. Transfer the eggplant slices to a plate and sprinkle the garlic and parsley on top before serving.

Roasted Ratatouille

Prep time: 10 minutes | Cook time: 12 minutes | Serves 6

1 medium zucchini, sliced ½-inch thick	1 small green bell pepper, cut into ½-inch chunks
1 small eggplant, peeled and sliced ½-inch thick	½ teaspoon dried oregano
2 teaspoons kosher salt, divided	¼ teaspoon freshly ground black pepper
4 tablespoons extra-virgin olive oil, divided	1 pint cherry tomatoes
3 garlic cloves, minced	2 tablespoons minced fresh basil
1 small onion, chopped	1 cup panko bread crumbs
1 small red bell pepper, cut into ½-inch chunks	½ cup grated Parmesan cheese (optional)

1. Season one side of the zucchini and eggplant slices with ¾ teaspoon of salt. Put the slices, salted side down, on a rack set over a baking sheet. Sprinkle the other sides with ¾ teaspoon of salt. Allow to sit for 10 minutes, or until the slices begin to exude water. When ready, rinse and dry them. Cut the zucchini slices into quarters and the eggplant slices into eighths.
2. Pour the zucchini and eggplant into a large bowl, along with 2 tablespoons of olive oil, garlic, onion, bell peppers, oregano, and black pepper. Toss to coat well. Arrange the vegetables on the sheet pan.
3. Select Roast, set temperature to 375°F (190°C), and set time to 12 minutes. Select Start to begin preheating.
4. Once preheated, place the pan into the air fryer.
5. Meanwhile, add the tomatoes and basil to the large bowl. Sprinkle with the remaining ½ teaspoon of salt and 1 tablespoon of olive oil. Toss well and set aside.
6. Stir together the remaining 1 tablespoon of olive oil, panko, and Parmesan cheese (if desired) in a small bowl.
7. After 6 minutes, remove the pan and add the tomato mixture to the sheet pan and stir to mix well. Scatter the panko mixture on top. Return the pan to the air fryer and continue cooking for 6 minutes, or until the vegetables are softened and the topping is golden brown.
8. Cool for 5 minutes before serving.

Potato and Asparagus with Cheese Sauce

Prep time: 5 minutes | Cook time: 26 minutes | Serves 5

4 medium potatoes, cut into wedges	Cheese Sauce:
Cooking spray	¼ cup crumbled cottage cheese
1 bunch asparagus, trimmed	¼ cup buttermilk
2 tablespoons olive oil	1 tablespoon whole-grain mustard
Salt and pepper, to taste	Salt and black pepper, to taste

1. Spritz the air fry basket with cooking spray.
2. Put the potatoes in the air fry basket.
3. Select Roast, set temperature to 400°F (205°C) and set time to 20 minutes. Select Start to begin preheating.
4. Once preheated, place the basket into the air fryer. Stir the potatoes halfway through.
5. When cooking is complete, the potatoes should be golden brown.
6. Remove the potatoes from the air fryer to a platter. Cover the potatoes with foil to keep warm. Set aside.
7. Place the asparagus in the air fry basket and drizzle with the olive oil. Sprinkle with salt and pepper.
8. Select Roast, set temperature to 400°F (205°C) and set time to 6 minutes. Place the basket into the air fryer. Stir the asparagus halfway through.
9. When cooking is complete, the asparagus should be crispy.
10. Meanwhile, make the cheese sauce by stirring together the cottage cheese, buttermilk, and mustard in a small bowl. Season as needed with salt and pepper.
11. Transfer the asparagus to the platter of potatoes and drizzle with the cheese sauce. Serve immediately.

Air-Fried Cheesy Cabbage Wedges

Prep time: 5 minutes | Cook time: 20 minutes | Serves 4

4 tablespoons melted butter
1 head cabbage, cut into wedges
1 cup shredded Parmesan cheese
Salt and black pepper, to taste
½ cup shredded Mozzarella cheese

1. Brush the melted butter over the cut sides of cabbage wedges and sprinkle both sides with the Parmesan cheese. Season with salt and pepper to taste.
2. Place the cabbage wedges in the air fry basket.
3. Select Air Fry, set temperature to 380ºF (193ºC), and set time to 20 minutes. Select Start to begin preheating.
4. Once preheated, place the air fry basket into the air fryer. Flip the cabbage halfway through the cooking time.
5. When cooking is complete, the cabbage wedges should be lightly browned. Transfer the cabbage wedges to a plate and serve with the Mozzarella cheese sprinkled on top.

Ratatouille

Prep time: 15 minutes | Cook time: 16 minutes | Serves 2

2 Roma tomatoes, thinly sliced
1 zucchini, thinly sliced
2 yellow bell peppers, sliced
2 garlic cloves, minced
2 tablespoons olive oil
2 tablespoons herbes de Prair fryerce
1 tablespoon vinegar
Salt and black pepper, to taste

1. Place the tomatoes, zucchini, bell peppers, garlic, olive oil, herbes de Prair fryerce, and vinegar in a large bowl and toss until the vegetables are evenly coated. Sprinkle with salt and pepper and toss again. Pour the vegetable mixture into a baking dish.
2. Select Roast, set temperature to 390ºF (199ºC) and set time to 16 minutes. Select Start to begin preheating.
3. Once preheated, place the baking dish into the air fryer. Stir the vegetables halfway through.
4. When cooking is complete, the vegetables should be tender.
5. Let the vegetable mixture stand for 5 minutes in the air fryer before removing and serving.

Cheesy Vegan Quesadilla

Prep time: 5 minutes | Cook time: 10 minutes | Serves 1

1 teaspoon olive oil
2 flour tortilla
¼ zucchini, sliced
¼ yellow bell pepper, sliced
¼ cup shredded gouda cheese
1 tablespoon chopped cilantro
½ green onion, sliced

1. Coat the air fry basket with 1 teaspoon of olive oil.
2. Arrange a flour tortilla in the air fry basket and scatter the top with zucchini, bell pepper, gouda cheese, cilantro, and green onion. Place the other flour tortilla on top.
3. Select Air Fry, set temperature to 390ºF (199ºC), and set time to 10 minutes. Select Start to begin preheating.
4. Once preheated, place the basket into the air fryer.
5. When cooking is complete, the tortillas should be lightly browned and the vegetables should be tender. Remove from the air fryer and cool for 5 minutes before slicing into wedges.

Rosemary Butternut Squash

Prep time: 5 minutes | Cook time: 20 minutes | Serves 2

1 pound (454 g) butternut squash, cut into wedges
2 tablespoons olive oil
1 tablespoon dried rosemary
Salt, to salt
1 cup crumbled goat cheese
1 tablespoon maple syrup

1. Toss the squash wedges with the olive oil, rosemary, and salt in a large bowl until well coated.
2. Transfer the squash wedges to the air fry basket, spreading them out in as even a layer as possible.
3. Select Air Fry, set temperature to 350°F (180°C), and set time to 20 minutes. Select Start to begin preheating.
4. Once preheated, place the air fry basket into the air fryer.
5. After 10 minutes, remove from the air fryer and flip the squash. eturn the basket to the air fryer and continue cooking for 10 minutes.
6. When cooking is complete, the squash should be golden brown. Remove the basket from the air fryer. Sprinkle the goat cheese on top and serve drizzled with the maple syrup.

Panko-Crusted Green Beans

Prep time: 5 minutes | Cook time: 15 minutes | Serves 4

½ cup flou
2 eggs
1 cup panko bread crumbs
½ cup grated Parmesan cheese
1 teaspoon cayenne pepper
Salt and black pepper, to taste
1½ pounds (680 g) green beans

1. In a bowl, place the flou . In a separate bowl, lightly beat the eggs. In a separate shallow bowl, thoroughly combine the bread crumbs, cheese, cayenne pepper, salt, and pepper.
2. Dip the green beans in the flou , then in the beaten eggs, finally in the bread crumb mixture to coat well. Transfer the green beans to the air fry basket.
3. Select Air Fry, set temperature to 400°F (205°C), and set time to 15 minutes. Select Start to begin preheating.
4. Once preheated, place the basket into the air fryer. Stir the green beans halfway through the cooking time.
5. When cooking is complete, remove from the air fryer to a bowl and serve.

Herbed Broccoli with Yellow Cheese

Prep time: 5 minutes | Cook time: 18 minutes | Serves 4

1 large-sized head broccoli, stemmed and cut into small floret
2½ tablespoons canola oil
2 teaspoons dried basil
2 teaspoons dried rosemary
Salt and ground black pepper, to taste
⅓ cup grated yellow cheese

1. Bring a pot of lightly salted water to a boil. Add the broccoli florets to the boiling water and let boil for about 3 minutes.
2. Drain the broccoli florets well and transfer to a large bowl. Add the canola oil, basil, rosemary, salt, and black pepper to the bowl and toss until the broccoli is fully coated. Place the broccoli in the air fry basket.
3. Select Air Fry, set temperature to 390°F (199°C), and set time to 15 minutes. Select Start to begin preheating.
4. Once preheated, place the air fry basket into the air fryer. Stir the broccoli halfway through the cooking time.
5. When cooking is complete, the broccoli should be crisp. Remove the basket from the air fryer. Serve the broccoli warm with grated cheese sprinkled on top.

Crispy Veggies with Mixed Herbs

Prep time: 5 minutes | Cook time: 14 minutes | Serves 2

2 zucchinis, cut into even chunks
1 large eggplant, peeled, cut into chunks
1 large carrot, cut into chunks
6 ounces (170 g) halloumi cheese, cubed
2 teaspoons olive oil
Salt and black pepper, to taste
1 teaspoon dried mixed herbs

1. Combine the zucchinis, eggplant, carrot, cheese, olive oil, salt, and pepper in a large bowl and toss to coat well.
2. Spread the mixture evenly in the air fry basket.
3. Select Air Fry, set temperature to 340°F (171°C), and set time to 14 minutes. Select Start to begin preheating.
4. Once preheated, place the basket into the air fryer. Stir the mixture once during cooking.
5. When cooking is complete, they should be crispy and golden. Remove from the air fryer and serve topped with mixed herbs.

Roasted Veggies and Rice

Prep time: 5 minutes | Cook time: 12 minutes | Serves 4

2 teaspoons melted butter
1 cup chopped mushrooms
1 cup cooked rice
1 cup peas
1 carrot, chopped
1 red onion, chopped
1 garlic clove, minced
Salt and black pepper, to taste
2 hard-boiled eggs, grated
1 tablespoon soy sauce

1. Coat a baking dish with melted butter.
2. Stir together the mushrooms, cooked rice, peas, carrot, onion, garlic, salt, and pepper in a large bowl until well mixed. Pour the mixture into the prepared baking dish.
3. Select Roast, set temperature to 380°F (193°C), and set time to 12 minutes. Select Start to begin preheating.
4. Once preheated, place the baking dish into the air fryer.
5. When cooking is complete, remove from the air fryer. Divide the mixture among four plates. Serve warm with a sprinkle of grated eggs and a drizzle of soy sauce.

Garlicky Carrots with Sesame

Prep time: 5 minutes | Cook time: 16 minutes | Serves 4 to 6

1 pound (454 g) baby carrots
1 tablespoon sesame oil
½ teaspoon dried dill
Pinch salt
Freshly ground black pepper, to taste
6 cloves garlic, peeled
3 tablespoons sesame seeds

1. In a medium bowl, drizzle the baby carrots with the sesame oil. Sprinkle with the dill, salt, and pepper and toss to coat well.
2. Place the baby carrots in the air fry basket.
3. Select Roast, set temperature to 380°F (193°C), and set time to 16 minutes. Select Start to begin preheating.
4. Once preheated, place the basket into the air fryer.
5. After 8 minutes, remove the basket from the air fryer and stir in the garlic. Return the basket to the air fryer and continue roasting for 8 minutes more.
6. When cooking is complete, the carrots should be lightly browned. Remove the basket from the air fryer and serve sprinkled with the sesame seeds.

Italian Spiced Tofu

Prep time: 5 minutes | Cook time: 10 minutes | Serves 2

1 tablespoon soy sauce
1 tablespoon water
⅓ teaspoon garlic powder
⅓ teaspoon onion powder
⅓ teaspoon dried oregano
⅓ teaspoon dried basil
Black pepper, to taste
6 ounces (170 g) extra firm tofu, pressed and cubed

1. In a large mixing bowl, whisk together the soy sauce, water, garlic powder, onion powder, oregano, basil, and black pepper. Add the tofu cubes, stirring to coat, and let them marinate for 10 minutes.
2. Arrange the tofu in the air fry basket.
3. Select Bake. Set temperature to 390°F (199°C) and set time to 10 minutes. Select Start to begin preheating.
4. Once preheated, place the basket into the air fryer. Flip the tofu halfway through the cooking time.
5. When cooking is complete, the tofu should be crisp.
6. Remove from the air fryer to a plate and serve.

Crispy Chili Okra

Prep time: 5 minutes | Cook time: 10 minutes | Serves 4

3 tablespoons sour cream
2 tablespoons flou
2 tablespoons semolina
½ teaspoon red chili powder
Salt and black pepper, to taste
1 pound (454 g) okra, halved
Cooking spray

1. Spray the air fry basket with cooking spray. Set aside.
2. In a shallow bowl, place the sour cream. In another shallow bowl, thoroughly combine the flou , semolina, red chili powder, salt, and pepper.
3. Dredge the okra in the sour cream, then roll in the flour mixture until e enly coated. Transfer the okra to the air fry basket.
4. Select Air Fry, set temperature to 400°F (205°C), and set time to 10 minutes. Select Start to begin preheating.
5. Once preheated, place the basket into the air fryer. Flip the okra halfway through the cooking time.
6. When cooking is complete, the okra should be golden brown and crispy. Remove the basket from the air fryer. Cool for 5 minutes before serving.

Panko Parmesan Zucchini Chips

Prep time: 5 minutes | Cook time: 14 minutes | Serves 4

2 egg whites
Salt and black pepper, to taste
½ cup seasoned bread crumbs
2 tablespoons grated Parmesan cheese
¼ teaspoon garlic powder
2 medium zucchini, sliced
Cooking spray

1. Spritz the air fry basket with cooking spray.
2. In a bowl, beat the egg whites with salt and pepper. In a separate bowl, thoroughly combine the bread crumbs, Parmesan cheese, and garlic powder.
3. Dredge the zucchini slices in the egg white, then coat in the bread crumb mixture.
4. Arrange the zucchini slices in the air fry basket.
5. Select Air Fry. Set temperature to 400°F (205°C) and set time to 14 minutes. Select Start to begin preheating.
6. Once preheated, place the basket into the air fryer. Flip the zucchini halfway through.
7. When cooking is complete, the zucchini should be tender.
8. Remove from the air fryer to a plate and serve.

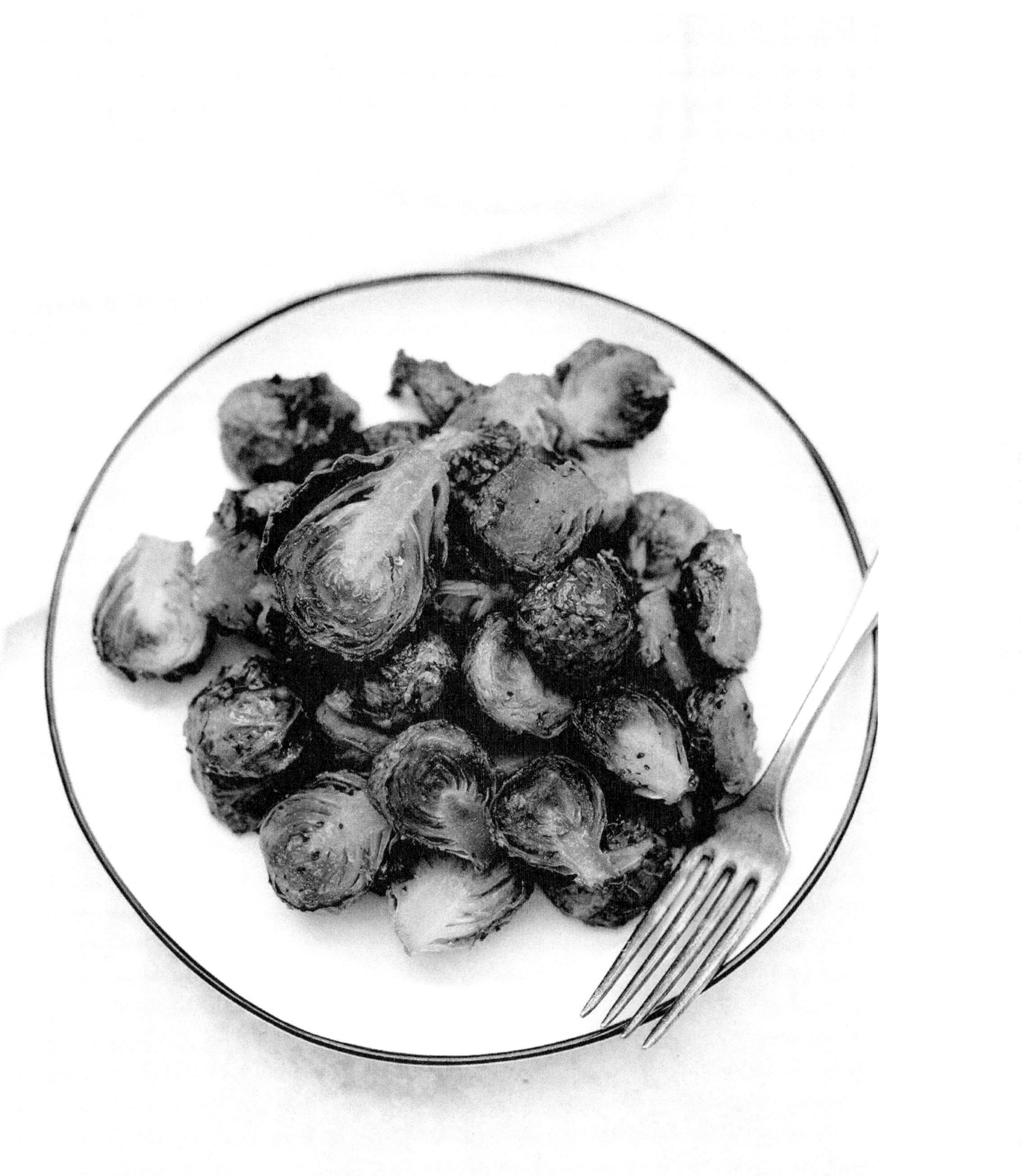

CHAPTER 8 *Vegetable Sides*

Air-Fried Broccoli with Hot Sauce

Prep time: 5 minutes | Cook time: 14 minutes | Serves 6

Broccoli:
1 medium-sized head broccoli, cut into floret
1½ tablespoons olive oil
1 teaspoon shallot powder
1 teaspoon porcini powder
½ teaspoon freshly grated lemon zest
½ teaspoon hot paprika
½ teaspoon granulated garlic
⅓ teaspoon fine sea salt
⅓ teaspoon celery seeds

Hot Sauce:
½ cup tomato sauce
1 tablespoon balsamic vinegar
½ teaspoon ground allspice

1. In a mixing bowl, combine all the ingredients for the broccoli and toss to coat. Transfer the broccoli to the air fry basket.
2. Select Air Fry, set temperature to 360ºF (182ºC), and set time to 14 minutes. Select Start to begin preheating.
3. Once preheated, place the basket into the air fryer.
4. Meanwhile, make the hot sauce by whisking together the tomato sauce, balsamic vinegar, and allspice in a small bowl.
5. When cooking is complete, remove the broccoli from the air fryer and serve with the hot sauce.

Maple Brussels Sprouts

Prep time: 10 minutes | Cook time: 11 minutes | Serves 4

2½ cups trimmed Brussels sprouts

Sauce:
1½ teaspoons mellow white miso
1½ tablespoons maple syrup
1 teaspoon toasted sesame oil
1 teaspoons tamari or shoyu
1 teaspoon grated fresh ginger
2 large garlic cloves, finely mince
¼ to ½ teaspoon red chili fla es
Cooking spray

1. Spritz the air fry basket with cooking spray.
2. Arrange the Brussels sprouts in the air fry basket and spray them with cooking spray.
3. Select Air Fry, set temperature to 392ºF (200ºC), and set time to 11 minutes. Select Start to begin preheating.
4. Once preheated, place the basket into the air fryer.
5. After 6 minutes, remove the basket from the air fryer. Flip the Brussels sprouts and spritz with cooking spray again. Return to the air fryer and continue cooking for 5 minutes more.
6. Meanwhile, make the sauce: Stir together the miso and maple syrup in a medium bowl. Add the sesame oil, tamari, ginger, garlic, and red chili fla es and whisk to combine.
7. When cooking is complete, the Brussels sprouts should be crisp-tender. Transfer the Brussels sprouts to the bowl of sauce, tossing to coat well. If you prefer a saltier taste, you can add additional ½ teaspoon tamari to the sauce. Serve immediately.

Baked Scalloped Potatoes

Prep time: 5 minutes | Cook time: 15 to 20 minutes | Serves 4

2 cup sliced frozen potatoes, thawed
3 cloves garlic, minced
Pinch salt
Freshly ground black pepper, to taste
¾ cup heavy cream

1. Toss the potatoes with the garlic, salt, and black pepper in a baking pan until evenly coated. Pour the heavy cream over the top.
2. Select Bake, set temperature to 380°F (193°C), and set time to 15 minutes. Select Start to begin preheating.
3. Once preheated, place the pan into the air fryer.
4. When cooking is complete, the potatoes should be tender and the top golden brown. Check for doneness and bake for another 5 minutes if needed. Remove from the air fryer and serve hot.

Roasted Spicy Cabbage

Prep time: 5 minutes | Cook time: 7 minutes | Serves 4

1 head cabbage, sliced into 1-inch-thick ribbons
1 tablespoon olive oil
1 teaspoon garlic powder
1 teaspoon red pepper fla es
1 teaspoon salt
1 teaspoon freshly ground black pepper

1. Toss the cabbage with the olive oil, garlic powder, red pepper fla es, salt, and pepper in a large mixing bowl until well coated.
2. Transfer the cabbage to the air fry basket.
3. Select Roast, set temperature to 350°F (180°C), and set time to 7 minutes. Select Start to begin preheating.
4. Once preheated, place the basket into the air fryer. Flip the cabbage with tongs halfway through the cooking time.
5. When cooking is complete, the cabbage should be crisp. Remove from the air fryer to a plate and serve warm.

Parmesan Buttered Broccoli

Prep time: 5 minutes | Cook time: 4 minutes | Serves 4

1 pound (454 g) broccoli floret
1 medium shallot, minced
2 tablespoons olive oil
2 tablespoons
unsalted butter, melted
2 teaspoons minced garlic
¼ cup grated Parmesan cheese

1. Combine the broccoli florets with the shallot, olive oil, butter, garlic, and Parmesan cheese in a medium bowl and toss until the broccoli florets are thoroughly coated.
2. Place the broccoli florets in the air fry basket in a single layer.
3. Select Roast, set temperature to 360°F (182°C), and set time to 4 minutes. Select Start to begin preheating.
4. Once preheated, place the basket into the air fryer.
5. When cooking is complete, the broccoli florets should be crisp-tende . Remove from the air fryer and serve warm.

Balsamic Asparagus

Prep time: 5 minutes | Cook time: 10 minutes | Serves 4

1 pound (454 g) asparagus, woody ends trimmed
2 tablespoons olive oil
1 tablespoon
balsamic vinegar
2 teaspoons minced garlic
Salt and freshly ground black pepper, to taste

1. In a large shallow bowl, toss the asparagus with the olive oil, balsamic vinegar, garlic, salt, and pepper until thoroughly coated. Put the asparagus in the air fry basket.
2. Select Roast, set temperature to 400°F (205°C), and set time to 10 minutes. Select Start to begin preheating.
3. Once preheated, place the basket into the air fryer. Flip the asparagus with tongs halfway through the cooking time.
4. When cooking is complete, the asparagus should be crispy. Remove the basket from the air fryer and serve warm.

Tangy Sweet Potatoes

Prep time: 5 minutes | Cook time: 22 minutes | Serves 4

5 garnet sweet potatoes, peeled and diced
1½ tablespoons fresh lime juice
1 tablespoon butter, melted
2 teaspoons tamarind paste
1½ teaspoon ground allspice
⅓ teaspoon white pepper
½ teaspoon turmeric powder
A few drops liquid stevia

1. In a large mixing bowl, combine all the ingredients and toss until the sweet potatoes are evenly coated. Place the sweet potatoes in the air fry basket.
2. Select Air Fry, set temperature to 400°F (205°C), and set time to 22 minutes. Select Start to begin preheating.
3. Once preheated, place the basket into the air fryer. Stir the potatoes twice during cooking.
4. When cooking is complete, the potatoes should be crispy on the outside and soft on the inside. Let the potatoes cool for 5 minutes before serving.

Cheesy Corn on the Cob

Prep time: 10 minutes | Cook time: 15 minutes | Serves 4

2 tablespoon olive oil, divided
2 tablespoons grated Parmesan cheese
1 teaspoon garlic powder
1 teaspoon chili powder
1 teaspoon ground cumin
1 teaspoon paprika
1 teaspoon salt
¼ teaspoon cayenne pepper (optional)
4 ears fresh corn, shucked

1. Grease the air fry basket with 1 tablespoon of olive oil. Set aside.
2. Combine the Parmesan cheese, garlic powder, chili powder, cumin, paprika, salt, and cayenne pepper (if desired) in a small bowl and stir to mix well.
3. Lightly coat the ears of corn with the remaining 1 tablespoon of olive oil. Rub the cheese mixture all over the ears of corn until completely coated.
4. Arrange the ears of corn in the greased basket in a single layer.
5. Select Air Fry, set temperature to 400°F (205°C), and set time to 15 minutes. Select Start to begin preheating.
6. Once preheated, place the basket into the air fryer. Flip the ears of corn halfway through the cooking time.
7. When cooking is complete, they should be lightly browned. Remove from the air fryer and let them cool for 5 minutes before serving.

Panko-Crusted Cheesy Broccoli

Prep time: 5 minutes | Cook time: 14 minutes | Serves 2

⅓ cup fat-free milk
1 tablespoon all-purpose or gluten-free flou
½ tablespoon olive oil
½ teaspoon ground sage
¼ teaspoon kosher salt
⅛ teaspoon freshly ground black pepper
2 cups roughly chopped broccoli floret
6 tablespoons shredded Cheddar cheese
2 tablespoons panko bread crumbs
1 tablespoon grated Parmesan cheese
Olive oil spray

1. Spritz a baking dish with olive oil spray.
2. Mix the milk, flou, olive oil, sage, salt, and pepper in a medium bowl and whisk to combine. Stir in the broccoli florets, Cheddar cheese, bread crumbs, and Parmesan cheese and toss to coat.
3. Pour the broccoli mixture into the prepared baking dish.
4. Select Bake, set temperature to 330°F (166°C), and set time to 14 minutes. Select Start to begin preheating.
5. Once preheated, place the baking dish into the air fryer.
6. When cooking is complete, the top should be golden brown and the broccoli should be tender. Remove from the air fryer and serve immediately.

Cheesy Corn Casserole

Prep time: 5 minutes | Cook time: 15 minutes | Serves 4

2 cups frozen yellow corn
1 egg, beaten
3 tablespoons flou
½ cup grated Swiss or Havarti cheese
½ cup light cream
¼ cup milk
Pinch salt
Freshly ground black pepper, to taste
2 tablespoons butter, cut into cubes
Nonstick cooking spray

1. Spritz a baking pan with nonstick cooking spray.
2. Stir together the remaining ingredients except the butter in a medium bowl until well incorporated. Transfer the mixture to the prepared baking pan and scatter with the butter cubes.
3. Select Bake, set temperature to 320ºF (160ºC), and set time to 15 minutes. Select Start to begin preheating.
4. Once preheated, place the pan into the air fryer.
5. When cooking is complete, the top should be golden brown and a toothpick inserted in the center should come out clean. Remove the pan from the air fryer. Let the casserole cool for 5 minutes before slicing into wedges and serving.

Air-Fried Acorn Squash

Prep time: 5 minutes | Cook time: 15 minutes | Serves 2

1 medium acorn squash, halved crosswise and deseeded
1 teaspoon coconut oil
1 teaspoon light brown sugar
Few dashes of ground cinnamon
Few dashes of ground nutmeg

1. On a clean work surface, rub the cut sides of the acorn squash with coconut oil. Scatter with the brown sugar, cinnamon, and nutmeg.
2. Put the squash halves in the air fry basket, cut-side up.
3. Select Air Fry, set temperature to 325ºF (163ºC), and set time to 15 minutes. Select Start to begin preheating.
4. Once preheated, place the basket into the air fryer.
5. When cooking is complete, the squash halves should be just tender when pierced in the center with a paring knife. Remove the basket from the air fryer. Rest for 5 to 10 minutes and serve warm.

Breaded Brussels Sprouts with Sage

Prep time: 5 minutes | Cook time: 15 minutes | Serves 4

1 pound (454 g) Brussels sprouts, halved
1 cup bread crumbs
2 tablespoons grated Grana Padano cheese
1 tablespoon paprika
2 tablespoons canola oil
1 tablespoon chopped sage

1. Line the air fry basket with parchment paper. Set aside.
2. In a small bowl, thoroughly mix the bread crumbs, cheese, and paprika. In a large bowl, place the Brussels sprouts and drizzle the canola oil over the top. Sprinkle with the bread crumb mixture and toss to coat.
3. Transfer the Brussels sprouts to the prepared basket.
4. Select Roast, set temperature to 400ºF (205ºC), and set time to 15 minutes. Select Start to begin preheating.
5. Once preheated, place the basket into the air fryer. Stir the Brussels a few times during cooking.
6. When cooking is complete, the Brussels sprouts should be lightly browned and crisp. Transfer the Brussels sprouts to a plate and sprinkle the sage on top before serving.

Crispy Parmesan Asparagus

Prep time: 15 minutes | Cook time: 6 minutes | Serves 4

2 egg whites
¼ cup water
¼ cup plus 2 tablespoons grated Parmesan cheese, divided
¾ cup panko bread crumbs
¼ teaspoon salt
12 ounces (340 g) fresh asparagus spears, woody ends trimmed
Cooking spray

1. In a shallow dish, whisk together the egg whites and water until slightly foamy. In a separate shallow dish, thoroughly combine ¼ cup of Parmesan cheese, bread crumbs, and salt.
2. Dip the asparagus in the egg white, then roll in the cheese mixture to coat well.
3. Place the asparagus in the air fry basket in a single layer, leaving space between each spear. Spritz the asparagus with cooking spray.
4. Select Air Fry, set temperature to 390°F (199°C), and set time to 6 minutes. Select Start to begin preheating.
5. Once preheated, place the basket into the air fryer.
6. When cooking is complete, the asparagus should be golden brown and crisp. Remove the basket from the air fryer. Sprinkle with the remaining 2 tablespoons of cheese and serve hot.

Arrowroot-Crusted Zucchini

Prep time: 5 minutes | Cook time: 14 minutes | Serves 4

2 small zucchini, cut into 2-inch × ½-inch sticks
3 tablespoons chickpea flou
2 teaspoons arrowroot (or cornstarch)
½ teaspoon garlic granules
¼ teaspoon sea salt
⅛ teaspoon freshly ground black pepper
1 tablespoon water
Cooking spray

1. Combine the zucchini sticks with the chickpea flou , arrowroot, garlic granules, salt, and pepper in a medium bowl and toss to coat. Add the water and stir to mix well.
2. Spritz the air fry basket with cooking spray and spread out the zucchini sticks in the basket. Mist the zucchini sticks with cooking spray.
3. Select Air Fry, set temperature to 392°F (200°C), and set time to 14 minutes. Select Start to begin preheating.
4. Once preheated, place the basket into the air fryer. Stir the sticks halfway through the cooking time.
5. When cooking is complete, the zucchini sticks should be crispy and nicely browned. Remove from the air fryer and serve warm.

Tangy Balsamic-Glazed Carrots

Prep time: 5 minutes | Cook time: 18 minutes | Serves 3

3 medium-size carrots, cut into 2-inch × ½-inch sticks
1 tablespoon orange juice
2 teaspoons balsamic vinegar
1 teaspoon maple syrup
1 teaspoon avocado oil
½ teaspoon dried rosemary
¼ teaspoon sea salt
¼ teaspoon lemon zest

1. Put the carrots in a baking pan and sprinkle with the orange juice, balsamic vinegar, maple syrup, avocado oil, rosemary, sea salt, finished y the lemon zest. Toss well.
2. Select Roast, set temperature to 392°F (200°C), and set time to 18 minutes. Select Start to begin preheating.
3. Once preheated, place the pan into the air fryer. Stir the carrots several times during the cooking process.
4. When cooking is complete, the carrots should be nicely glazed and tender. Remove from the air fryer and serve hot.

Russet Potatoes with Yogurt and Chives

Prep time: 5 minutes | Cook time: 35 minutes | Serves 4

4 (7-ounce / 198-g) russet potatoes, rinsed
Olive oil spray
½ teaspoon kosher salt, divided
½ cup 2% plain Greek yogurt
¼ cup minced fresh chives
Freshly ground black pepper, to taste

1. Pat the potatoes dry and pierce them all over with a fork. Spritz the potatoes with olive oil spray. Sprinkle with ¼ teaspoon of the salt.
2. Transfer the potatoes to the air fry basket.
3. Select Bake, set temperature to 400°F (205°C), and set time to 35 minutes. Select Start to begin preheating.
4. Once preheated, place the basket into the air fryer.
5. When cooking is complete, the potatoes should be fork-tender. Remove from the air fryer and split open the potatoes. Top with the yogurt, chives, the remaining ¼ teaspoon of salt, and finish with the black pepper. Serve immediately.

Rosemary Red Potatoes

Prep time: 5 minutes | Cook time: 20 minutes | Serves 4

1½ pounds (680 g) small red potatoes, cut into 1-inch cubes
2 tablespoons olive oil
2 tablespoons minced fresh rosemary
1 tablespoon minced garlic
1 teaspoon salt, plus additional as needed
½ teaspoon freshly ground black pepper, plus additional as needed

1. Toss the potato cubes with the olive oil, rosemary, garlic, salt, and pepper in a large bowl until thoroughly coated.
2. Arrange the potato cubes in the air fry basket in a single layer.
3. Select Roast, set temperature to 400°F (205°C), and set time to 20 minutes. Select Start to begin preheating.
4. Once preheated, place the basket into the air fryer. Stir the potatoes a few times during cooking for even cooking.
5. When cooking is complete, the potatoes should be tender. Remove from the air fryer to a plate. Taste and add additional salt and pepper as needed.

Golden Butternut Squash Croquettes

Prep time: 5 minutes | Cook time: 17 minutes | Serves 4

⅓ butternut squash, peeled and grated
⅓ cup all-purpose flou
2 eggs, whisked
4 cloves garlic, minced
1½ tablespoons olive oil
1 teaspoon fine sea salt
⅓ teaspoon freshly ground black pepper, or more to taste
⅓ teaspoon dried sage
A pinch of ground allspice

1. Line the air fry basket with parchment paper. Set aside.
2. In a mixing bowl, stir together all the ingredients until well combined.
3. Make the squash croquettes: Use a small cookie scoop to drop tablespoonfuls of the squash mixture onto a lightly floured surface and shape into balls with your hands. Transfer them to the air fry basket.
4. Select Air Fry, set temperature to 345°F (174°C), and set time to 17 minutes. Select Start to begin preheating.
5. Once preheated, place the basket into the air fryer.
6. When cooking is complete, the squash croquettes should be golden brown. Remove from the air fryer to a plate and serve warm.

Chapter 8 Vegetable Sides | 123

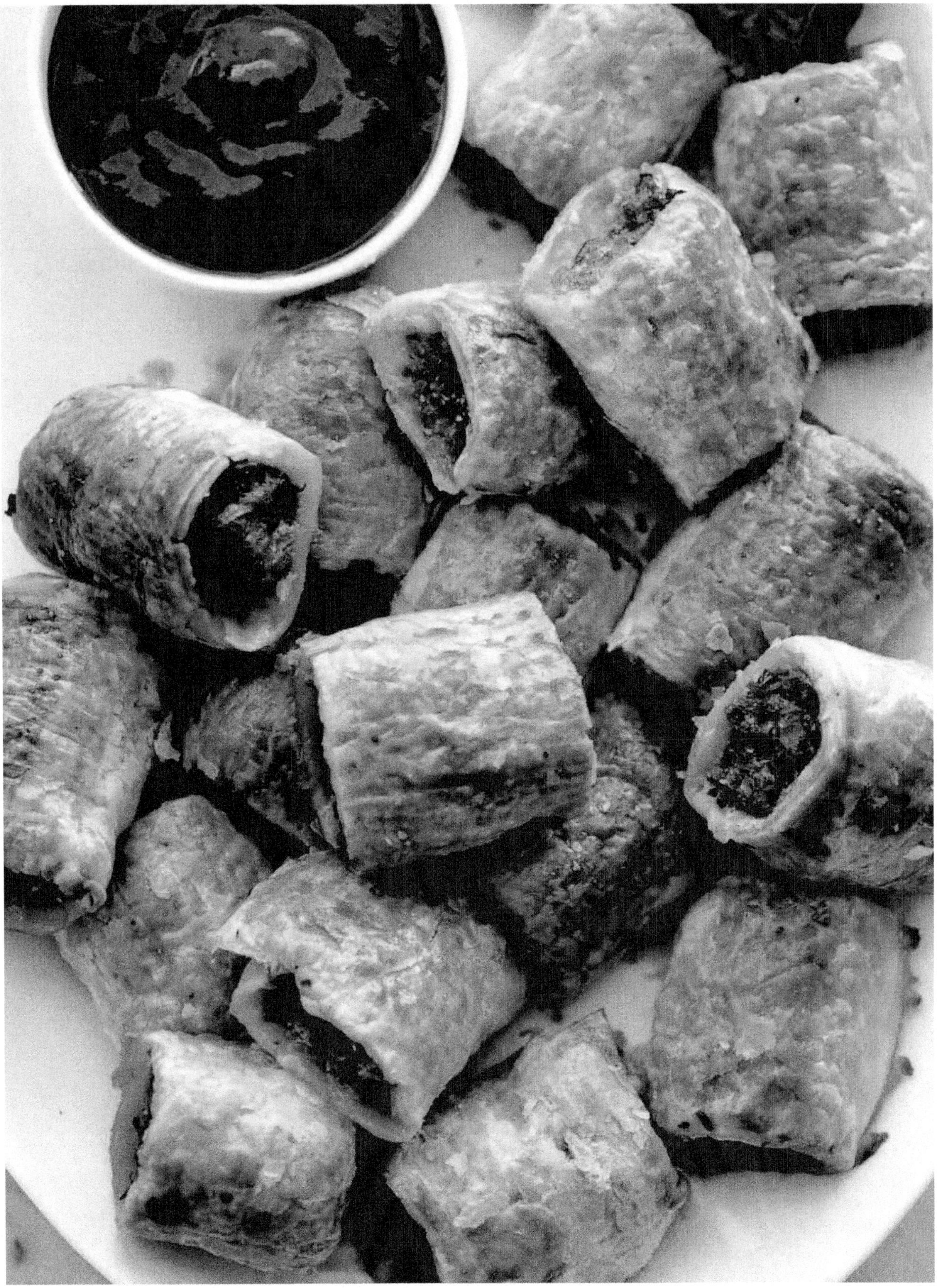

CHAPTER 9 Appetizers and Snacks

Roasted Tuna Melts

Prep time: 10 minutes | Cook time: 6 minutes | Serves 6

2 (5- to 6-ounce / 142- to 170-g) cans oil-packed tuna, drained
1 large scallion, chopped
1 small stalk celery, chopped
⅓ cup mayonnaise
1 tablespoon chopped fresh dill
1 tablespoon capers, drained
¼ teaspoon celery salt
12 slices cocktail rye bread
2 tablespoons butter, melted
6 slices sharp Cheddar cheese

1. In a medium bowl, stir together the tuna, scallion, celery, mayonnaise, dill, capers and celery salt.
2. Brush one side of the bread slices with the butter. Arrange the bread slices on the sheet pan, buttered-side down. Scoop a heaping tablespoon of the tuna mixture on each slice of bread, spreading it out evenly to the edges.
3. Cut the cheese slices to fit the dimensions of the bread and place a cheese slice on each piece.
4. Select Roast, set temperature to 375°F (190°C) and set time to 6 minutes. Select Start to begin preheating.
5. Once the unit has preheated, place the pan into the air fryer.
6. After 4 minutes, remove the pan from the air fryer and check the tuna melts. The tuna melts are done when the cheese has melted and the tuna is heated through. If needed, continue cooking.
7. When cooking is complete, remove the pan from the air fryer. Use a spatula to transfer the tuna melts to a clean work surface and slice each one in half diagonally. Serve warm.

Roasted Sausage and Onion Rolls

Prep time: 15 minutes | Cook time: 15 minutes | Serves 12

1 pound (454 g) bulk breakfast sausage
½ cup finely chopped onion
½ cup fresh bread crumbs
½ teaspoon dried mustard
½ teaspoon dried sage
¼ teaspoon cayenne pepper
1 large egg, beaten
1 garlic clove, minced
2 sheets (1 package) frozen puff pastry, thawed
All-purpose flou , for dusting

1. In a medium bowl, break up the sausage. Stir in the onion, bread crumbs, mustard, sage, cayenne pepper, egg and garlic. Divide the sausage mixture in half and tightly wrap each half in plastic wrap. Refrigerate for 5 to 10 minutes.
2. Lay the pastry sheets on a lightly floured work surface. Using a rolling pin, lightly roll out the pastry to smooth out the dough. Take out one of the sausage packages and form the sausage into a long roll. Remove the plastic wrap and place the sausage on top of the puff pastry about 1 inch from one of the long edges. Roll the pastry around the sausage and pinch the edges of the dough together to seal. Repeat with the other pastry sheet and sausage.
3. Slice the logs into lengths about 1½ inches long. Place the sausage rolls on the sheet pan, cut-side down.
4. Select Roast, set temperature to 350°F (180°C) and set time to 15 minutes. Select Start to begin preheating.
5. Once the unit has preheated, place the pan into the air fryer.
6. After 7 or 8 minutes, rotate the pan and continue cooking.
7. When cooking is complete, the rolls will be golden brown and sizzling. Remove the pan from the air fryer and let cool for 5 minutes.

Deviled Eggs with Paprika

Prep time: 20 minutes | Cook time: 16 minutes | Serves 12

3 cups ice
12 large eggs
½ cup mayonnaise
10 hamburger dill pickle chips, diced
¼ cup diced onion
2 teaspoons salt
2 teaspoons yellow mustard
1 teaspoon freshly ground black pepper
½ teaspoon paprika

1. Put the ice in a large bowl and set aside. Carefully place the eggs in the air fry basket.
2. Select Bake, set temperature to 250°F (121°C), and set time to 16 minutes. Select Start to begin preheating.
3. Once preheated, place the basket into the air fryer.
4. When cooking is complete, transfer the eggs to the large bowl of ice to cool.
5. When cool enough to handle, peel the eggs. Slice them in half lengthwise and scoop out yolks into a small bowl. Stir in the mayonnaise, pickles, onion, salt, mustard, and pepper. Mash the mixture with a fork until well combined.
6. Fill each egg white half with 1 to 2 teaspoons of the egg yolk mixture.
7. Sprinkle the paprika on top and serve immediately.

Homemade Baked Almonds

Prep time: 5 minutes | Cook time: 25 minutes | Serves 4

1 cup raw almonds
1 egg white, beaten
½ teaspoon coarse sea salt

1. Spread the almonds on the sheet pan in an even layer.
2. Select Bake, set temperature to 350°F (180°C) and set time to 20 minutes. Select Start to begin preheating.
3. When the unit has preheated, place the pan into the air fryer.
4. When cooking is complete, the almonds should be lightly browned and fragrant. Remove the pan from the air fryer.
5. Coat the almonds with the egg white and sprinkle with the salt. Return the pan to the air fryer.
6. Select Bake, set temperature to 350°F (180°C) and set time to 5 minutes.
7. When cooking is complete, the almonds should be dried. Cool completely before serving.

Stuffed Mushrooms with Cheese

Prep time: 10 minutes | Cook time: 18 minutes | Serves 12

24 medium raw white button mushrooms, rinsed and drained
4 ounces (113 g) shredded extra-sharp Cheddar cheese
2 ounces (57 g) cream cheese, at room temperature
1 ounce (28 g) chopped jarred pimientos
2 tablespoons grated onion
⅛ teaspoon smoked paprika
⅛ teaspoon hot sauce
2 tablespoons butter, melted, divided
⅓ cup panko bread crumbs
2 tablespoons grated Parmesan cheese

1. Gently pull out the stems of the mushrooms and discard. Set aside.
2. In a medium bowl, stir together the Cheddar cheese, cream cheese, pimientos, onion, paprika and hot sauce.
3. Brush the sheet pan with 1 tablespoon of the melted butter. Arrange the mushrooms evenly on the pan, hollow-side up.
4. Place the cheese mixture into a large heavy plastic bag and cut off the end. Fill the mushrooms with the cheese mixture.
5. In a small bowl, whisk together the remaining 1 tablespoon of the melted butter, bread crumbs and Parmesan cheese. Sprinkle the panko mixture over each mushroom.
6. Select Roast, set temperature to 350°F (180°C) and set time to 18 minutes. Select Start to begin preheating.
7. When the unit has preheated, place the pan into the air fryer.
8. After about 9 minutes, rotate the pan and continue cooking.
9. When cooking is complete, let the stuffed mushrooms rest for 2 minutes before serving.

Sardines with Tomato Sauce

Prep time: 10 minutes | Cook time: 20 minutes | Serves 4

2 pounds (907 g) fresh sardines
3 tablespoons olive oil, divided
4 Roma tomatoes, peeled and chopped
1 small onion, sliced thinly
Zest of 1 orange
Sea salt and freshly ground pepper, to taste
2 tablespoons whole-wheat bread crumbs
½ cup white wine

1. Brush the sheet pan with a little olive oil. Set aside.
2. Rinse the sardines under running water. Slit the belly, remove the spine and butterfly the fish. Set asid
3. Heat the remaining olive oil in a large skillet. Add the tomatoes, onion, orange zest, salt and pepper to the skillet and simmer for 20 minutes, or until the mixture thickens and softens.
4. Place half the sauce in the bottom of the sheet pan. Arrange the sardines on top and spread the remaining half the sauce over the fish. Sprinkle with the bread crumbs and drizzle with the white wine.
5. Select Bake, set temperature to 425°F (220°C) and set time to 20 minutes. Select Start to begin preheating.
6. When the unit has preheated, place the pan into the air fryer.
7. When cooking is complete, remove the pan from the air fryer. Serve immediately.

Stuffed Jalapeño Poppers with Cheese

Prep time: 10 minutes | Cook time: 15 minutes | Serves 8

6 ounces (170 g) cream cheese, at room temperature
4 ounces (113 g) shredded Cheddar cheese
1 teaspoon chili powder
12 large jalapeño peppers, deseeded and sliced in half lengthwise
2 slices cooked bacon, chopped
¼ cup panko bread crumbs
1 tablespoon butter, melted

1. In a medium bowl, whisk together the cream cheese, Cheddar cheese and chili powder. Spoon the cheese mixture into the jalapeño halves and arrange them on the sheet pan.
2. In a small bowl, stir together the bacon, bread crumbs and butter. Sprinkle the mixture over the jalapeño halves.
3. Select Roast, set temperature to 375°F (190°C) and set time to 15 minutes. Select Start to begin preheating.
4. When the unit has preheated, place the pan into the air fryer.
5. After 7 or 8 minutes, rotate the pan and continue cooking until the peppers are softened, the filling is bubbling and the bread crumbs are browned.
6. When cooking is complete, remove the pan from the air fryer. Let the poppers cool for 5 minutes before serving.

Air-Fried Cheesy Zucchini Tots

Prep time: 15 minutes | Cook time: 6 minutes | Serves 8

2 medium zucchini (about 12 ounces / 340 g), shredded
1 large egg, whisked
½ cup grated pecorino romano cheese
½ cup panko bread crumbs
¼ teaspoon black pepper
1 clove garlic, minced
Cooking spray

1. Using your hands, squeeze out as much liquid from the zucchini as possible. In a large bowl, mix the zucchini with the remaining ingredients except the oil until well incorporated.
2. Make the zucchini tots: Use a spoon or cookie scoop to place tablespoonfuls of the zucchini mixture onto a lightly floured cutt ng board and form into 1-inch logs.
3. Spritz the air fry basket with cooking spray. Place the zucchini tots in the pan.
4. Select Air Fry, set temperature to 375°F (190°C), and set time to 6 minutes. Select Start to begin preheating.
5. Once preheated, place the basket into the air fryer.
6. When cooking is complete, the tots should be golden brown. Remove from the air fryer to a serving plate and serve warm.

Lemon-Pepper Chicken Wings

Prep time: 5 minutes | Cook time: 24 minutes | Serves 10

2 pounds (907 g) chicken wings
4½ teaspoons salt-free lemon pepper seasoning
1½ teaspoons baking powder
1½ teaspoons kosher salt

1. In a large bowl, toss together all the ingredients until well coated. Place the wings on the sheet pan, making sure they don't crowd each other too much.
2. Select Air Fry, set temperature to 375°F (190°C) and set time to 24 minutes. Select Start to begin preheating.
3. Once preheated, slide the pan into the air fryer.
4. After 12 minutes, remove the pan from the air fryer. Use tongs to turn the wings over. Rotate the pan and return the pan to the air fryer to continue cooking.
5. When cooking is complete, the wings should be dark golden brown and a bit charred in places. Remove the pan from the air fryer and let rest for 5 minutes before serving.

Cheesy Green Chiles Nachos

Prep time: 10 minutes | Cook time: 10 minutes | Serves 6

8 ounces (227 g) tortilla chips
3 cups shredded Monterey Jack cheese, divided
2 (7-ounce / 198-g) cans chopped green chiles, drained
1 (8-ounce / 227-g) can tomato sauce
¼ teaspoon dried oregano
¼ teaspoon granulated garlic
¼ teaspoon freshly ground black pepper
Pinch cinnamon
Pinch cayenne pepper

1. Arrange the tortilla chips close together in a single layer on the sheet pan. Sprinkle 1½ cups of the cheese over the chips. Arrange the green chiles over the cheese as evenly as possible. Top with the remaining 1½ cups of the cheese.
2. Select Roast, set temperature to 375°F (190°C) and set time to 10 minutes. Select Start to begin preheating.
3. When the unit has preheated, place the pan into the air fryer.
4. After 5 minutes, rotate the pan and continue cooking.
5. Meanwhile, stir together the remaining ingredients in a bowl.
6. When cooking is complete, the cheese will be melted and starting to crisp around the edges of the pan. Remove the pan from the air fryer. Drizzle the sauce over the nachos and serve warm.

Mozzarella Pepperoni Rolls

Prep time: 5 minutes | Cook time: 12 minutes | Serves 8

1 cup finely shredded Mozzarella cheese
½ cup chopped pepperoni
¼ cup Marinara sauce
1 (8-ounce / 227-g) can crescent roll dough
All-purpose flou , for dusting

1. In a small bowl, stir together the cheese, pepperoni and Marinara sauce.
2. Lay the dough on a lightly floured work surface. Separate it into 4 rectangles. Firmly pinch the perforations together and pat the dough pieces flat
3. Divide the cheese mixture evenly between the rectangles and spread it out over the dough, leaving a ¼-inch border. Roll a rectangle up tightly, starting with the short end. Pinch the edge down to seal the roll. Repeat with the remaining rolls.
4. Slice the rolls into 4 or 5 even slices. Place the slices on the sheet pan, leaving a few inches between each slice.
5. Select Roast, set temperature to 350°F (180°C) and set time to 12 minutes. Select Start to begin preheating.
6. Once the unit has preheated, place the pan into the air fryer.
7. After 6 minutes, rotate the pan and continue cooking.
8. When cooking is complete, the rolls will be golden brown with crisp edges. Remove the pan from the air fryer. Serve hot.

Cheesy Sausage Balls

Prep time: 10 minutes | Cook time: 10 minutes | Serves 8

12 ounces (340 g) mild ground sausage
1½ cups baking mix
1 cup shredded mild Cheddar cheese
3 ounces (85 g) cream cheese, at room temperature
1 to 2 tablespoons olive oil

1. Line the air fry basket with parchment paper. Set aside.
2. Mix together the ground sausage, baking mix, Cheddar cheese, and cream cheese in a large bowl and stir to incorporate.
3. Divide the sausage mixture into 16 equal portions and roll them into 1-inch balls with your hands. Arrange the sausage balls on the parchment, leaving space between each ball. Brush the sausage balls with the olive oil.
4. Select Air Fry, set temperature to 325°F (163°C), and set time to 10 minutes. Select Start to begin preheating.
5. Once preheated, place the basket into the air fryer. Flip the balls halfway through the cooking time.
6. When cooking is complete, the balls should be firm and lightly browned on both sides. Remove from the air fryer to a plate and serve warm.

Parmesan Cauliflower Florets

Prep time: 15 minutes | Cook time: 15 minutes | Makes 5 cups

8 cups small cauliflower floret (about 1¼ pounds / 567 g)
3 tablespoons olive oil
1 teaspoon garlic powder
½ teaspoon salt
½ teaspoon turmeric
¼ cup shredded Parmesan cheese

1. In a bowl, combine the cauliflower florets, oli e oil, garlic powder, salt, and turmeric and toss to coat. Transfer to the air fry basket.
2. Select Air Fry, set temperature to 390°F (199°C), and set time to 15 minutes. Select Start to begin preheating.
3. Once preheated, place the basket into the air fryer.
4. After 5 minutes, remove from the air fryer and stir the cauliflower florets Return the basket to the air fryer and continue cooking.
5. After 6 minutes, remove from the air fryer and stir the cauliflowe . Return the basket to the air fryer and continue cooking for 4 minutes. The cauliflower florets should be crisp-tende .
6. When cooking is complete, remove from the air fryer to a plate. Sprinkle with the shredded Parmesan cheese and toss well. Serve warm.

Air-Fried Edamame

Prep time: 5 minutes | Cook time: 9 minutes | Serves 4

1 (16-ounce / 454-g) bag frozen edamame in pods
2 tablespoon olive oil, divided
½ teaspoon garlic salt
½ teaspoon salt
¼ teaspoon freshly ground black pepper
½ teaspoon red pepper fla es (optional)

1. Place the edamame in a medium bowl and drizzle with 1 tablespoon of olive oil. Toss to coat well.
2. Stir together the garlic salt, salt, pepper, and red pepper fla es (if desired) in a small bowl. Pour the mixture into the bowl of edamame and toss until the edamame is fully coated.
3. Grease the air fry basket with the remaining 1 tablespoon of olive oil.
4. Place the edamame in the greased basket.
5. Select Air Fry, set temperature to 375°F (190°C), and set time to 9 minutes. Select Start to begin preheating.
6. Once preheated, place the basket into the air fryer. Stir the edamame once halfway through the cooking time.
7. When cooking is complete, the edamame should be crisp. Remove from the air fryer to a plate and serve warm.

Garlicky Button Mushrooms

Prep time: 5 minutes | Cook time: 27 minutes | Serves 4

16 garlic cloves, peeled
2 teaspoons olive oil, divided
16 button mushrooms
½ teaspoon dried marjoram
⅛ teaspoon freshly ground black pepper
1 tablespoon white wine

1. Place the garlic cloves on the sheet pan and drizzle with 1 teaspoon of the olive oil. Toss to coat well.
2. Select Roast, set temperature to 350°F (180°C) and set time to 12 minutes. Select Start to begin preheating.
3. Once the unit has preheated, place the pan into the air fryer.
4. When cooking is complete, remove the pan from the air fryer. Stir in the mushrooms, marjoram and pepper. Drizzle with the remaining 1 teaspoon of the olive oil and the white wine. Toss to coat well. Return the pan to the air fryer.
5. Select Roast, set temperature to 350°F (180°C) and set time to 15 minutes. Place the pan into the air fryer.
6. Once done, the mushrooms and garlic cloves will be softened. Remove the pan from the air fryer.
7. Serve warm.

Roasted Honey Grapes

Prep time: 5 minutes | Cook time: 10 minutes | Serves 6

2 cups seedless red grapes, rinsed and patted dry
1 tablespoon apple cider vinegar
1 tablespoon honey
1 cup low-fat Greek yogurt
2 tablespoons 2 percent milk
2 tablespoons minced fresh basil

1. Spread the red grapes in the air fry basket and drizzle with the cider vinegar and honey. Lightly toss to coat.
2. Select Roast, set temperature to 380°F (193°C) and set time to 10 minutes. Select Start to begin preheating.
3. Once the unit has preheated, place the basket into the air fryer.
4. When cooking is complete, the grapes will be wilted but still soft. Remove the pan from the air fryer.
5. In a medium bowl, whisk together the yogurt and milk. Gently fold in the grapes and basil.
6. Serve immediately.

Golden Hush Puppies

Prep time: 45 minutes | Cook time: 10 minutes | Serves 12

1 cup self-rising yellow cornmeal
½ cup all-purpose flou
1 teaspoon sugar
1 teaspoon salt
1 teaspoon freshly ground black pepper
1 large egg
⅓ cup canned creamed corn
1 cup minced onion
2 teaspoons minced jalapeño pepper
2 tablespoons olive oil, divided

1. Thoroughly combine the cornmeal, flou , sugar, salt, and pepper in a large bowl.
2. Whisk together the egg and corn in a small bowl. Pour the egg mixture into the bowl of cornmeal mixture and stir to combine. Stir in the minced onion and jalapeño. Cover the bowl with plastic wrap and place in the refrigerator for 30 minutes.
3. Line the air fry basket with parchment paper and lightly brush it with 1 tablespoon of olive oil.
4. Scoop out the cornmeal mixture and form into 24 balls, about 1 inch.
5. Arrange the balls on the parchment, leaving space between each ball.
6. Select Air Fry, set temperature to 375°F (190°C), and set time to 10 minutes. Select Start to begin preheating.
7. Once preheated, place the basket into the air fryer.
8. After 5 minutes, remove the basket from the air fryer. Flip the balls and brush them with the remaining 1 tablespoon of olive oil. Return to the air fryer and continue cooking for 5 minutes until golden brown.
9. When cooking is complete, remove the balls (hush puppies) from the air fryer and serve on a plate.

Browned Ricotta Capers

Prep time: 10 minutes | Cook time: 8 minutes | Serves 4 to 6

1½ cups whole milk ricotta cheese
2 tablespoons extra-virgin olive oil
2 tablespoons capers, rinsed
Zest of 1 lemon, plus more for garnish
1 teaspoon finely chopped fresh rosemary
Pinch crushed red pepper flakes
Salt and freshly ground black pepper, to taste
1 tablespoon grated Parmesan cheese

1. In a mixing bowl, stir together the ricotta cheese, olive oil, capers, lemon zest, rosemary, red pepper flakes, salt, and pepper until well combined.
2. Spread the mixture evenly in a baking dish.
3. Select Air Fry, set temperature to 380°F (193°C), and set time to 8 minutes. Select Start to begin preheating.
4. Once preheated, place the baking dish in the air fryer.
5. When cooking is complete, the top should be nicely browned. Remove from the air fryer and top with a sprinkle of grated Parmesan cheese. Garnish with the lemon zest and serve warm.

Homemade Paprika Potato Chips

Prep time: 5 minutes | Cook time: 22 minutes | Serves 3

2 medium potatoes, preferably Yukon Gold, scrubbed
Cooking spray
2 teaspoons olive oil
½ teaspoon garlic granules
¼ teaspoon paprika
¼ teaspoon plus ⅛ teaspoon sea salt
¼ teaspoon freshly ground black pepper
Ketchup or hot sauce, for serving

1. Spritz the air fry basket with cooking spray.
2. On a flat work surface, cut the potatoes into ¼-inch-thick slices. Transfer the potato slices to a medium bowl, along with the olive oil, garlic granules, paprika, salt, and pepper and toss to coat well. Transfer the potato slices to the air fry basket.
3. Select Air Fry, set temperature to 392°F (200°C), and set time to 22 minutes. Select Start to begin preheating.
4. Once preheated, place the basket into the air fryer. Stir the potato slices twice during the cooking process.
5. When cooking is complete, the potato chips should be tender and nicely browned. Remove from the air fryer and serve alongside the ketchup for dipping.

Smoked Sausage and Mushroom Empanadas

Prep time: 5 minutes | Cook time: 12 minutes | Serves 4

½ pound (227 g) Kielbasa smoked sausage, chopped
4 chopped canned mushrooms
2 tablespoons chopped onion
½ teaspoon ground cumin
¼ teaspoon paprika
Salt and black pepper, to taste
½ package puff pastry dough, at room temperature
1 egg, beaten
Cooking spray

1. Combine the sausage, mushrooms, onion, cumin, paprika, salt, and pepper in a bowl and stir to mix well.
2. Make the empanadas: Place the puff pastry dough on a lightly floured surface. Cut circles into the dough with a glass. Place 1 tablespoon of the sausage mixture into the center of each pastry circle. Fold each in half and pinch the edges to seal. Using a fork, crimp the edges. Brush them with the beaten egg and mist with cooking spray.
3. Spritz the air fry basket with cooking spray. Place the empanadas in the air fry basket.
4. Select Air Fry, set temperature to 360°F (182°C), and set time to 12 minutes. Select Start to begin preheating.
5. Once preheated, place the basket into the air fryer. Flip the empanadas halfway through the cooking time.
6. When cooking is complete, the empanadas should be golden brown. Remove the basket from the air fryer. Allow them to cool for 5 minutes and serve hot.

Parma Prosciutto-Wrapped Pear

Prep time: 12 minutes | Cook time: 6 minutes | Serves 8

2 large, ripe Anjou pears
4 thin slices Parma prosciutto
2 teaspoons aged balsamic vinegar

1. Peel the pears. Slice into 8 wedges and cut out the core from each wedge.
2. Cut the prosciutto into 8 long strips. Wrap each pear wedge with a strip of prosciutto. Place the wrapped pears in the sheet pan.
3. Select Broil, set temperature to High and set time to 6 minutes. Select Start to begin preheating.
4. When the unit has preheated, place the pan into the air fryer.
5. After 2 or 3 minutes, check the pears. The pears should be turned over if the prosciutto is beginning to crisp up and brown. Return the pan to the air fryer and continue cooking.
6. When cooking is complete, remove the pan from the air fryer. Drizzle the pears with the balsamic vinegar and serve warm.

Air-Fried Polenta Fries with Mayo

Prep time: 10 minutes | Cook time: 28 minutes | Serves 4

Polenta Fries:
2 teaspoons vegetable or olive oil
¼ teaspoon paprika
1 pound (454 g) prepared polenta, cut into 3-inch × ½-inch strips
Salt and freshly ground black pepper, to taste

Chili-Lime Mayo:
½ cup mayonnaise
1 teaspoon chili powder
1 teaspoon chopped fresh cilantro
¼ teaspoon ground cumin
Juice of ½ lime
Salt and freshly ground black pepper, to taste

1. Mix the oil and paprika in a bowl. Add the polenta strips and toss until evenly coated. Transfer the polenta strips to the air fry basket.
2. Select Air Fry, set temperature to 400ºF (205ºC), and set time to 28 minutes. Select Start to begin preheating.
3. Once preheated, place the basket into the air fryer. Stir the polenta strips halfway through the cooking time.
4. Meanwhile, whisk together all the ingredients for the chili-lime mayo in a small bowl.
5. When cooking is complete, remove the polenta fries from the air fryer to a plate. Season as desired with salt and pepper. Serve alongside the chili-lime mayo as a dipping sauce.

Air-Fried Pickle Spears

Prep time: 5 minutes | Cook time: 15 minutes | Serves 6

2 jars sweet and sour pickle spears, patted dry
2 medium-sized eggs
⅓ cup milk
1 teaspoon garlic powder
1 teaspoon sea salt
½ teaspoon shallot powder
⅓ teaspoon chili powder
⅓ cup all-purpose flour
Cooking spray

1. Spritz the air fry basket with cooking spray.
2. In a bowl, beat together the eggs with milk. In another bowl, combine garlic powder, sea salt, shallot powder, chili powder and all-purpose flour until well blended.
3. One by one, roll the pickle spears in the powder mixture, then dredge them in the egg mixture. Dip them in the powder mixture a second time for additional coating.
4. Place the coated pickles in the air fry basket.
5. Select Air Fry, set temperature to 385ºF (196ºC), and set time to 15 minutes. Select Start to begin preheating.
6. Once preheated, place the basket into the air fryer. Stir the pickles halfway through the cooking time.
7. When cooking is complete, they should be golden and crispy. Transfer to a plate and let cool for 5 minutes before serving.

Honey Snack Mix

Prep time: 5 minutes | Cook time: 10 minutes | Makes about 10 cups

3 tablespoons butter, melted
½ cup honey
1 teaspoon salt
2 cups granola
2 cups sesame sticks
2 cups crispy corn puff cereal
2 cups mini pretzel crisps
1 cup cashews
1 cup pepitas
1 cup dried cherries

1. In a small mixing bowl, mix together the butter, honey, and salt until well incorporated.
2. In a large bowl, combine the granola, sesame sticks, corn puff cereal and pretzel crisps, cashews, and pepitas. Drizzle with the butter mixture and toss until evenly coated. Transfer the snack mix to a sheet pan.
3. Select Air Fry, set temperature to 370°F (188°C), and set time to 10 minutes. Select Start to begin preheating.
4. Once preheated, slide the pan into the air fryer. Stir the snack mix halfway through the cooking time.
5. When cooking is complete, they should be lightly toasted. Remove from the air fryer and allow to cool completely. Scatter with the dried cherries and mix well. Serve immediately.

Sweet Roasted Mixed Nuts

Prep time: 5 minutes | Cook time: 20 minutes | Serves 6

2 cups mixed nuts (walnuts, pecans, and almonds)
2 tablespoons egg white
2 tablespoons sugar
1 teaspoon paprika
1 teaspoon ground cinnamon
Cooking spray

1. Line the air fry basket with parchment paper and spray with cooking spray.
2. Stir together the mixed nuts, egg white, sugar, paprika, and cinnamon in a small bowl until the nuts are fully coated. Place the nuts in the air fry basket.
3. Select Roast, set temperature to 300°F (150°C), and set time to 20 minutes. Select Start to begin preheating.
4. Once preheated, place the basket into the air fryer. Stir the nuts halfway through the cooking time.
5. When cooking is complete, remove the basket from the air fryer. Transfer the nuts to a bowl and serve warm.

Shrimp Toasts with Thai Chili Sauce

Prep time: 15 minutes | Cook time: 8 minutes | Serves 4 to 6

½ pound (227 g) raw shrimp, peeled and deveined
1 egg, beaten
2 scallions, chopped, plus more for garnish
2 tablespoons chopped fresh cilantro
2 teaspoons grated fresh ginger
1 to 2 teaspoons sriracha sauce
1 teaspoon soy sauce
½ teaspoon toasted sesame oil
6 slices thinly sliced white sandwich bread
½ cup sesame seeds
Cooking spray
Thai chili sauce, for serving

1. In a food processor, add the shrimp, egg, scallions, cilantro, ginger, sriracha sauce, soy sauce and sesame oil, and pulse until chopped finel . You'll need to stop the food processor occasionally to scrape down the sides. Transfer the shrimp mixture to a bowl.
2. On a clean work surface, cut the crusts off the sandwich bread. Using a brush, generously brush one side of each slice of bread with shrimp mixture.
3. Place the sesame seeds on a plate. Press bread slices, shrimp-side down, into sesame seeds to coat evenly. Cut each slice diagonally into quarters.
4. Spritz the air fry basket with cooking spray. Spread the coated slices in a single layer in the air fry basket.
5. Select Air Fry, set temperature to 400°F (205°C), and set time to 8 minutes. Select Start to begin preheating.
6. Once preheated, place the basket into the air fryer. Flip the bread slices halfway through.
7. When cooking is complete, they should be golden and crispy. Remove from the air fryer to a plate and let cool for 5 minutes. Top with the chopped scallions and serve warm with Thai chili sauce.

Crispy Cinnamon Apple Chips

Prep time: 10 minutes | Cook time: 10 minutes | Serves 4

2 apples, cored and cut into thin slices
2 heaped teaspoons ground cinnamon
Cooking spray

1. Spritz the air fry basket with cooking spray.
2. In a medium bowl, sprinkle the apple slices with the cinnamon. Toss until evenly coated. Spread the coated apple slices on the pan in a single layer.
3. Select Air Fry, set temperature to 350°F (180°C) and set time to 10 minutes. Select Start to begin preheating.
4. Once preheated, place the basket into the air fryer.
5. After 5 minutes, remove the basket from the air fryer. Stir the apple slices and return the basket to the air fryer to continue cooking.
6. When cooking is complete, the slices should be until crispy Remove the basket from the air fryer and let rest for 5 minutes before serving.

Apple Wedges with Yogurt

Prep time: 10 minutes | Cook time: 12 minutes | Serves 4

2 medium apples, cored and sliced into ¼-inch wedges
1 teaspoon canola oil
2 teaspoons peeled and grated fresh ginger
½ teaspoon ground cinnamon
½ cup low-fat Greek vanilla yogurt, for serving

1. In a large bowl, toss the apple wedges with the canola oil, ginger, and cinnamon until evenly coated. Put the apple wedges in the air fry basket.
2. Select Air Fry, set temperature to 360°F (182°C), and set time to 12 minutes. Select Start to begin preheating.
3. Once preheated, place the basket into the air fryer.
4. When cooking is complete, the apple wedges should be crisp-tender. Remove the apple wedges from the air fryer and serve drizzled with the yogurt.

Fast Carrot Chips

Prep time: 15 minutes | Cook time: 10 minutes | Serves 4

4 to 5 medium carrots, trimmed and thinly sliced
1 tablespoon olive oil, plus more for greasing
1 teaspoon seasoned salt

1. Toss the carrot slices with 1 tablespoon of olive oil and salt in a medium bowl until thoroughly coated.
2. Grease the air fry basket with the olive oil. Place the carrot slices in the greased pan.
3. Select Air Fry, set temperature to 390°F (199°C), and set time to 10 minutes. Select Start to begin preheating.
4. Once preheated, place the basket into the air fryer. Stir the carrot slices halfway through the cooking time.
5. When cooking is complete, the chips should be crisp-tender. Remove the basket from the air fryer and allow to cool for 5 minutes before serving.

Crispy Spiced Apple Chips

Prep time: 10 minutes | Cook time: 10 minutes | Serves 4

4 medium apples (any type will work), cored and thinly sliced
¼ teaspoon nutmeg
¼ teaspoon cinnamon
Cooking spray

1. Place the apple slices in a large bowl and sprinkle the spices on top. Toss to coat.
2. Put the apple slices in the air fry basket in a single layer and spray them with cooking spray.
3. Select Air Fry, set temperature to 360°F (182°C), and set time to 10 minutes. Select Start to begin preheating.
4. Once preheated, place the basket into the air fryer. Stir the apple slices halfway through.
5. When cooking is complete, the apple chips should be crispy. Transfer the apple chips to a paper towel-lined plate and rest for 5 minutes before serving.

Stuffed Mushroom with Ham

Prep time: 15 minutes | Cook time: 12 minutes | Serves 8

4 ounces (113 g) Mozzarella cheese, cut into pieces
½ cup diced ham
2 green onions, chopped
2 tablespoons bread crumbs
½ teaspoon garlic powder
¼ teaspoon ground oregano
¼ teaspoon ground black pepper
1 to 2 teaspoons olive oil
16 fresh Baby Bella mushrooms, stemmed removed

1. Process the cheese, ham, green onions, bread crumbs, garlic powder, oregano, and pepper in a food processor until finely chopped
2. With the food processor running, slowly drizzle in 1 to 2 teaspoons olive oil until a thick paste has formed. Transfer the mixture to a bowl.
3. Evenly divide the mixture into the mushroom caps and lightly press down the mixture.
4. Lay the mushrooms in the air fry basket in a single layer.
5. Select Roast, set temperature to 390ºF (199ºC), and set time to 12 minutes. Select Start to begin preheating.
6. Once preheated, place the basket into the air fryer.
7. When cooking is complete, the mushrooms should be lightly browned and tender. Remove from the air fryer to a plate. Let the mushrooms cool for 5 minutes and serve warm.

Caramelized Cinnamon Peach

Prep time: 5 minutes | Cook time: 10 minutes | Serves 4

2 tablespoons sugar
¼ teaspoon ground cinnamon
4 peaches, cut into wedges
Cooking spray

1. Spritz the air fry basket with cooking spray.
2. In a large bowl, stir together the sugar and cinnamon. Add the peaches to the bowl and toss to coat evenly.
3. Spread the coated peaches in a single layer in the air fry basket.
4. Select Air Fry, set temperature to 350ºF (180ºC) and set time to 10 minutes. Select Start to begin preheating.
5. Once preheated, place the basket into the air fryer.
6. After 5 minutes, remove the basket from the air fryer. Use tongs to turn the peaches skin side down. Lightly mist them with cooking spray. Return the basket to the air fryer to continue cooking.
7. When cooking is complete, the peaches will be lightly browned and caramelized. Remove the basket from the air fryer and let rest for 5 minutes before serving.

Air-Fried Crunchy Chickpeas

Prep time: 5 minutes | Cook time: 18 minutes | Serves 4

½ teaspoon chili powder
½ teaspoon ground cumin
¼ teaspoon cayenne pepper
¼ teaspoon salt
1 (19-ounce / 539-g) can chickpeas, drained and rinsed
Cooking spray

1. Lina the air fry basket with parchment paper and lightly spritz with cooking spray.
2. Mix the chili powder, cumin, cayenne pepper, and salt in a small bowl.
3. Place the chickpeas in a medium bowl and lightly mist with cooking spray.
4. Add the spice mixture to the chickpeas and toss until evenly coated. Transfer the chickpeas to the parchment.
5. Select Air Fry, set temperature to 390ºF (199ºC), and set time to 18 minutes. Select Start to begin preheating.
6. Once preheated, place the basket into the air fryer. Stir the chickpeas twice during cooking.
7. When cooking is complete, the chickpeas should be crunchy. Remove the basket from the air fryer. Let the chickpeas cool for 5 minutes before serving.

Spicy-Sweet Walnut

Prep time: 5 minutes | Cook time: 15 minutes | Makes 4 cups

1 pound (454 g) walnut halves and pieces	3 tablespoons vegetable oil
½ cup granulated sugar	1 teaspoon cayenne pepper
	½ teaspoon fine sal

1. Soak the walnuts in a large bowl with boiling water for a minute or two. Drain the walnuts. Stir in the sugar, oil and cayenne pepper to coat well. Spread the walnuts in a single layer on the sheet pan.
2. Select Roast, set temperature to 325°F (163°C) and set time to 15 minutes. Select Start to begin preheating.
3. When the unit has preheated, place the pan into the air fryer.
4. After 7 or 8 minutes, remove the pan from the air fryer. Stir the nuts. Return the pan to the air fryer and continue cooking, check frequently.
5. When cooking is complete, the walnuts should be dark golden brown. Remove the pan from the air fryer. Sprinkle the nuts with the salt and let cool. Serve.

Panko-Crusted Avocado Chips

Prep time: 15 minutes | Cook time: 10 minutes | Serves 4

1 egg	crumbs
1 tablespoon lime juice	¼ cup cornmeal
⅛ teaspoon hot sauce	¼ teaspoon salt
2 tablespoons flou	1 large avocado, pitted, peeled, and cut into ½-inch slices
¾ cup panko bread	Cooking spray

1. Whisk together the egg, lime juice, and hot sauce in a small bowl.
2. On a sheet of wax paper, place the flou . In a separate sheet of wax paper, combine the bread crumbs, cornmeal, and salt.
3. Dredge the avocado slices one at a time in the flou , then in the egg mixture, finally roll them in the bread crumb mixture to coat well.
4. Place the breaded avocado slices in the air fry basket and mist them with cooking spray.
5. Select Air Fry, set temperature to 390°F (199°C), and set time to 10 minutes. Select Start to begin preheating.
6. Once preheated, place the basket into the air fryer.
7. When cooking is complete, the slices should be nicely browned and crispy. Transfer the avocado slices to a plate and serve.

Muffuletta Sliders with Olives

Prep time: 10 minutes | Cook time: 6 minutes | Makes 8 sliders

¼ pound (113 g) thinly sliced deli ham	cheese, grated
¼ pound (113 g) thinly sliced pastrami	8 slider buns, split in half
4 ounces (113 g) low-fat Mozzarella	Cooking spray
	1 tablespoon sesame seeds

Olive Mix:

½ cup sliced green olives with pimentos	1 teaspoon red wine vinegar
¼ cup sliced black olives	¼ teaspoon basil
¼ cup chopped kalamata olives	⅛ teaspoon garlic powder

1. Combine all the ingredients for the olive mix in a small bowl and stir well.
2. Stir together the ham, pastrami, and cheese in a medium bowl and divide the mixture into 8 equal portions.
3. Assemble the sliders: Top each bottom bun with 1 portion of meat and cheese, 2 tablespoons of olive mix, finished y the remaining buns. Lightly spritz the tops with cooking spray. Scatter the sesame seeds on top.
4. Arrange the sliders in the air fry basket.
5. Select Bake, set temperature to 360°F (182°C), and set time to 6 minutes. Select Start to begin preheating.
6. Once preheated, place the basket into the air fryer.
7. When cooking is complete, the cheese should be melted. Remove the basket from the air fryer and serve.

Spicy Kale Chips

Prep time: 15 minutes | Cook time: 8 minutes | Serves 5

8 cups deribbed kale leaves, torn into 2-inch pieces
1½ tablespoons olive oil
¾ teaspoon chili powder
¼ teaspoon garlic powder
½ teaspoon paprika
2 teaspoons sesame seeds

1. In a large bowl, toss the kale with the olive oil, chili powder, garlic powder, paprika, and sesame seeds until well coated.
2. Transfer the kale to the air fry basket.
3. Select Air Fry, set temperature to 350°F (180°C), and set time to 8 minutes. Select Start to begin preheating.
4. Once preheated, place the basket into the air fryer. Flip the kale twice during cooking.
5. When cooking is complete, the kale should be crispy. Remove from the air fryer and serve warm.

Green Tomato with Horseradish

Prep time: 18 minutes | Cook time: 13 minutes | Serves 4

2 eggs
¼ cup buttermilk
½ cup bread crumbs
½ cup cornmeal
¼ teaspoon salt

Horseradish Sauce:
¼ cup sour cream
¼ cup mayonnaise
2 teaspoons prepared horseradish
½ teaspoon lemon juice
½ teaspoon Worcestershire sauce
⅛ teaspoon black pepper

1½ pounds (680 g) firm green tomatoes, cut into ¼-inch slices
Cooking spray

1. Spritz the air fry basket with cooking spray. Set aside.
2. In a small bowl, whisk together all the ingredients for the horseradish sauce until smooth. Set aside.
3. In a shallow dish, beat the eggs and buttermilk.
4. In a separate shallow dish, thoroughly combine the bread crumbs, cornmeal, and salt.
5. Dredge the tomato slices, one at a time, in the egg mixture, then roll in the bread crumb mixture until evenly coated.
6. Place the tomato slices in the air fry basket in a single layer. Spray them with cooking spray.
7. Select Air Fry, set temperature to 390°F (199°C), and set time to 13 minutes. Select Start to begin preheating.
8. Once preheated, place the basket into the air fryer. Flip the tomato slices halfway through the cooking time.
9. When cooking is complete, the tomato slices should be nicely browned and crisp. Remove from the air fryer to a platter and serve drizzled with the prepared horseradish sauce.

Easy Spicy Tortilla Chips

Prep time: 5 minutes | Cook time: 5 minutes | Serves 4

½ teaspoon ground cumin
½ teaspoon paprika
½ teaspoon chili powder
½ teaspoon salt
Pinch cayenne pepper
8 (6-inch) corn tortillas, each cut into 6 wedges
Cooking spray

1. Lightly spritz the air fry basket with cooking spray.
2. Stir together the cumin, paprika, chili powder, salt, and pepper in a small bowl.
3. Place the tortilla wedges in the air fry basket in a single layer. Lightly mist them with cooking spray. Sprinkle the seasoning mixture on top of the tortilla wedges.
4. Select Air Fry, set temperature to 375°F (190°C), and set time to 5 minutes. Select Start to begin preheating.
5. Once preheated, place the basket into the air fryer. Stir the tortilla wedges halfway through the cooking time.
6. When cooking is complete, the chips should be lightly browned and crunchy. Remove the basket from the air fryer. Let the tortilla chips cool for 5 minutes and serve.

Chapter 9 Appetizers and Snacks |137

Air-Fried Old Bay Chicken Wings

Prep time: 10 minutes | Cook time: 13 minutes | Serves 4

2 tablespoons Old Bay seasoning
2 teaspoons baking powder
2 teaspoons salt
2 pounds (907 g) chicken wings, patted dry
Cooking spray

1. Combine the Old Bay seasoning, baking powder, and salt in a large zip-top plastic bag. Add the chicken wings, seal, and shake until the wings are thoroughly coated in the seasoning mixture.
2. Lightly spray the air fry basket with cooking spray. Lay the chicken wings in the air fry basket in a single layer and lightly mist them with cooking spray.
3. Select Air Fry, set temperature to 400°F (205°C), and set time to 13 minutes. Select Start to begin preheating.
4. Once preheated, place the basket into the air fryer. Flip the wings halfway through the cooking time.
5. When cooking is complete, the wings should reach an internal temperature of 165°F (74°C) on a meat thermometer. Remove from the air fryer to a plate and serve hot.

Roasted Parmesan Snack Mix

Prep time: 5 minutes | Cook time: 6 minutes | Makes 6 cups

2 cups oyster crackers
2 cups Chex rice
1 cup sesame sticks
2/3 cup finely g ated Parmesan cheese
8 tablespoons unsalted butter, melted
1½ teaspoons granulated garlic
½ teaspoon kosher salt

1. Toss together all the ingredients in a large bowl until well coated. Spread the mixture on the sheet pan in an even layer.
2. Select Roast, set temperature to 350°F (180°C) and set time to 6 minutes. Select Start to begin preheating.
3. When the unit has preheated, place the pan into the air fryer.
4. After 3 minutes, remove the pan and stir the mixture. Return the pan to the air fryer and continue cooking.
5. When cooking is complete, the mixture should be lightly browned and fragrant. Let cool before serving.

Golden Italian Rice Balls

Prep time: 20 minutes | Cook time: 10 minutes | Makes 8 rice balls

1½ cups cooked sticky rice
½ teaspoon Italian seasoning blend
¾ teaspoon salt, divided
8 black olives, pitted
1 ounce (28 g) Mozzarella cheese, cut into tiny pieces (small enough to stuff into olives)
2 eggs
1/3 cup Italian bread crumbs
¾ cup panko bread crumbs
Cooking spray

1. Stuff each black olive with a piece of Mozzarella cheese.
2. In a bowl, combine the cooked sticky rice, Italian seasoning blend, and ½ teaspoon of salt and stir to mix well. Form the rice mixture into a log with your hands and divide it into 8 equal portions. Mold each portion around a black olive and roll into a ball.
3. Transfer to the freezer to chill for 10 to 15 minutes until firm
4. In a shallow dish, place the Italian bread crumbs. In a separate shallow dish, whisk the eggs. In a third shallow dish, combine the panko bread crumbs and remaining salt.
5. One by one, roll the rice balls in the Italian bread crumbs, then dip in the whisked eggs, finally coat them with the panko bread crumbs.
6. Arrange the rice balls in the air fry basket and spritz both sides with cooking spray.
7. Select Air Fry, set temperature to 390°F (199°C), and set time to 10 minutes. Select Start to begin preheating.
8. Once preheated, place the basket into the air fryer. Flip the balls halfway through the cooking time.
9. When cooking is complete, the rice balls should be golden brown. Remove from the air fryer and serve warm.

Fast Cripsy Artichoke Bites

Prep time: 10 minutes | Cook time: 8 minutes | Serves 4

14 whole artichoke hearts packed in water
½ cup all-purpose flou
1 egg
⅓ cup panko bread crumbs
1 teaspoon Italian seasoning
Cooking spray

1. Drain the artichoke hearts and dry thoroughly with paper towels.
2. Place the flour on a plate. Beat the egg in a shallow bowl until frothy. Thoroughly combine the bread crumbs and Italian seasoning in a separate shallow bowl.
3. Dredge the artichoke hearts in the flou , then in the beaten egg, and finally roll in the bread crumb mixture until evenly coated.
4. Place the artichoke hearts in the air fry basket and mist them with cooking spray.
5. Select Air Fry, set temperature to 375°F (190°C), and set time to 8 minutes. Select Start to begin preheating.
6. Once preheated, place the basket into the air fryer. Flip the artichoke hearts halfway through the cooking time.
7. When cooking is complete, the artichoke hearts should start to brown and the edges should be crispy. Remove the basket from the air fryer. Let the artichoke hearts sit for 5 minutes before serving.

Barbecue Herby Sausage Pizza

Prep time: 5 minutes | Cook time: 8 minutes | Serves 1

1 piece naan bread
¼ cup Barbecue sauce
¼ cup shredded Monterrey Jack cheese
¼ cup shredded Mozzarella cheese
½ chicken herby sausage, sliced
2 tablespoons red onion, thinly sliced
Chopped cilantro or parsley, for garnish
Cooking spray

1. Spritz the bottom of naan bread with cooking spray, then transfer to the air fry basket.
2. Brush with the Barbecue sauce. Top with the cheeses, sausage, and finish with the red onion.
3. Select Air Fry, set temperature to 400°F (205°C), and set time to 8 minutes. Select Start to begin preheating.
4. Once preheated, place the basket into the air fryer.
5. When cooking is complete, the cheese should be melted. Remove the basket from the air fryer. Garnish with the chopped cilantro or parsley before slicing to serve.

Air-Fried Breaded Chicken Wings

Prep time: 1 hour 20 minutes | Cook time: 18 minutes | Serves 4

2 pounds (907 g) chicken wings
Cooking spray
Marinade:
1 cup buttermilk
½ teaspoon salt
½ teaspoon black pepper

Coating:
1 cup flou
1 cup panko bread crumbs
2 tablespoons poultry seasoning
2 teaspoons salt

1. Whisk together all the ingredients for the marinade in a large bowl.
2. Add the chicken wings to the marinade and toss well. Transfer to the refrigerator to marinate for at least an hour.
3. Spritz the air fry basket with cooking spray. Set aside.
4. Thoroughly combine all the ingredients for the coating in a shallow bowl.
5. Remove the chicken wings from the marinade and shake off any excess. Roll them in the coating mixture.
6. Place the chicken wings in the air fry basket in a single layer. Mist the wings with cooking spray.
7. Select Air Fry, set temperature to 360°F (182°C), and set time to 18 minutes. Select Start to begin preheating.
8. Once preheated, place the basket into the air fryer. Flip the wings halfway through the cooking time.
9. When cooking is complete, the wings should be crisp and golden brown on the outside. Remove from the air fryer to a plate and serve hot.

Bacon-Wrapped Stuffed Dates

Prep time: 10 minutes | Cook time: 6 minutes | Makes 16 appetizers

16 whole dates, pitted
16 whole almonds
6 to 8 strips turkey bacon, cut in half

Special Equipment:
16 toothpicks, soaked in water for at least 30 minutes

1.
2. On a flat work surface, stuff each pitted date with a whole almond.
3. Wrap half slice of bacon around each date and secure it with a toothpick.
4. Place the bacon-wrapped dates in the air fry basket.
5. Select Air Fry, set temperature to 390ºF (199ºC), and set time to 6 minutes. Select Start to begin preheating.
6. Once preheated, place the basket into the air fryer.
7. When cooking is complete, transfer the dates to a paper towel-lined plate to drain. Serve hot.

Super Cheesy Sandwiches

Prep time: 10 minutes | Cook time: 6 minutes | Serves 4 to 8

8 ounces (227 g) Brie
8 slices oat nut bread
1 large ripe pear, cored and cut into ½-inch-thick slices
2 tablespoons butter, melted

1. Make the sandwiches: Spread each of 4 slices of bread with ¼ of the Brie. Top the Brie with the pear slices and remaining 4 bread slices.
2. Brush the melted butter lightly on both sides of each sandwich.
3. Arrange the sandwiches in the air fry basket.
4. Select Bake, set temperature to 360ºF (182ºC), and set time to 6 minutes. Select Start to begin preheating.
5. Once preheated, place the basket into the air fryer.
6. When cooking is complete, the cheese should be melted. Remove the basket from the air fryer and serve warm.

Golden Mushroom and Spinach Calzones

Prep time: 15 minutes | Cook time: 26 to 27 minutes | Serves 4

2 tablespoons olive oil
1 onion, chopped
2 garlic cloves, minced
¼ cup chopped mushrooms
1 pound (454 g) spinach, chopped
1 tablespoon Italian seasoning
½ teaspoon oregano
Salt and black pepper, to taste
1½ cups marinara sauce
1 cup ricotta cheese, crumbled
1 (13-ounce / 369-g) pizza crust
Cooking spray

Make the Filling:
1. Heat the olive oil in a pan over medium heat until shimmering.
2. Add the onion, garlic, and mushrooms and sauté for 4 minutes, or until softened.
3. Stir in the spinach and sauté for 2 to 3 minutes, or until the spinach is wilted. Sprinkle with the Italian seasoning, oregano, salt, and pepper and mix well.
4. Add the marinara sauce and cook for about 5 minutes, stirring occasionally, or until the sauce is thickened.
5. Remove the pan from the heat and stir in the ricotta cheese. Set aside.

Make the Calzones:
1. Spritz the air fry basket with cooking spray. Set aside.
2. Roll the pizza crust out with a rolling pin on a lightly floured work surface, then cut it into 4 rectangles.
3. Spoon ¼ of the filling into each rectangle and fold in half. Crimp the edges with a fork to seal. Mist them with cooking spray. Transfer the calzones to the air fry basket.
4. Select Air Fry, set temperature to 375ºF (190ºC), and set time to 15 minutes. Select Start to begin preheating.
5. Once preheated, place the basket into the air fryer. Flip the calzones halfway through the cooking time.
6. When cooking is complete, the calzones should be golden brown and crisp. Transfer the calzones to a paper towel-lined plate and serve.

Cheesy Crab Meat Toasts

Prep time: 10 minutes | Cook time: 5 minutes | Makes 15 to 18 toasts

1 (6-ounce / 170-g) can fl ked crab meat, well drained
3 tablespoons light mayonnaise
¼ cup shredded Parmesan cheese
¼ cup shredded Cheddar cheese
1 teaspoon Worcestershire sauce
½ teaspoon lemon juice
1 loaf artisan bread, French bread, or baguette, cut into ⅜-inch-thick slices

1. In a large bowl, stir together all the ingredients except the bread slices.
2. On a clean work surface, lay the bread slices. Spread ½ tablespoon of crab mixture onto each slice of bread.
3. Arrange the bread slices in the air fry basket in a single layer.
4. Select Bake, set temperature to 360°F (182°C), and set time to 5 minutes. Select Start to begin preheating.
5. Once preheated, place the basket into the air fryer.
6. When cooking is complete, the tops should be lightly browned. Remove the basket from the air fryer. Serve warm.

Cod Fingers Gratin

Prep time: 5 minutes | Cook time: 12 minutes | Serves 4

2 eggs
2 tablespoons milk
2 cups flou
1 cup cornmeal
1 teaspoon seafood seasoning
Salt and black pepper, to taste
1 cup bread crumbs
1 pound (454 g) cod fillets, cut into 1-inch strips

1. Beat the eggs with the milk in a shallow bowl. In another shallow bowl, combine the flou , cornmeal, seafood seasoning, salt, and pepper. On a plate, place the bread crumbs.
2. Dredge the cod strips, one at a time, in the flour mixture, then in the egg mixture, finally roll in the bread crumb to coat evenly.
3. Transfer the cod strips to the air fry basket.
4. Select Air Fry, set temperature to 400°F (205°C), and set time to 12 minutes. Select Start to begin preheating.
5. Once preheated, place the basket into the air fryer.
6. When cooking is complete, the cod strips should be crispy. Remove from the air fryer to a paper towel-lined plate and serve warm.

Bruschetta with Tomato Sauce

Prep time: 5 minutes | Cook time: 3 minutes | Serves 6

4 tomatoes, diced
⅓ cup shredded fresh basil
¼ cup shredded Parmesan cheese
1 tablespoon balsamic vinegar
1 tablespoon minced garlic
1 teaspoon olive oil
1 teaspoon salt
1 teaspoon freshly ground black pepper
1 loaf French bread, cut into 1-inch-thick slices
Cooking spray

1. Mix together the tomatoes and basil in a medium bowl. Add the cheese, vinegar, garlic, olive oil, salt, and pepper and stir until well incorporated. Set aside.
2. Spritz the air fry basket with cooking spray and lay the bread slices in the pan in a single layer. Spray the slices with cooking spray.
3. Select Bake, set temperature to 250°F (121°C), and set time to 3 minutes. Select Start to begin preheating.
4. Once preheated, place the basket into the air fryer.
5. When cooking is complete, remove from the air fryer to a plate. Top each slice with a generous spoonful of the tomato mixture and serve.

Cheesy Corn and Black Bean Salsa

Prep time: 10 minutes | Cook time: 10 minutes | Serves 4

½ (15-ounce / 425-g) can corn, drained and rinsed
½ (15-ounce / 425-g) can black beans, drained and rinsed
¼ cup chunky salsa
2 ounces (57 g) reduced-fat cream cheese, softened
¼ cup shredded reduced-fat Cheddar cheese
½ teaspoon paprika
½ teaspoon ground cumin
Salt and freshly ground black pepper, to taste

1. Combine the corn, black beans, salsa, cream cheese, Cheddar cheese, paprika, and cumin in a medium bowl. Sprinkle with salt and pepper and stir until well blended.
2. Pour the mixture into a baking dish.
3. Select Air Fry, set temperature to 325ºF (163ºC), and set time to 10 minutes. Select Start to begin preheating.
4. Once preheated, place the baking dish in the air fryer.
5. When cooking is complete, the mixture should be heated through. Rest for 5 minutes and serve warm.

Cuban Turkey Sandwiches

Prep time: 20 minutes | Cook time: 8 minutes | Makes 4 sandwiches

8 slices ciabatta bread, about ¼-inch thick

Toppings:
6 to 8 ounces (170 to 227 g) thinly sliced leftover roast pork
4 ounces (113 g) thinly sliced deli turkey
Cooking spray
1 tablespoon brown mustard
⅓ cup bread and butter pickle slices
2 to 3 ounces (57 to 85 g) Pepper Jack cheese slices

1. On a clean work surface, spray one side of each slice of bread with cooking spray. Spread the other side of each slice of bread evenly with brown mustard.
2. Top 4 of the bread slices with the roast pork, turkey, pickle slices, cheese, and finish with remaining bread slices. Transfer to the air fry basket.
3. Select Air Fry, set temperature to 390ºF (199ºC), and set time to 8 minutes. Select Start to begin preheating.
4. Once preheated, place the basket into the air fryer.
5. When cooking is complete, remove the basket from the air fryer. Cool for 5 minutes and serve warm.

Caramelized Peach Wedge

Prep time: 10 minutes | Cook time: 10 to 13 minutes | Serves 4

2 tablespoons sugar
¼ teaspoon ground cinnamon
4 peaches, cut into wedges
Cooking spray

1. Toss the peaches with the sugar and cinnamon in a medium bowl until evenly coated.
2. Lightly spray the air fry basket with cooking spray. Place the peaches in the air fry basket in a single layer. Lightly mist the peaches with cooking spray.
3. Select Air Fry, set temperature to 350ºF (180ºC), and set time to 10 minutes. Select Start to begin preheating.
4. Once preheated, place the basket into the air fryer.
5. After 5 minutes, remove from the air fryer and flip the peaches. eturn to the air fryer and continue cooking for 5 minutes.
6. When cooking is complete, the peaches should be caramelized. If necessary, continue cooking for 3 minutes. Remove the basket from the air fryer. Let the peaches cool for 5 minutes and serve warm.

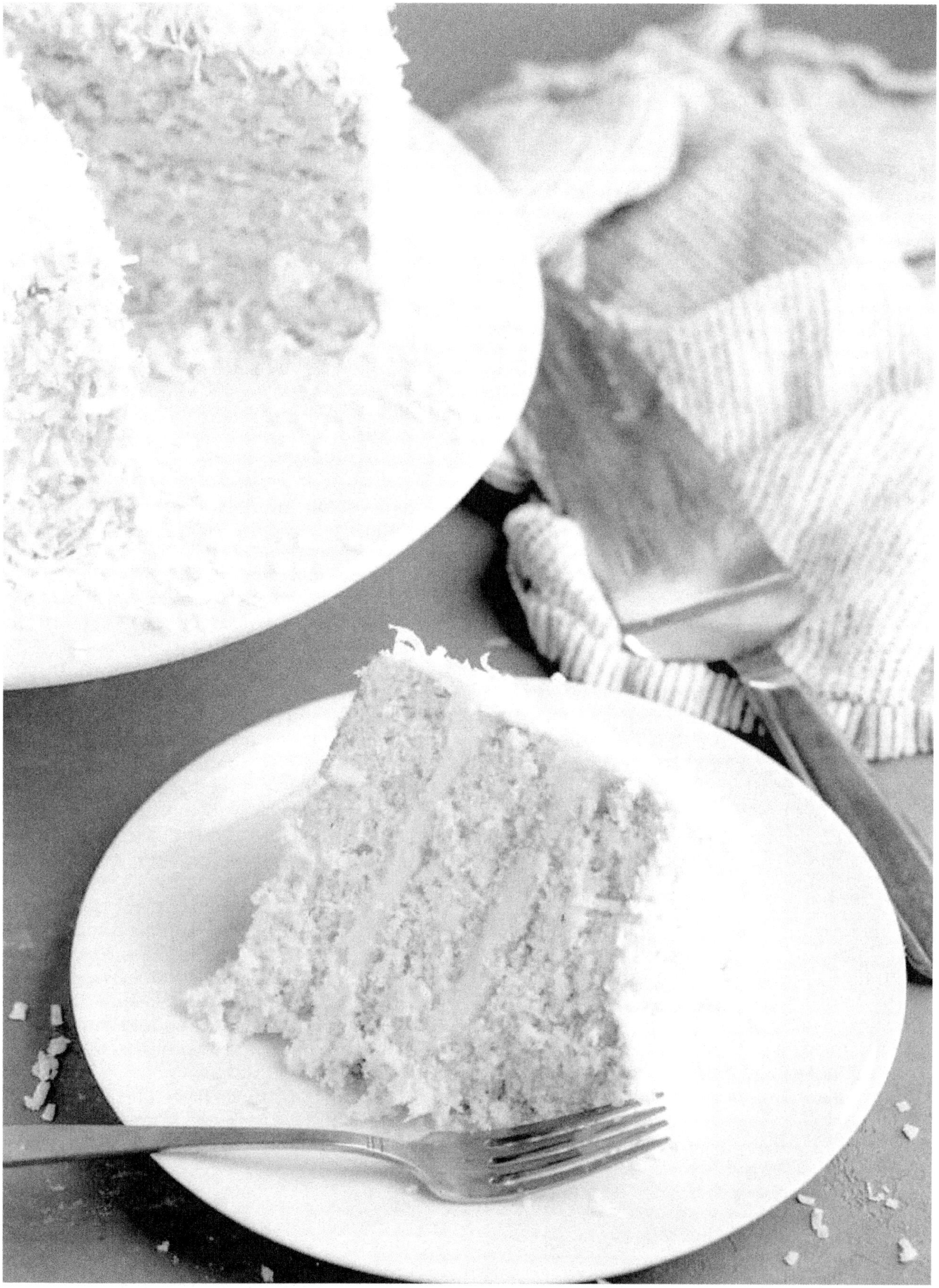

CHAPTER 10 *Desserts*

Tangy Cake

Prep time: 5 minutes | Cook time: 20 minutes | Serves 6

1 stick butter, at room temperature
5 tablespoons liquid monk fruit
2 eggs plus 1 egg yolk, beaten
⅓ cup hazelnuts, roughly chopped
3 tablespoons sugar-free orange marmalade
6 ounces (170 g) unbleached almond flou
1 teaspoon baking soda
½ teaspoon baking powder
½ teaspoon ground cinnamon
½ teaspoon ground allspice
½ ground anise seed
Cooking spray

1. Lightly spritz a baking pan with cooking spray.
2. In a mixing bowl, whisk the butter and liquid monk fruit until the mixture is pale and smooth. Mix in the beaten eggs, hazelnuts, and marmalade and whisk again until well incorporated.
3. Add the almond flou , baking soda, baking powder, cinnamon, allspice, anise seed and stir to mix well.
4. Scrape the batter into the prepared baking pan.
5. Select Bake, set temperature to 310ºF (154ºC), and set time to 20 minutes. Select Start to begin preheating.
6. Once the air fryer has preheated, place the pan into the air fryer.
7. When cooking is complete, the top of the cake should spring back when gently pressed with your fingers
8. Transfer to a wire rack and let the cake cool to room temperature. Serve immediately.

Blueberry Cupcakes

Prep time: 5 minutes | Cook time: 15 minutes | Serves 6

¾ cup granulated erythritol
1¼ cups almond flo r
1 teaspoon unsweetened baking powder
3 teaspoons cocoa powder
½ teaspoon baking soda
½ teaspoon ground cinnamon
¼ teaspoon grated nutmeg
⅛ teaspoon salt
½ cup milk
1 stick butter, at room temperature
3 eggs, whisked
1 teaspoon pure rum extract
½ cup blueberries
Cooking spray

1. Spray a 6-cup muffin tin with cooking spray.
2. In a mixing bowl, combine the erythritol, almond flou , baking powder, cocoa powder, baking soda, cinnamon, nutmeg, and salt and stir until well blended.
3. In another mixing bowl, mix together the milk, butter, egg, and rum extract until thoroughly combined. Slowly and carefully pour this mixture into the bowl of dry mixture. Stir in the blueberries.
4. Spoon the batter into the greased muffin cups, filling each about three-quarters full.
5. Select Bake, set temperature to 345ºF (174ºC), and set time to 15 minutes. Select Start to begin preheating.
6. Once the air fryer has preheated, place the muffin tin into the air fr er.
7. When done, the center should be springy and a toothpick inserted in the middle should come out clean.
8. Remove from the air fryer and place on a wire rack to cool. Serve immediately.

Buttery Shortbread

Prep time: 10 minutes | Cook time: 36 to 40 minutes | Makes 4 dozen cookies

1 tablespoon grated lemon zest
1 cup granulated sugar
1 pound (454 g) unsalted butter, at room temperature
¼ teaspoon fine sal
4 cups all-purpose flou
⅓ cup cornstarch
Cooking spray

1. Add the lemon zest and sugar to a stand mixer fitted with the paddle attachment and beat on medium speed for 1 to 2 minute. Let stand for about 5 minutes. Fold in the butter and salt and blend until fluf y.
2. Mix together the flour and cornstarch in a large bowl. Add to the butter mixture and mix to combine.
3. Spritz the sheet pan with cooking spray and spread a piece of parchment paper onto the pan. Scrape the dough into the pan until even and smooth.
4. Select Bake, set temperature to 325°F (160°C), and set time to 36 minutes. Select Start to begin preheating.
5. Once the unit has preheated, place the pan into the air fryer.
6. After 20 minutes, check the shortbread, rotating the pan if it is not browning evenly. Continue cooking for another 16 minutes until lightly browned.
7. When done, remove the pan from the air fryer. Slice and allow to cool for 5 minutes before serving.

Rhubarb Oatmeal Crumble

Prep time: 10 minutes | Cook time: 12 to 17 minutes | Serves 6

1½ cups sliced fresh strawberries
⅓ cup sugar
¾ cup sliced rhubarb
⅔ cup quick-cooking oatmeal
¼ cup packed brown sugar
½ cup whole-wheat pastry flou
½ teaspoon ground cinnamon
3 tablespoons unsalted butter, melted

1. Place the strawberries, sugar, and rhubarb in a baking pan and toss to coat.
2. Combine the oatmeal, brown sugar, pastry flou , and cinnamon in a medium bowl.
3. Add the melted butter to the oatmeal mixture and stir until crumbly. Sprinkle this generously on top of the strawberries and rhubarb.
4. Select Bake, set temperature to 370°F (188°C), and set the time to 12 minutes. Select Start to begin preheating.
5. Once the unit has preheated, place the pan into the air fryer.
6. Bake until the fruit is bubbly and the topping is golden brown. Continue cooking for an additional 2 to 5 minutes if needed.
7. When cooking is complete, remove from the air fryer and serve warm.

Baked Coconut Cake

Prep time: 5 minutes | Cook time: 15 minutes | Serves 10

1¼ cups unsweetened bakers' chocolate
1 stick butter
1 teaspoon liquid stevia
⅓ cup shredded coconut
2 tablespoons coconut milk
2 eggs, beaten
Cooking spray

1. Lightly spritz a baking pan with cooking spray.
2. Place the chocolate, butter, and stevia in a microwave-safe bowl. Microwave for about 30 seconds until melted. Let the chocolate mixture cool to room temperature.
3. Add the remaining ingredients to the chocolate mixture and stir until well incorporated. Pour the batter into the prepared baking pan.
4. Select Bake, set temperature to 330°F (166°C), and set time to 15 minutes. Select Start to begin preheating.
5. Once the air fryer has preheated, place the pan into the air fryer.
6. When cooking is complete, a toothpick inserted in the center should come out clean.
7. Remove from the air fryer and allow to cool for about 10 minutes before serving.

Baked Apple Fritters

Prep time: 30 minutes | Cook time: 7 minutes | Serves 6

1 cup chopped, peeled Granny Smith apple
½ cup granulated sugar
1 teaspoon ground cinnamon
1 cup all-purpose flou
1 teaspoon baking powder
1 teaspoon salt
2 tablespoons milk
2 tablespoons butter, melted
1 large egg, beaten
Cooking spray
¼ cup confectioners' sugar (optional)

1. Mix together the apple, granulated sugar, and cinnamon in a small bowl. Allow to sit for 30 minutes.
2. Combine the flou , baking powder, and salt in a medium bowl. Add the milk, butter, and egg and stir to incorporate.
3. Pour the apple mixture into the bowl of flour mixture and stir with a spatula until a dough forms.
4. Make the fritters: On a clean work surface, divide the dough into 12 equal portions and shape into 1-inch balls. Flatten them into patties with your hands.
5. Line the air fry basket with parchment paper and spray it with cooking spray.
6. Transfer the apple fritters onto the parchment paper, evenly spaced but not too close together. Spray the fritters with cooking spray.
7. Select Bake, set temperature to 350°F (180°C), and set time to 7 minutes. Select Start to begin preheating.
8. Once the air fryer has preheated, place the basket into the air fryer. Flip the fritters halfway through the cooking time.
9. When cooking is complete, the fritters should be lightly browned.
10. Remove from the air fryer to a plate and serve with the confectioners' sugar sprinkled on top, if desired.

Buttery Chocolate Cookies

Prep time: 10 minutes | Cook time: 22 minutes | Makes 30 cookies

⅓ cup (80g) organic brown sugar
⅓ cup (80g) organic cane sugar
4 ounces (112g) cashew-based vegan butter
½ cup coconut cream
1 teaspoon vanilla extract
2 tablespoons ground flaxsee
1 teaspoon baking powder
1 teaspoon baking soda
Pinch of salt
2¼ cups (220g) almond flou
½ cup (90g) dairy-free dark chocolate chips

1. Line a baking sheet with parchment paper.
2. Mix together the brown sugar, cane sugar, and butter in a medium bowl or the bowl of a stand mixer. Cream together with a mixer.
3. Fold in the coconut cream, vanilla, flaxseed, baking powde , baking soda, and salt. Stir well.
4. Add the almond flou , a little at a time, mixing after each addition until fully incorporated. Stir in the chocolate chips with a spatula.
5. Scoop the dough onto the prepared baking sheet.
6. Select Bake, set temperature to 325°F (160°C), and set the time to 22 minutes. Select Start to begin preheating.
7. Once the unit has preheated, place the baking sheet into the air fryer.
8. Bake until the cookies are golden brown.
9. When cooking is complete, transfer the baking sheet onto a wire rack to cool completely before serving.

Walnut Butter Baklava

Prep time: 10 minutes | Cook time: 16 minutes | Serves 10

1 cup walnut pieces
1 cup shelled raw pistachios
½ cup unsalted butter, melted
¼ cup plus 2 tablespoons honey, divided
3 tablespoons granulated sugar
1 teaspoon ground cinnamon
2 (1.9-ounce / 54-g) packages frozen miniature phyllo tart shells

1. Place the walnuts and pistachios in the air fry basket in an even layer.
2. Select Air Fry, set the temperature to 350°F (180°C), and set the time for 4 minutes. Select Start to begin preheating.
3. Once the unit has preheated, place the basket into the air fryer.
4. After 2 minutes, remove the basket and stir the nuts. Transfer the basket back to the air fryer and cook for another 1 to 2 minutes until the nuts are golden brown and fragrant.
5. Meanwhile, stir together the butter, ¼ cup of honey, sugar, and cinnamon in a medium bowl.
6. When done, remove the basket from the air fryer and place the nuts on a cutting board and allow to cool for 5 minutes. Finely chop the nuts. Add the chopped nuts and all the "nut dust" to the butter mixture and stir well.
7. Arrange the phyllo cups on the basket. Evenly fill the p yllo cups with the nut mixture, mounding it up. As you work, stir the nuts in the bowl frequently so that the syrup is evenly distributed throughout the filling
8. Select Bake, set temperature to 350°F (180°C), and set time to 12 minutes. Select Start to begin preheating.
9. Once the unit has preheated, place the basket into the air fryer. After about 8 minutes, check the cups. Continue cooking until the cups are golden brown and the syrup is bubbling.
10. When cooking is complete, remove the baklava from the air fryer, drizzle each cup with about ⅛ teaspoon of the remaining honey over the top.
11. Allow to cool for 5 minutes before serving.

Blueberry and Peach Galette

Prep time: 10 minutes | Cook time: 20 minutes | Serves 6

1 pint blueberries, rinsed and picked through (about 2 cups)
2 large peaches or nectarines, peeled and cut into ½-inch slices (about 2 cups)
⅓ cup plus 2 tablespoons granulated sugar, divided
2 tablespoons unbleached all-purpose flou
½ teaspoon grated lemon zest (optional)
¼ teaspoon ground allspice or cinnamon
Pinch kosher or fine salt
1 (9-inch) refrigerated piecrust (or use homemade)
2 teaspoons unsalted butter, cut into pea-size pieces
1 large egg, beaten

1. Mix together the blueberries, peaches, ⅓ cup of sugar, flou , lemon zest (if desired), allspice, and salt in a medium bowl.
2. Unroll the crust on the sheet pan, patching any tears if needed. Place the fruit in the center of the crust, leaving about 1½ inches of space around the edges. Scatter the butter pieces over the fruit. Fold the outside edge of the crust over the outer circle of the fruit, making pleats as needed.
3. Brush the egg over the crust. Sprinkle the crust and fruit with the remaining 2 tablespoons of sugar.
4. Select Bake, set temperature to 350°F (180°C), and set time to 20 minutes. Select Start to begin preheating.
5. Once the unit has preheated, place the pan into the air fryer.
6. After about 15 minutes, check the galette, rotating the pan if the crust is not browning evenly. Continue cooking until the crust is deep golden brown and the fruit is bubbling.
7. When cooking is complete, remove the pan from the air fryer and allow to cool for 10 minutes before slicing and serving.

Berry Crisp with Coconut Chip

Prep time: 5 minutes | Cook time: 20 minutes | Serves 6

1 tablespoon butter, melted
12 ounces (340 g) mixed berries
⅓ cup granulated Swerve
1 teaspoon pure vanilla extract
½ teaspoon ground cinnamon
¼ teaspoon ground cloves
¼ teaspoon grated nutmeg
½ cup coconut chips, for garnish

1. Coat a baking pan with melted butter.
2. Put the remaining ingredients except the coconut chips in the prepared baking pan.
3. Select Bake, set temperature to 330ºF (166ºC), and set time to 20 minutes. Select Start to begin preheating.
4. Once the air fryer has preheated, place the pan into the air fryer.
5. When cooking is complete, remove from the air fryer. Serve garnished with the coconut chips.

Pecans Nuts Cookies

Prep time: 10 minutes | Cook time: 25 minutes | Serves 10

1½ cups coconut flou
1½ cups extra-fine almond flou
½ teaspoon baking powder
⅓ teaspoon baking soda
3 eggs plus an egg yolk, beaten
¾ cup coconut oil, at room temperature
1 cup unsalted pecan nuts, roughly chopped
¾ cup monk fruit
¼ teaspoon freshly grated nutmeg
⅓ teaspoon ground cloves
½ teaspoon pure vanilla extract
½ teaspoon pure coconut extract
⅛ teaspoon fine sea salt

1. Line the air fry basket with parchment paper.
2. Mix the coconut flou , almond flou , baking powder, and baking soda in a large mixing bowl.
3. In another mixing bowl, stir together the eggs and coconut oil. Add the wet mixture to the dry mixture.
4. Mix in the remaining ingredients and stir until a soft dough forms.
5. Drop about 2 tablespoons of dough on the parchment paper for each cookie and flatten each biscuit until i 's 1 inch thick.
6. Select Bake, set temperature to 370ºF (188ºC), and set time to 25 minutes. Select Start to begin preheating.
7. Once the air fryer has preheated, place the basket into the air fryer.
8. When cooking is complete, the cookies should be golden and firm to the touch
9. Remove from the air fryer to a plate. Let the cookies cool to room temperature and serve.

Creamy Raspberry Muffin

Prep time: 5 minutes | Cook time: 15 minutes | Serves 6

2 cups almond flou
¾ cup Swerve
1¼ teaspoons baking powder
⅓ teaspoon ground allspice
⅓ teaspoon ground anise star
½ teaspoon grated lemon zest
¼ teaspoon salt
2 eggs
1 cup sour cream
½ cup coconut oil
½ cup raspberries

1. Line a muffin pan with 6 paper liners
2. In a mixing bowl, mix the almond flou , Swerve, baking powder, allspice, anise, lemon zest, and salt.
3. In another mixing bowl, beat the eggs, sour cream, and coconut oil until well mixed. Add the egg mixture to the flour mixture and stir to combine. Mix in the raspberries.
4. Scrape the batter into the prepared muffin cups, filling each about thre quarters full.
5. Select Bake, set temperature to 345ºF (174ºC), and set time to 15 minutes. Select Start to begin preheating.
6. Once the air fryer has preheated, place the muffin pan into the air fr er.
7. When cooking is complete, the tops should be golden and a toothpick inserted in the middle should come out clean.
8. Allow the muffins to cool for 10 minutes in the muffin pan before rem ving and serving.

Baked Apple-Peach Crisp

Prep time: 10 minutes | Cook time: 10 to 12 minutes | Serves 4

2 peaches, peeled, pitted, and chopped
1 apple, peeled and chopped
2 tablespoons honey
3 tablespoons packed brown sugar
2 tablespoons unsalted butter, at room temperature
½ cup quick-cooking oatmeal
⅓ cup whole-wheat pastry flou
½ teaspoon ground cinnamon

1. Place the peaches, apple, and honey in a baking pan and toss until thoroughly combined.
2. Mix together the brown sugar, butter, oatmeal, pastry flou, and cinnamon in a medium bowl and stir until crumbly. Sprinkle this mixture generously on top of the peaches and apples.
3. Select Bake, set temperature to 380ºF (193ºC), and set the time to 10 minutes. Select Start to begin preheating.
4. Once the unit has preheated, place the pan into the air fryer.
5. Bake until the fruit is bubbling and the topping is golden brown.
6. Once cooking is complete, remove the pan from the air fryer and allow to cool for 5 minutes before serving.

Buttery Chocolate Cheesecake

Prep time: 5 minutes | Cook time: 18 minutes | Serves 6

Crust:
½ cup butter, melted
½ cup coconut flou
2 tablespoons stevia
Cooking spray

Topping:
4 ounces (113 g) unsweetened baker's chocolate
1 cup mascarpone cheese, at room temperature
1 teaspoon vanilla extract
2 drops peppermint extract

1. Lightly coat a baking pan with cooking spray.
2. In a mixing bowl, whisk together the butter, flou, and stevia until well combined. Transfer the mixture to the prepared baking pan.
3. Select Bake, set temperature to 350ºF (180ºC), and set time to 18 minutes. Select Start to begin preheating.
4. Once the air fryer has preheated, place the pan into the air fryer.
5. When done, a toothpick inserted in the center should come out clean.
6. Remove the crust from the air fryer to a wire rack to cool.
7. Once cooled completely, place it in the freezer for 20 minutes.
8. When ready, combine all the ingredients for the topping in a small bowl and stir to incorporate.
9. Spread this topping over the crust and let it sit for another 15 minutes in the freezer.
10. Serve chilled.

Buttermilk Cake

Prep time: 5 minutes | Cook time: 30 minutes | Serves 8

1 stick butter, at room temperature
1 cup Swerve
4 eggs
1½ cups coconut flou
½ cup buttermilk
½ teaspoon baking soda
½ teaspoon baking powder
¼ teaspoon salt
1 teaspoon vanilla essence
A pinch of ground star anise
A pinch of freshly grated nutmeg
Cooking spray

1. Spray a baking pan with cooking spray.
2. With an electric mixer or hand mixer, beat the butter and Swerve until creamy. One at a time, mix in the eggs and whisk until fluf y. Add the remaining ingredients and stir to combine.
3. Transfer the batter to the prepared baking pan.
4. Select Bake, set temperature to 320ºF (160ºC), and set time to 30 minutes. Select Start to begin preheating.
5. Once the air fryer has preheated, place the pan into the air fryer. Rotate the pan halfway through the cooking time.
6. When cooking is complete, the center of the cake should be springy.
7. Allow the cake to cool in the pan for 10 minutes before removing and serving.

Pumpkin Pudding with Vanilla Wafers

Prep time: 10 minutes | Cook time: 15 minutes | Serves 4

1 cup canned no-salt-added pumpkin purée (not pumpkin pie filling
¼ cup packed brown sugar
3 tablespoons all-purpose flou
1 egg, whisked
2 tablespoons milk
1 tablespoon unsalted butter, melted
1 teaspoon pure vanilla extract
4 low-fat vanilla wafers, crumbled
Cooking spray

1. Coat a baking pan with cooking spray. Set aside.
2. Mix the pumpkin purée, brown sugar, flou , whisked egg, milk, melted butter, and vanilla in a medium bowl and whisk to combine. Transfer the mixture to the baking pan.
3. Select Bake, set temperature to 350°F (180°C), and set time to 15 minutes. Select Start to begin preheating.
4. Once the air fryer has preheated, place the pan into the air fryer.
5. When cooking is complete, the pudding should be set.
6. Remove the pudding from the air fryer to a wire rack to cool.
7. Divide the pudding into four bowls and serve with the vanilla wafers sprinkled on top.

Coffee Coconut Cake

Prep time: 5 minutes | Cook time: 30 minutes | Serves 8

Dry Ingredients:
1½ cups almond flo r
½ cup coconut meal
⅔ cup Swerve
1 teaspoon baking powder
¼ teaspoon salt

Wet Ingredients:
1 egg
1 stick butter, melted
½ cup hot strongly brewed coffee

Topping:
½ cup confectioner's Swerve
¼ cup coconut flou
3 tablespoons coconut oil
1 teaspoon ground cinnamon
½ teaspoon ground cardamom

1. In a medium bowl, combine the almond flou , coconut meal, Swerve, baking powder, and salt.
2. In a large bowl, whisk the egg, melted butter, and coffee until smooth.
3. Add the dry mixture to the wet and stir until well incorporated. Transfer the batter to a greased baking pan.
4. Stir together all the ingredients for the topping in a small bowl. Spread the topping over the batter and smooth the top with a spatula.
5. Select Bake, set temperature to 330°F (166°C), and set time to 30 minutes. Select Start to begin preheating.
6. Once the air fryer has preheated, place the pan into the air fryer.
7. When cooking is complete, the cake should spring back when gently pressed with your fingers
8. Rest for 10 minutes before serving.

Baked Walnuts Tart

Prep time: 5 minutes | Cook time: 13 minutes | Serves 6

1 cup coconut milk
½ cup walnuts, ground
½ cup Swerve
½ cup almond flou
½ stick butter, at room temperature
2 eggs
1 teaspoon vanilla essence
¼ teaspoon ground cardamom
¼ teaspoon ground cloves
Cooking spray

1. Coat a baking pan with cooking spray.
2. Combine all the ingredients except the oil in a large bowl and stir until well blended. Spoon the batter mixture into the baking pan.
3. Select Bake, set temperature to 360°F (182°C), and set time to 13 minutes. Select Start to begin preheating.
4. Once the air fryer has preheated, place the pan into the air fryer.
5. When cooking is complete, a toothpick inserted into the center of the tart should come out clean.
6. Remove from the air fryer and place on a wire rack to cool. Serve immediately.

Peach-Blueberry Tart

Prep time: 10 minutes | Cook time: 30 minutes | Serves 6 to 8

4 peaches, pitted and sliced
1 cup fresh blueberries
2 tablespoons cornstarch
3 tablespoons sugar
1 tablespoon freshly squeezed lemon juice
Cooking spray
1 sheet frozen puff pastry, thawed
1 tablespoon nonfat or low-fat milk
Confectioners' sugar, for dusting

1. Add the peaches, blueberries, cornstarch, sugar, and lemon juice to a large bowl and toss to coat.
2. Spritz a round baking pan with cooking spray.
3. Unfold the pastry and put on the prepared baking pan.
4. Lay the peach slices on the pan, slightly overlapping them. Scatter the blueberries over the peach.
5. Drape the pastry over the outside of the fruit and press pleats firmly togethe . Brush the milk over the pastry.
6. Select Bake, set temperature to 400ºF (205ºC), and set time to 30 minutes. Select Start to begin preheating.
7. Once the unit has preheated, place the pan into the air fryer.
8. Bake until the crust is golden brown and the fruit is bubbling.
9. When cooking is complete, remove the pan from the air fryer and allow to cool for 10 minutes.
10. Serve the tart with the confectioners' sugar sprinkled on top.

Chocolate Cake

Prep time: 5 minutes | Cook time: 15 minutes | Serves 6

½ cup unsweetened chocolate, chopped
½ stick butter, at room temperature
1 tablespoon liquid stevia
1½ cups coconut flou
2 eggs, whisked
½ teaspoon vanilla extract
A pinch of fine sea salt
Cooking spray

1. Place the chocolate, butter, and stevia in a microwave-safe bowl. Microwave for about 30 seconds until melted.
2. Let the chocolate mixture cool for 5 to 10 minutes.
3. Add the remaining ingredients to the bowl of chocolate mixture and whisk to incorporate.
4. Lightly spray a baking pan with cooking spray.
5. Scrape the chocolate mixture into the prepared baking pan.
6. Select Bake, set temperature to 330ºF (166ºC), and set time to 15 minutes. Select Start to begin preheating.
7. Once the air fryer has preheated, place the pan into the air fryer.
8. When cooking is complete, the top should spring back lightly when gently pressed with your fingers
9. Let the cake cool for 5 minutes and serve.

Baked Sweet Apple

Prep time: 15 minutes | Cook time: 12 minutes | Serves 4

1 cup packed light brown sugar
2 teaspoons ground cinnamon
2 medium Granny Smith apples, peeled and diced

1. Thoroughly combine the brown sugar and cinnamon in a medium bowl.
2. Add the apples to the bowl and stir until well coated. Transfer the apples to a baking pan.
3. Select Bake, set temperature to 350ºF (180ºC), and set time to 12 minutes. Select Start to begin preheating.
4. Once the air fryer has preheated, place the pan into the air fryer.
5. After about 9 minutes, stir the apples and bake for an additional 3 minutes. When cooking is complete, the apples should be softened.
6. Serve warm.

Apple Wedges with Apricots

Prep time: 5 minutes | Cook time: 15 to 18 minutes | Serves 4

4 large apples, peeled and sliced into 8 wedges
2 tablespoons olive oil
½ cup dried apricots, chopped
1 to 2 tablespoons sugar
½ teaspoon ground cinnamon

1. Toss the apple wedges with the olive oil in a mixing bowl until well coated.
2. Place the apple wedges in the air fry basket.
3. Select Air Fry, set temperature to 350°F (180°C), and set time to 15 minutes. Select Start to begin preheating.
4. Once the air fryer has preheated, place the basket into the air fryer.
5. After about 12 minutes, remove from the air fryer. Sprinkle with the dried apricots and air fry for another 3 minutes.
6. Meanwhile, thoroughly combine the sugar and cinnamon in a small bowl.
7. Remove the apple wedges from the air fryer to a plate. Serve sprinkled with the sugar mixture.

Caramelized Fruit Kebabs

Prep time: 10 minutes | Cook time: 4 minutes | Serves 4

2 peaches, peeled, pitted, and thickly sliced
3 plums, halved and pitted
3 nectarines, halved and pitted
1 tablespoon honey
½ teaspoon ground cinnamon
¼ teaspoon ground allspice
Pinch cayenne pepper

Special Equipment:
8 metal skewers

1. Thread, alternating peaches, plums, and nectarines onto the metal skewers that fit into the air fr er.
2. Thoroughly combine the honey, cinnamon, allspice, and cayenne in a small bowl. Brush generously the glaze over the fruit skewers.
3. Transfer the fruit skewers to the air fry basket.
4. Select Air Fry, set temperature to 400°F (205°C), and set time to 4 minutes. Select Start to begin preheating.
5. Once the air fryer has preheated, place the basket into the air fryer.
6. When cooking is complete, the fruit should be caramelized.
7. Remove the fruit skewers from the air fryer and let rest for 5 minutes before serving.

Tangy Cake

Prep time: 5 minutes | Cook time: 17 minutes | Serves 6

1 stick butter, melted
¾ cup granulated Swerve
2 eggs, beaten
¾ cup coconut flou
¼ teaspoon salt
⅓ teaspoon grated nutmeg
⅓ cup coconut milk
1¼ cups almond flo r
½ teaspoon baking powder
2 tablespoons unsweetened orange jam
Cooking spray

1. Coat a baking pan with cooking spray. Set aside.
2. In a large mixing bowl, whisk together the melted butter and granulated Swerve until fluf y.
3. Mix in the beaten eggs and whisk again until smooth. Stir in the coconut flou , salt, and nutmeg and gradually pour in the coconut milk. Add the remaining ingredients and stir until well incorporated.
4. Scrape the batter into the baking pan.
5. Select Bake, set temperature to 355°F (179°C), and set time to 17 minutes. Select Start to begin preheating.
6. Once the air fryer has preheated, place the pan into the air fryer.
7. When cooking is complete, the top of the cake should spring back when gently pressed with your fingers
8. Remove from the air fryer to a wire rack to cool. Serve chilled.

Breaded Banana with Chocolate Sauce

Prep time: 10 minutes | Cook time: 7 minutes | Serves 6

¼ cup cornstarch
¼ cup plain bread crumbs
1 large egg, beaten
3 bananas, halved crosswise
Cooking spray
Chocolate sauce, for serving

1. Place the cornstarch, bread crumbs, and egg in three separate bowls.
2. Roll the bananas in the cornstarch, then in the beaten egg, and finally in the bread crumbs to coat well.
3. Spritz the air fry basket with cooking spray.
4. Arrange the banana halves in the air fry basket and mist them with cooking spray.
5. Select Air Fry, set temperature to 350°F (180°C), and set time to 7 minutes. Select Start to begin preheating.
6. Once the air fryer has preheated, place the basket into the air fryer.
7. After about 5 minutes, flip the bananas and continue to air fry for another 2 minutes.
8. When cooking is complete, remove the bananas from the air fryer to a serving plate. Serve with the chocolate sauce drizzled over the top.

Lemony Cheese Cake

Prep time: 5 minutes | Cook time: 25 minutes | Serves 6

17.5 ounces (496 g) ricotta cheese
5.4 ounces (153 g) sugar
3 eggs, beaten
3 tablespoons flou
1 lemon, juiced and zested
2 teaspoons vanilla extract

1. In a large mixing bowl, stir together all the ingredients until the mixture reaches a creamy consistency.
2. Pour the mixture into a baking pan and place in the air fryer.
3. Select Bake, set temperature to 320°F (160°C), and set time to 25 minutes. Select Start to begin preheating.
4. Once the air fryer has preheated, place the pan into the air fryer.
5. When cooking is complete, a toothpick inserted in the center should come out clean.
6. Allow to cool for 10 minutes on a wire rack before serving.

Baked Chocolate Pie

Prep time: 20 minutes | Cook time: 25 minutes | Serves 8

1 (9-inch) unbaked pie crust
Filling:
2 large eggs
⅓ cup butter, melted
1 cup sugar
½ cup all-purpose flou
1 cup milk chocolate chips
1½ cups coarsely chopped pecans
2 tablespoons bourbon

1. Whisk the eggs and melted butter in a large bowl until creamy.
2. Add the sugar and flour and stir to incorporate. Mix in the milk chocolate chips, pecans, and bourbon and stir until well combined.
3. Use a fork to prick holes in the bottom and sides of the pie crust. Pour the prepared filling into the pie crust. Place the pie crust in the air fry basket.
4. Select Bake, set temperature to 350°F (180°C), and set time to 25 minutes. Select Start to begin preheating.
5. Once the air fryer has preheated, place the basket into the air fryer.
6. When cooking is complete, a toothpick inserted in the center should come out clean.
7. Allow the pie cool for 10 minutes in the basket before serving.

Chapter 10 Desserts | 153

Fudge Pie

Prep time: 15 minutes | Cook time: 26 minutes | Serves 8

1½ cups sugar
½ cup self-rising flou
⅓ cup unsweetened cocoa powder
3 large eggs, beaten
12 tablespoons (1½ sticks) butter, melted
1½ teaspoons vanilla extract
1 (9-inch) unbaked pie crust
¼ cup confectioners' sugar (optional)

1. Thoroughly combine the sugar, flou , and cocoa powder in a medium bowl. Add the beaten eggs and butter and whisk to combine. Stir in the vanilla.
2. Pour the prepared filling into the pie crust and transfer to the air fry basket.
3. Select Bake, set temperature to 350°F (180°C), and set time to 26 minutes. Select Start to begin preheating.
4. Once the air fryer has preheated, place the basket into the air fryer.
5. When cooking is complete, the pie should be set.
6. Allow the pie to cool for 5 minutes. Sprinkle with the confectioners' sugar, if desired. Serve warm.

Blackberry Butter Cake

Prep time: 10 minutes | Cook time: 22 minutes | Serves 8

½ cup butter, at room temperature
2 ounces (57 g) Swerve
4 eggs
1 cup almond flou
1 teaspoon baking soda
⅓ teaspoon baking powder
½ cup cocoa powder
1 teaspoon orange zest
⅓ cup fresh blackberries

1. With an electric mixer or hand mixer, beat the butter and Swerve until creamy.
2. One at a time, mix in the eggs and beat again until fluf y.
3. Add the almond flou , baking soda, baking powder, cocoa powder, orange zest and mix well. Add the butter mixture to the almond flour mixture and stir until well blended. Fold in the blackberries.
4. Scrape the batter into a baking pan.
5. Select Bake, set temperature to 335°F (168°C), and set time to 22 minutes. Select Start to begin preheating.
6. Once the air fryer has preheated, place the pan into the air fryer.
7. When cooking is complete, a toothpick inserted into the center of the cake should come out clean.
8. Allow the cake cool on a wire rack to room temperature. Serve immediately.

Air Fried Pineapple Rings

Prep time: 5 minutes | Cook time: 7 minutes | Serves 6

1 cup rice milk
⅔ cup flou
½ cup water
¼ cup unsweetened fla ed coconut
4 tablespoons sugar
½ teaspoon baking soda
½ teaspoon baking powder
½ teaspoon vanilla essence
½ teaspoon ground cinnamon
¼ teaspoon ground anise star
Pinch of kosher salt
1 medium pineapple, peeled and sliced

1. In a large bowl, stir together all the ingredients except the pineapple.
2. Dip each pineapple slice into the batter until evenly coated.
3. Arrange the pineapple slices in the air fry basket.
4. Select Air Fry, set temperature to 380°F (193°C), and set time to 7 minutes. Select Start to begin preheating.
5. Once the air fryer has preheated, place the basket into the air fryer.
6. When cooking is complete, the pineapple rings should be golden brown.
7. Remove from the air fryer to a plate and cool for 5 minutes before serving.

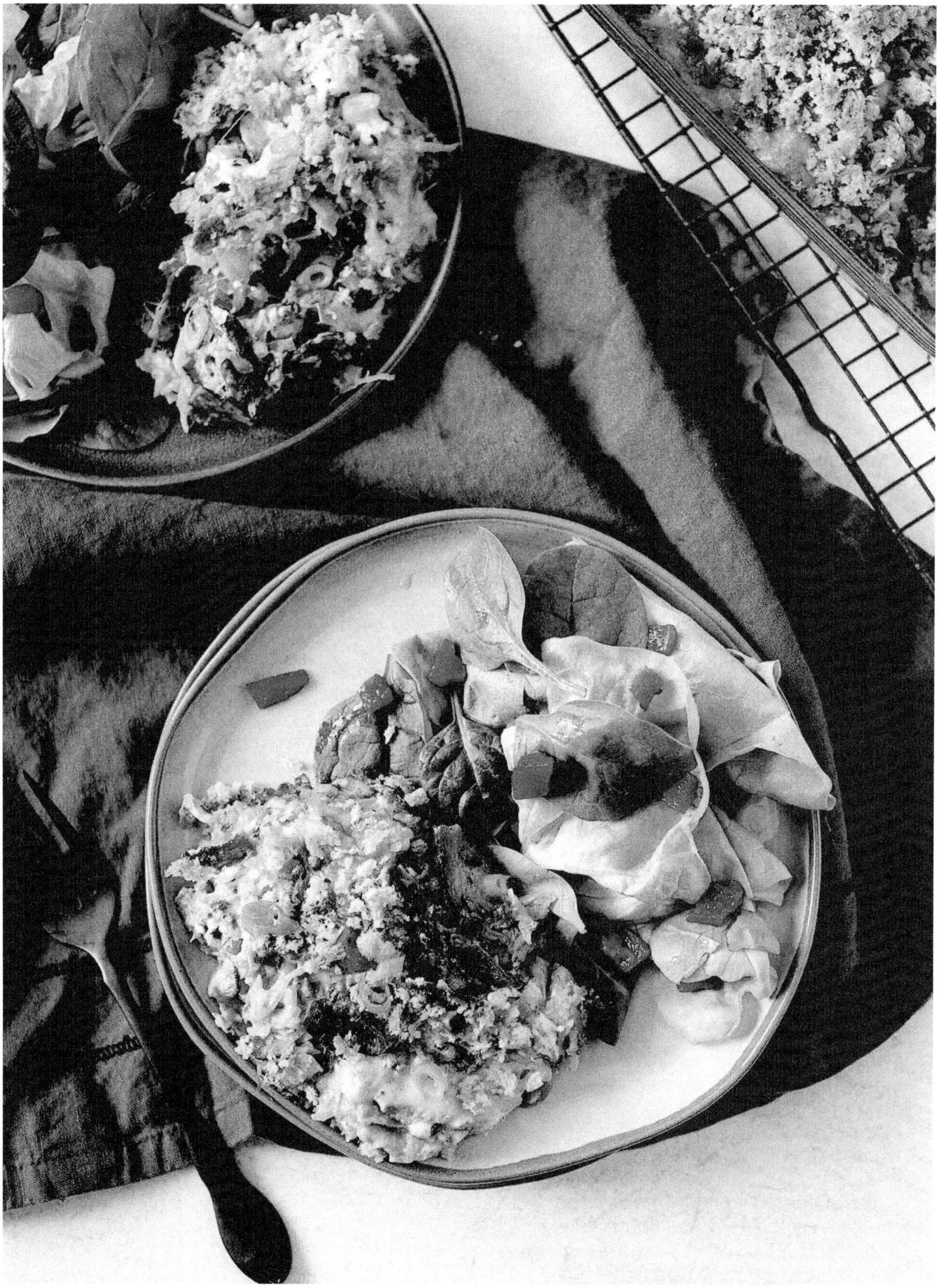

CHAPTER 11 *Casseroles, Frittata, and Quiche*

Cauliflower and Chicken Casserole

Prep time: 15 minutes | Cook time: 50 minutes | Serves 6

1 cup chicken broth
2 cups cauliflower floret
1 cup canned pumpkin purée
¼ cup heavy cream
1 teaspoon vanilla extract
2 large eggs, beaten
1/3 cup unsalted butter, melted, plus more for greasing the pan
¼ cup sugar
1 teaspoon fine sea salt
Chopped fresh parsley leaves, for garnish

TOPPING:
½ cup blanched almond flou
1 cup chopped pecans
1/3 cup unsalted butter, melted
½ cup sugar

1. Pour the chicken broth in a baking pan, then add the cauliflowe .
2. Select Bake, set temperature to 350ºF (180ºC) and set time to 20 minutes. Press Start to begin preheating.
3. Once preheated, place the pan into the air fryer.
4. When cooking is complete, the cauliflower should be soft
5. Meanwhile, combine the ingredients for the topping in a large bowl. Stir to mix well.
6. Pat the cauliflower dry with paper towels, then place in a food processor and pulse with pumpkin purée, heavy cream, vanilla extract, eggs, butter, sugar, and salt until smooth.
7. Clean the baking pan and grease with more butter, then pour the purée mixture in the pan. Spread the topping over the mixture.
8. Place the baking pan back to the air fryer. Select Bake and set time to 30 minutes.
9. When baking is complete, the topping of the casserole should be lightly browned.
10. Remove the casserole from the air fryer and serve with fresh parsley on top.

Cheesy Chicken Crouton

Prep time: 5 minutes | Cook time: 24 minutes | Serves 4

4 chicken breasts
Salt and ground black pepper, to taste
1 head broccoli, cut into floret
½ cup cream of mushroom soup
1 cup shredded Cheddar cheese
½ cup croutons
Cooking spray

1. Spritz the air fry basket with cooking spray.
2. Put the chicken breasts in the air fry basket and sprinkle with salt and ground black pepper.
3. Select Air Fry. Set temperature to 390ºF (199ºC) and set time to 14 minutes. Press Start to begin preheating.
4. Once preheated, place the basket into the air fryer. Flip the breasts halfway through the cooking time.
5. When cooking is complete, the breasts should be well browned and tender.
6. Remove the breasts from the air fryer and allow to cool for a few minutes on a plate, then cut the breasts into bite-size pieces.
7. Combine the chicken, broccoli, mushroom soup, and Cheddar cheese in a large bowl. Stir to mix well.
8. Spritz a baking pan with cooking spray. Pour the chicken mixture into the pan. Spread the croutons over the mixture.
9. Select Bake. Set time to 10 minutes. Place the pan into the air fryer.
10. When cooking is complete, the croutons should be lightly browned and the mixture should be set.
11. Remove the baking pan from the air fryer and serve immediately.

Spinach and Chickpea Casserole

Prep time: 10 minutes | Cook time: 21 to 22 minutes | Serves 4

2 tablespoons olive oil
2 garlic cloves, minced
1 tablespoon ginger, minced
1 onion, chopped
1 chili pepper, minced
Salt and ground black pepper, to taste
1 pound (454 g) spinach
1 can coconut milk
½ cup dried tomatoes, chopped
1 (14-ounce / 397-g) can chickpeas, drained

1. Heat the olive oil in a saucepan over medium heat. Sauté the garlic and ginger in the olive oil for 1 minute, or until fragrant.
2. Add the onion, chili pepper, salt and pepper to the saucepan. Sauté for 3 minutes.
3. Mix in the spinach and sauté for 3 to 4 minutes or until the vegetables become soft. Remove from heat.
4. Pour the vegetable mixture into a baking pan. Stir in coconut milk, dried tomatoes and chickpeas until well blended.
5. Select Bake, set temperature to 370°F (188°C) and set time to 15 minutes. Press Start to begin preheating.
6. Once preheated, place the pan into the air fryer.
7. When cooking is complete, transfer the casserole to a serving dish. Let cool for 5 minutes before serving.

Beef and Mushroom Casserole

Prep time: 10 minutes | Cook time: 25 minutes | Serves 4

1½ pounds (680 g) beef steak
1 ounce (28 g) dry onion soup mix
2 cups sliced mushrooms
1 (14.5-ounce / 411-g) can cream of mushroom soup
½ cup beef broth
¼ cup red wine
3 garlic cloves, minced
1 whole onion, chopped

1. Put the beef steak in a large bowl, then sprinkle with dry onion soup mix. Toss to coat well.
2. Combine the mushrooms with mushroom soup, beef broth, red wine, garlic, and onion in a large bowl. Stir to mix well.
3. Transfer the beef steak in a baking pan, then pour in the mushroom mixture.
4. Select Bake, set temperature to 360°F (182°C) and set time to 25 minutes. Press Start to begin preheating.
5. Once preheated, place the pan into the air fryer.
6. When cooking is complete, the mushrooms should be soft and the beef should be well browned.
7. Remove the baking pan from the air fryer and serve immediately.

Baked Corn Casserole

Prep time: 10 minutes | Cook time: 20 minutes | Serves 4

1 cup corn kernels
¼ cup bell pepper, finely choppe
½ cup low-fat milk
1 large egg, beaten
½ cup yellow cornmeal
½ cup all-purpose flou
½ teaspoon baking powder
2 tablespoons melted unsalted butter
1 tablespoon granulated sugar
Pinch of cayenne pepper
¼ teaspoon kosher salt
Cooking spray

1. Spritz a baking pan with cooking spray.
2. Combine all the ingredients in a large bowl. Stir to mix well. Pour the mixture into the baking pan.
3. Select Bake, set temperature to 330°F (166°C) and set time to 20 minutes. Press Start to begin preheating.
4. Once preheated, place the pan into the air fryer.
5. When cooking is complete, the casserole should be lightly browned and set.
6. Remove the baking pan from the air fryer and serve immediately.

Cheesy Green Bean Casserole

Prep time: 4 minutes | Cook time: 6 minutes | Serves 4

1 tablespoon melted butter
1 cup green beans
6 ounces (170 g) Cheddar cheese, shredded
7 ounces (198 g) Parmesan cheese, shredded
¼ cup heavy cream
Sea salt, to taste

1. Grease a baking pan with the melted butter.
2. Add the green beans, Cheddar, salt, and black pepper to the prepared baking pan. Stir to mix well, then spread the Parmesan and cream on top.
3. Select Bake, set temperature to 400°F (205°C) and set time to 6 minutes. Press Start to begin preheating.
4. Once preheated, place the pan into the air fryer.
5. When cooking is complete, the beans should be tender and the cheese should be melted.
6. Serve immediately.

Chessy Sausage and Broccoli Casserole

Prep time: 10 minutes | Cook time: 20 minutes | Serves 8

10 eggs
1 cup Cheddar cheese, shredded and divided
¾ cup heavy whipping cream
1 (12-ounce / 340-g) package cooked chicken sausage
1 cup broccoli, chopped
2 cloves garlic, minced
½ tablespoon salt
¼ tablespoon ground black pepper
Cooking spray

1. Spritz a baking pan with cooking spray.
2. Whisk the eggs with Cheddar and cream in a large bowl to mix well.
3. Combine the cooked sausage, broccoli, garlic, salt, and ground black pepper in a separate bowl. Stir to mix well.
4. Pour the sausage mixture into the baking pan, then spread the egg mixture over to cover.
5. Select Bake, set temperature to 400°F (205°C) and set time to 20 minutes. Press Start to begin preheating.
6. Once preheated, place the pan into the air fryer.
7. When cooking is complete, the egg should be set and a toothpick inserted in the center should come out clean.
8. Serve immediately.

Ritzy Chicken and Vegetable Casserole

Prep time: 15 minutes | Cook time: 15 minutes | Serves 4

4 boneless and skinless chicken breasts, cut into cubes
2 carrots, sliced
1 yellow bell pepper, cut into strips
1 red bell pepper, cut into strips
15 ounces (425 g) broccoli floret
1 cup snow peas
1 scallion, sliced
Cooking spray

Sauce:
1 teaspoon Sriracha
3 tablespoons soy sauce
2 tablespoons oyster sauce
1 tablespoon rice wine vinegar
1 teaspoon cornstarch
1 tablespoon grated ginger
2 garlic cloves, minced
1 teaspoon sesame oil
1 tablespoon brown sugar

1. Spritz a baking pan with cooking spray.
2. Combine the chicken, carrot, and bell peppers in a large bowl. Stir to mix well.
3. Combine the ingredients for the sauce in a separate bowl. Stir to mix well.
4. Pour the chicken mixture into the baking pan, then pour the sauce over. Stir to coat well.
5. Select Bake, set temperature to 370°F (188°C) and set time to 13 minutes. Press Start to begin preheating.
6. Once preheated, place the pan into the air fryer. Add the broccoli and snow peas to the pan halfway through.
7. When cooking is complete, the vegetables should be tender.
8. Remove the pan from the air fryer and sprinkle with sliced scallion before serving.

Smoked Trout and Crème Fraiche Frittata

Prep time: 8 minutes | Cook time: 17 minutes | Serves 4

2 tablespoons olive oil
1 onion, sliced
1 egg, beaten
½ tablespoon horseradish sauce
6 tablespoons crème fraiche
1 cup diced smoked trout
2 tablespoons chopped fresh dill
Cooking spray

1. Spritz a baking pan with cooking spray.
2. Heat the olive oil in a nonstick skillet over medium heat until shimmering.
3. Add the onion and sauté for 3 minutes or until translucent.
4. Combine the egg, horseradish sauce, and crème fraiche in a large bowl. Stir to mix well, then mix in the sautéed onion, smoked trout, and dill.
5. Pour the mixture in the prepared baking pan.
6. Select Bake, set temperature to 350°F (180°C) and set time to 14 minutes. Press Start to begin preheating.
7. Once preheated, place the pan into the air fryer. Stir the mixture halfway through.
8. When cooking is complete, the egg should be set and the edges should be lightly browned.
9. Serve immediately.

Pastrami Cheese Casserole

Prep time: 10 minutes | Cook time: 8 minutes | Serves 2

1 cup pastrami, sliced
1 bell pepper, chopped
¼ cup Greek yogurt
2 spring onions, chopped
½ cup Cheddar cheese, grated
4 eggs
¼ teaspoon ground black pepper
Sea salt, to taste
Cooking spray

1. Spritz a baking pan with cooking spray.
2. Whisk together all the ingredients in a large bowl. Stir to mix well. Pour the mixture into the baking pan.
3. Select Bake, set temperature to 330°F (166°C) and set time to 8 minutes. Press Start to begin preheating.
4. Once preheated, place the pan into the air fryer.
5. When cooking is complete, the eggs should be set and the casserole edges should be lightly browned.
6. Remove the baking pan from the air fryer and allow to cool for 10 minutes before serving.

Cheesy Vegetable Frittata

Prep time: 15 minutes | Cook time: 20 minutes | Serves 2

4 eggs
⅓ cup milk
2 teaspoons olive oil
1 large zucchini, sliced
2 asparagus, sliced thinly
⅓ cup sliced mushrooms
1 cup baby spinach
1 small red onion, sliced
⅓ cup crumbled feta cheese
⅓ cup grated Cheddar cheese
¼ cup chopped chives
Salt and ground black pepper, to taste

1. Line a baking pan with parchment paper.
2. Whisk together the eggs, milk, salt, and ground black pepper in a large bowl. Set aside.
3. Heat the olive oil in a nonstick skillet over medium heat until shimmering.
4. Add the zucchini, asparagus, mushrooms, spinach, and onion to the skillet and sauté for 5 minutes or until tender.
5. Pour the sautéed vegetables into the prepared baking pan, then spread the egg mixture over and scatter with cheeses.
6. Select Bake, set temperature to 380°F (193°C) and set time to 15 minutes. Press Start to begin preheating.
7. Once preheated, place the pan into the air fryer. Stir the mixture halfway through.
8. When cooking is complete, the egg should be set and the edges should be lightly browned.
9. Remove the frittata from the air fryer and sprinkle with chives before serving.

Riced Cauliflower Okra Casserole

Prep time: 8 minutes | Cook time: 12 minutes | Serves 4

1 head cauliflowe , cut into floret
1 cup okra, chopped
1 yellow bell pepper, chopped
2 eggs, beaten
½ cup chopped onion
1 tablespoon soy sauce
2 tablespoons olive oil
Salt and ground black pepper, to taste

1. Spritz a baking pan with cooking spray.
2. Put the cauliflower in a food processor and pulse to rice the cauliflowe .
3. Pour the cauliflower rice in the baking pan and add the remaining ingredients. Stir to mix well.
4. Select Bake, set temperature to 380ºF (193ºC) and set time to 12 minutes. Press Start to begin preheating.
5. Once preheated, place the pan into the air fryer.
6. When cooking is complete, the eggs should be set.
7. Remove the baking pan from the air fryer and serve immediately.

Cheesy Chicken Ham Casserole

Prep time: 15 minutes | Cook time: 15 minutes | Serves 4 to 6

2 cups diced cooked chicken
1 cup diced ham
¼ teaspoon ground nutmeg
½ cup half-and-half
½ teaspoon ground black pepper
6 slices Swiss cheese
Cooking spray

1. Spritz a baking pan with cooking spray.
2. Combine the chicken, ham, nutmeg, half-and-half, and ground black pepper in a large bowl. Stir to mix well.
3. Pour half of the mixture into the baking pan, then top the mixture with 3 slices of Swiss cheese, then pour in the remaining mixture and top with remaining cheese slices.
4. Select Bake, set temperature to 350ºF (180ºC) and set time to 15 minutes. Press Start to begin preheating.
5. Once preheated, place the pan into the air fryer.
6. When cooking is complete, the egg should be set and the cheese should be melted.
7. Serve immediately.

Ritzy Turkey Breast Casserole

Prep time: 5 minutes | Cook time: 32 minutes | Serves 4

1 pound (454 g) turkey breasts
1 tablespoon olive oil
2 boiled eggs, chopped
2 tablespoons chopped pimentos
¼ cup slivered almonds, chopped
¼ cup mayonnaise
½ cup diced celery
2 tablespoons chopped green onion
¼ cup cream of chicken soup
¼ cup bread crumbs
Salt and ground black pepper, to taste

1. Put the turkey breasts in a large bowl. Sprinkle with salt and ground black pepper and drizzle with olive oil. Toss to coat well.
2. Transfer the turkey in the air fry basket.
3. Select Air Fry. Set temperature to 390ºF (199ºC) and set time to 12 minutes. Press Start to begin preheating.
4. Once preheated, place the basket into the air fryer. Flip the turkey halfway through.
5. When cooking is complete, the turkey should be well browned.
6. Remove the turkey breasts from the air fryer and cut into cubes, then combine the chicken cubes with eggs, pimentos, almonds, mayo, celery, green onions, and chicken soup in a large bowl. Stir to mix.
7. Pour the mixture into a baking pan, then spread with bread crumbs.
8. Select Bake. Set time to 20 minutes. Place the pan into the air fryer.
9. When cooking is complete, the eggs should be set.
10. Remove the baking pan from the air fryer and serve immediately.

160 | Chapter 11 Casseroles, Frittata, and Quiche

Tilapia and Rockfish Casserole

Prep time: 8 minutes | Cook time: 22 minutes | Serves 2

1 tablespoon olive oil
1 small yellow onion, chopped
2 garlic cloves, minced
4 ounces (113 g) tilapia pieces
4 ounces (113 g) rockfish piece
½ teaspoon dried basil
Salt and ground white pepper, to taste
4 eggs, lightly beaten
1 tablespoon dry sherry
4 tablespoons cheese, shredded

1. Heat the olive oil in a nonstick skillet over medium-high heat until shimmering.
2. Add the onion and garlic and sauté for 2 minutes or until fragrant.
3. Add the tilapia, rockfish, basil, salt, and white pepper to the skillet. Sauté to combine well and transfer them on a baking pan.
4. Combine the eggs, sherry and cheese in a large bowl. Stir to mix well. Pour the mixture in the baking pan over the fish mixture.
5. Select Bake, set temperature to 360°F (182°C) and set time to 20 minutes. Press Start to begin preheating.
6. Once preheated, place the pan into the air fryer.
7. When cooking is complete, the eggs should be set and the casserole edges should be lightly browned.
8. Serve immediately.

Goat Cheese and Asparagus Frittata

Prep time: 5 minutes | Cook time: 25 minutes | Serves 2 to 4

1 cup asparagus spears, cut into 1-inch pieces
1 teaspoon vegetable oil
1 tablespoon milk
6 eggs, beaten
2 ounces (57 g) goat cheese, crumbled
1 tablespoon minced chives, optional
Kosher salt and pepper, to taste

1. Add the asparagus spears to a small bowl and drizzle with the vegetable oil. Toss until well coated and transfer to the air fry basket.
2. Select Air Fry. Set temperature to 400°F (205°C) and set time to 5 minutes. Press Start to begin preheating.
3. Once preheated, place the basket into the air fryer. Flip the asparagus halfway through.
4. When cooking is complete, the asparagus should be tender and slightly wilted.
5. Remove the asparagus from the air fryer to a baking pan.
6. Stir together the milk and eggs in a medium bowl. Pour the mixture over the asparagus in the pan. Sprinkle with the goat cheese and the chives (if using) over the eggs. Season with salt and pepper.
7. Select Bake, set temperature to 320°F (160°C) and set time to 20 minutes. Press Start. Place the pan into the air fryer
8. When cooking is complete, the top should be golden and the eggs should be set.
9. Transfer to a serving dish. Slice and serve.

Broccoli Cheese Casserole

Prep time: 5 minutes | Cook time: 30 minutes | Serves 6

4 cups broccoli floret
¼ cup heavy whipping cream
½ cup sharp Cheddar cheese, shredded
¼ cup ranch dressing
Kosher salt and ground black pepper, to taste

1. Combine all the ingredients in a large bowl. Toss to coat well broccoli well.
2. Pour the mixture into a baking pan.
3. Select Bake, set temperature to 375°F (190°C) and set time to 30 minutes. Press Start to begin preheating.
4. Once preheated, place the pan into the air fryer.
5. When cooking is complete, the broccoli should be tender.
6. Remove the baking pan from the air fryer and serve immediately.

Chapter 11 Casseroles, Frittata, and Quiche | 161

Cheesy Spinach and Mushroon Frittata

Prep time: 7 minutes | Cook time: 8 minutes | Serves 2

1 cup chopped mushrooms
2 cups spinach, chopped
4 eggs, lightly beaten
3 ounces (85 g) feta cheese, crumbled
2 tablespoons heavy cream
A handful of fresh parsley, chopped
Salt and ground black pepper, to taste
Cooking spray

1. Spritz a baking pan with cooking spray.
2. Whisk together all the ingredients in a large bowl. Stir to mix well.
3. Pour the mixture in the prepared baking pan.
4. Select Bake, set temperature to 350°F (180°C) and set time to 8 minutes. Press Start to begin preheating.
5. Once preheated, place the pan into the air fryer. Stir the mixture halfway through.
6. When cooking is complete, the eggs should be set.
7. Serve immediately.

Grits and Asparagus Casserole

Prep time: 5 minutes | Cook time: 30 minutes | Serves 4

10 fresh asparagus spears, cut into 1-inch pieces
2 cups cooked grits, cooled to room temperature
2 teaspoons Worcestershire sauce
1 egg, beaten
½ teaspoon garlic powder
¼ teaspoon salt
2 slices provolone cheese, crushed
Cooking spray

1. Spritz a baking pan with cooking spray.
2. Set the asparagus in the air fry basket. Spritz the asparagus with cooking spray.
3. Select Air Fry. Set temperature to 390°F (199°C) and set time to 5 minutes. Press Start to begin preheating.
4. Once preheated, place the basket into the air fryer. Flip the asparagus halfway through.
5. When cooking is complete, the asparagus should be lightly browned and crispy.
6. Meanwhile, combine the grits, Worcestershire sauce, egg, garlic powder, and salt in a bowl. Stir to mix well.
7. Pour half of the grits mixture in the prepared baking pan, then spread with fried asparagus.
8. Spread the cheese over the asparagus and pour the remaining grits over.
9. Select Bake. Set time to 25 minutes. Place the pan into the air fryer.
10. When cooking is complete, the egg should be set.
11. Serve immediately.

Beef and Chile Cheese Casserole

Prep time: 10 minutes | Cook time: 15 minutes | Serves 4

1 pound (454 g) 85% lean ground beef
1 tablespoon taco seasoning
1 (7-ounce / 198-g) can diced mild green chiles
½ cup milk
2 large eggs
1 cup shredded Mexican cheese blend
2 tablespoons all-purpose flou
½ teaspoon kosher salt
Cooking spray

1. Spritz a baking pan with cooking spray.
2. Toss the ground beef with taco seasoning in a large bowl to mix well. Pour the seasoned ground beef in the prepared baking pan.
3. Combing the remaining ingredients in a medium bowl. Whisk to mix well, then pour the mixture over the ground beef.
4. Select Bake, set temperature to 350°F (180°C) and set time to 15 minutes. Press Start to begin preheating.
5. Once preheated, place the pan into the air fryer.
6. When cooking is complete, a toothpick inserted in the center should come out clean.
7. Remove the casserole from the air fryer and allow to cool for 5 minutes, then slice to serve.

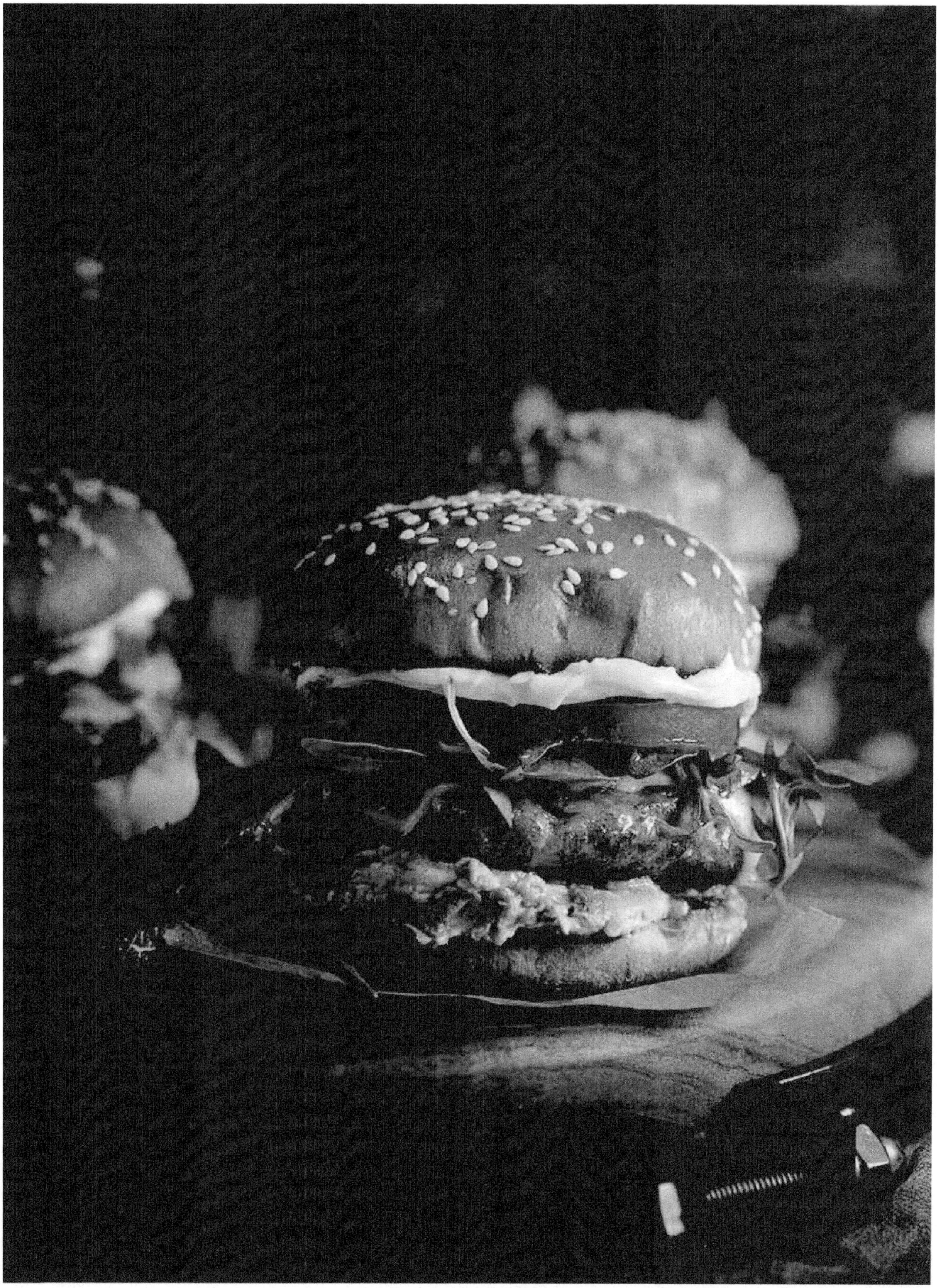

Chapter 12 Wraps and Sandwiches

Prawn and Cabbage Egg Rolls Wraps

Prep time: 20 minutes | Cook time: 18 minutes | Serves 4

2 tablespoons olive oil
1 carrot, cut into strips
1-inch piece fresh ginger, grated
1 tablespoon minced garlic
2 tablespoons soy sauce
¼ cup chicken broth
1 tablespoon sugar
1 cup shredded Napa cabbage
1 tablespoon sesame oil
8 cooked prawns, minced
8 egg roll wrappers
1 egg, beaten
Cooking spray

1. Spritz the air fry basket with cooking spray. Set aside.
2. Heat the olive oil in a nonstick skillet over medium heat until shimmering.
3. Add the carrot, ginger, and garlic and sauté for 2 minutes or until fragrant.
4. Pour in the soy sauce, broth, and sugar. Bring to a boil. Keep stirring.
5. Add the cabbage and simmer for 4 minutes or until the cabbage is tender.
6. Turn off the heat and mix in the sesame oil. Let sit for 15 minutes.
7. Use a strainer to remove the vegetables from the liquid, then combine with the minced prawns.
8. Unfold the egg roll wrappers on a clean work surface, then divide the prawn mixture in the center of wrappers.
9. Dab the edges of a wrapper with the beaten egg, then fold a corner over the filling and tuck the corner under the filling. old the left and right corner into the center. Roll the wrapper up and press to seal. Repeat with remaining wrappers.
10. Arrange the wrappers in the basket and spritz with cooking spray.
11. Select Air Fry, set temperature to 370°F (188°C) and set time to 12 minutes. Select Start to begin preheating.
12. Once the air fryer has preheated, place the basket into the air fryer. Flip the wrappers halfway through the cooking time.
13. When cooking is complete, the wrappers should be golden.
14. Serve immediately.

Golden Cod Tacos with Salsa

Prep time: 5 minutes | Cook time: 15 minutes | Serves 4

2 eggs
1¼ cups Mexican beer
1½ cups coconut flou
1½ cups almond flo r
½ tablespoon chili powder
1 tablespoon cumin
Salt, to taste
1 pound (454 g) cod fillet, slice into large pieces
4 toasted corn tortillas
4 large lettuce leaves, chopped
¼ cup salsa
Cooking spray

1. Spritz the air fry basket with cooking spray.
2. Break the eggs in a bowl, then pour in the beer. Whisk to combine well.
3. Combine the coconut flou , almond flou , chili powder, cumin, and salt in a separate bowl. Stir to mix well.
4. Dunk the cod pieces in the egg mixture, then shake the excess off and dredge into the flour mixture to coat well. Arrange the cod in the basket.
5. Select Air Fry, set temperature to 375°F (190°C) and set time to 15 minutes. Select Start to begin preheating.
6. Once the air fryer has preheated, place the basket into the air fryer. Flip the cod halfway through the cooking time.
7. When cooking is complete, the cod should be golden brown.
8. Unwrap the toasted tortillas on a large plate, then divide the cod and lettuce leaves on top. Baste with salsa and wrap to serve.

Air Fried Avocado Tacos

Prep time: 15 minutes | Cook time: 6 minutes | Serves 4

¼ cup all-purpose flou
¼ teaspoon salt, plus more as needed
¼ teaspoon ground black pepper
2 large egg whites
1¼ cups panko bread crumbs
2 tablespoons olive oil
2 avocados, peeled and halved, cut into ½-inch-thick slices
½ small red cabbage, thinly sliced
1 deseeded jalapeño, thinly sliced
2 green onions, thinly sliced
½ cup cilantro leaves
¼ cup mayonnaise
Juice and zest of 1 lime
4 corn tortillas, warmed
½ cup sour cream
Cooking spray

1. Spritz the air fry basket with cooking spray.
2. Pour the flour in a large bowl and sprinkle with salt and black pepper, then stir to mix well.
3. Whisk the egg whites in a separate bowl. Combine the panko with olive oil on a shallow dish.
4. Dredge the avocado slices in the bowl of flou , then into the egg to coat. Shake the excess off, then roll the slices over the panko.
5. Arrange the avocado slices in a single layer in the basket and spritz the cooking spray.
6. Select Air Fry, set temperature to 400ºF (205ºC) and set time to 6 minutes. Select Start to begin preheating.
7. Once preheated, place the basket into the air fryer. Flip the slices halfway through with tongs.
8. When cooking is complete, the avocado slices should be tender and lightly browned.
9. Combine the cabbage, jalapeño, onions, cilantro leaves, mayo, lime juice and zest, and a touch of salt in a separate large bowl. Toss to mix well.
10. Unfold the tortillas on a clean work surface, then spread with cabbage slaw and air fried avocados. Top with sour cream and serve.

Beer Cod Tacos

Prep time: 15 minutes | Cook time: 17 minutes | Makes 6 tacos

1 egg
5 ounces (142 g) Mexican beer
¾ cup all-purpose flou
¾ cup cornstarch
¼ teaspoon chili powder
½ teaspoon ground cumin
½ pound (227 g) cod, cut into large pieces
6 corn tortillas
Cooking spray

Salsa:
1 mango, peeled and diced
¼ red bell pepper, diced
½ small jalapeño, diced
¼ red onion, minced
Juice of half a lime
Pinch chopped fresh cilantro
¼ teaspoon salt
¼ teaspoon ground black pepper

1. Spritz the air fry basket with cooking spray.
2. Whisk the egg with beer in a bowl. Combine the flou , cornstarch, chili powder, and cumin in a separate bowl.
3. Dredge the cod in the egg mixture first, then in the flour mixture to coat well. Shake the excess off.
4. Arrange the cod in the air fry basket and spritz with cooking spray.
5. Select Air Fry, set temperature to 380ºF (193ºC) and set time to 17 minutes. Select Start to begin preheating.
6. Once preheated, place the basket into the air fryer. Flip the cod halfway through the cooking time.
7. When cooked, the cod should be golden brown and crunchy.
8. Meanwhile, combine the ingredients for the salsa in a small bowl. Stir to mix well.
9. Unfold the tortillas on a clean work surface, then divide the fish on the tortillas and spread the salsa on top. Fold to serve.

Chapter 12 Wraps and Sandwiches | 165

Cheesy Bacon and Egg Wraps

Prep time: 15 minutes | Cook time: 10 minutes | Serves 3

3 corn tortillas
3 slices bacon, cut into strips
2 scrambled eggs
3 tablespoons salsa
1 cup grated Pepper Jack cheese
3 tablespoons cream cheese, divided
Cooking spray

1. Spritz the air fry basket with cooking spray.
2. Unfold the tortillas on a clean work surface, divide the bacon and eggs in the middle of the tortillas, then spread with salsa and scatter with cheeses. Fold the tortillas over.
3. Arrange the tortillas in the basket.
4. Select Air Fry, set temperature to 390°F (199°C) and set time to 10 minutes. Select Start to begin preheating.
5. Once the air fryer has preheated, place the basket into the air fryer. Flip the tortillas halfway through the cooking time.
6. When cooking is complete, the cheeses will be melted and the tortillas will be lightly browned.
7. Serve immediately.

Spinach and Cheese Pockets

Prep time: 20 minutes | Cook time: 10 minutes | Makes 8 pockets

2 large eggs, divided
1 tablespoon water
1 cup baby spinach, roughly chopped
¼ cup sun-dried tomatoes, finely chopped
1 cup ricotta cheese
1 cup basil, chopped
¼ teaspoon red pepper fla es
¼ teaspoon kosher salt
2 refrigerated rolled pie crusts
2 tablespoons sesame seeds

1. Spritz the air fry basket with cooking spray.
2. Whisk an egg with water in a small bowl.
3. Combine the spinach, tomatoes, the other egg, ricotta cheese, basil, red pepper fla es, and salt in a large bowl. Whisk to mix well.
4. Unfold the pie crusts on a clean work surface and slice each crust into 4 wedges. Scoop up 3 tablespoons of the spinach mixture on each crust and leave ½ inch space from edges.
5. Fold the crust wedges in half to wrap the filling and press the edges with a fork to seal.
6. Arrange the wraps in the basket and spritz with cooking spray. Sprinkle with sesame seeds.
7. Select Air Fry, set temperature to 380°F (193°C) and set time to 10 minutes. Select Start to begin preheating.
8. Once the air fryer has preheated, place the basket into the air fryer. Flip the wraps halfway through the cooking time.
9. When cooked, the wraps will be crispy and golden.
10. Serve immediately.

Pork and Carrot Momos

Prep time: 20 minutes | Cook time: 20 minutes | Serves 4

2 tablespoons olive oil
1 pound (454 g) ground pork
1 shredded carrot
1 onion, chopped
1 teaspoon soy sauce
16 wonton wrappers
Salt and ground black pepper, to taste
Cooking spray

1. Heat the olive oil in a nonstick skillet over medium heat until shimmering.
2. Add the ground pork, carrot, onion, soy sauce, salt, and ground black pepper and sauté for 10 minutes or until the pork is well browned and carrots are tender.
3. Unfold the wrappers on a clean work surface, then divide the cooked pork and vegetables on the wrappers. Fold the edges around the filling to form momos. Nip the top to seal the momos.
4. Arrange the momos in the air fry basket and spritz with cooking spray.
5. Select Air Fry, set temperature to 320°F (160°C) and set time to 10 minutes. Select Start to begin preheating.
6. Once the air fryer has preheated, place the basket into the air fryer.
7. When cooking is complete, the wrappers will be lightly browned.
8. Serve immediately.

Cheesy Potato and Black Bean Burritos

Prep time: 15 minutes | Cook time: 30 minutes | Makes 6 burritos

2 sweet potatoes, peeled and cut into a small dice
1 tablespoon vegetable oil
Kosher salt and ground black pepper, to taste
6 large flour tortilla
1 (16-ounce / 454-g) can refried black beans, divided
1½ cups baby spinach, divided
6 eggs, scrambled
¾ cup grated Cheddar cheese, divided
¼ cup salsa
¼ cup sour cream
Cooking spray

1. Put the sweet potatoes in a large bowl, then drizzle with vegetable oil and sprinkle with salt and black pepper. Toss to coat well.
2. Place the potatoes in the air fry basket.
3. Select Air Fry, set temperature to 400°F (205°C) and set time to 10 minutes. Select Start to begin preheating.
4. Once preheated, place the basket into the air fryer. Flip the potatoes halfway through the cooking time.
5. When done, the potatoes should be lightly browned. Remove the potatoes from the air fryer.
6. Unfold the tortillas on a clean work surface. Divide the black beans, spinach, air fried sweet potatoes, scrambled eggs, and cheese on top of the tortillas.
7. Fold the long side of the tortillas over the filling, then fold in the shorter side to wrap the filling to ma e the burritos.
8. Wrap the burritos in the aluminum foil and put in the basket.
9. Select Air Fry, set temperature to 350°F (180°C) and set time to 20 minutes. Place the basket into the air fryer. Flip the burritos halfway through the cooking time.
10. Remove the burritos from the air fryer and spread with sour cream and salsa. Serve immediately.

Air Fried Cheesy Steak

Prep time: 20 minutes | Cook time: 20 minutes | Serves 2

12 ounces (340 g) boneless rib-eye steak, sliced thinly
½ teaspoon Worcestershire sauce
½ teaspoon soy sauce
Kosher salt and ground black pepper, to taste
½ green bell pepper, stemmed, deseeded, and thinly sliced
½ small onion, halved and thinly sliced
1 tablespoon vegetable oil
2 soft hoagie rolls, split three-fourths of the way through
1 tablespoon butter, softened
2 slices provolone cheese, halved

1. Combine the steak, Worcestershire sauce, soy sauce, salt, and ground black pepper in a large bowl. Toss to coat well. Set aside.
2. Combine the bell pepper, onion, salt, ground black pepper, and vegetable oil in a separate bowl. Toss to coat the vegetables well.
3. Pour the steak and vegetables in the air fry basket.
4. Select Air Fry, set temperature to 400°F (205°C) and set time to 15 minutes. Select Start to begin preheating.
5. Once preheated, place the basket into the air fryer.
6. When cooked, the steak will be browned and vegetables will be tender. Transfer them on a plate. Set aside.
7. Brush the hoagie rolls with butter and place in the basket.
8. Select Toast and set time to 3 minutes. Place the basket on the toast position. When done, the rolls should be lightly browned.
9. Transfer the rolls to a clean work surface and divide the steak and vegetable mix in between the rolls. Spread with cheese. Place the stuffed rolls back in the basket.
10. Select Air Fry and set time to 2 minutes. Place the basket into the air fryer. When done, the cheese should be melted.
11. Serve immediately.

Chapter 12 Wraps and Sandwiches

Sumptuous Spring Roll

Prep time: 20 minutes | Cook time: 14 minutes | Makes 14 spring rolls

2 tablespoons vegetable oil
4 cups sliced Napa cabbage
5 ounces (142 g) shiitake mushrooms, diced
3 carrots, cut into thin matchsticks
1 tablespoon minced fresh ginger
1 tablespoon minced garlic
1 bunch scallions, white and light green parts only, sliced
2 tablespoons soy sauce
1 (4-ounce / 113-g) package cellophane noodles
¼ teaspoon cornstarch
1 (12-ounce / 340-g) package frozen spring roll wrappers, thawed
Cooking spray

1. Heat the olive oil in a nonstick skillet over medium-high heat until shimmering.
2. Add the cabbage, mushrooms, and carrots and sauté for 3 minutes or until tender.
3. Add the ginger, garlic, and scallions and sauté for 1 minutes or until fragrant.
4. Mix in the soy sauce and turn off the heat. Discard any liquid remains in the skillet and allow to cool for a few minutes.
5. Bring a pot of water to a boil, then turn off the heat and pour in the noodles. Let sit for 10 minutes or until the noodles are al dente. Transfer 1 cup of the noodles in the skillet and toss with the cooked vegetables. Reserve the remaining noodles for other use.
6. Dissolve the cornstarch in a small dish of water, then place the wrappers on a clean work surface. Dab the edges of the wrappers with cornstarch.
7. Scoop up 3 tablespoons of filling in the center of each wrapper, then fold the corner in front of you over the filling. Tuck the wrapper under the filling, then fold the corners on both sides into the center. Keep rolling to seal the wrapper. Repeat with remaining wrappers.
8. Spritz the air fry basket with cooking spray. Arrange the wrappers in the basket and spritz with cooking spray.
9. Select Air Fry, set temperature to 400ºF (205ºC) and set time to 10 minutes. Select Start to begin preheating.
10. Once preheated, place the basket into the air fryer. Flip the wrappers halfway through the cooking time.
11. When cooking is complete, the wrappers will be golden brown.
12. Serve immediately.

Aromatic Beef and Onion Tacos

Prep time: 1 hour 15 minutes | Cook time: 12 minutes | Serves 6

2 tablespoons gochujang
1 tablespoon soy sauce
2 tablespoons sesame seeds
2 teaspoons minced fresh ginger
2 cloves garlic, minced
2 tablespoons toasted sesame oil
2 teaspoons sugar
½ teaspoon kosher salt
1½ pounds (680 g) thinly sliced beef chuck
1 medium red onion, sliced
6 corn tortillas, warmed
¼ cup chopped fresh cilantro
½ cup kimchi
½ cup chopped green onions

1. Combine the gochujang, soy sauce, sesame seeds, ginger, garlic, sesame oil, sugar, and salt in a large bowl. Stir to mix well.
2. Dunk the beef chunk in the large bowl. Press to submerge, then wrap the bowl in plastic and refrigerate to marinate for at least 1 hour.
3. Remove the beef chunk from the marinade and transfer to the air fry basket. Add the onion to the basket.
4. Select Air Fry, set temperature to 400ºF (205ºC) and set time to 12 minutes. Select Start to begin preheating.
5. Once preheated, place the basket into the air fryer. Stir the mixture halfway through the cooking time.
6. When cooked, the beef will be well browned.
7. Unfold the tortillas on a clean work surface, then divide the fried beef and onion on the tortillas. Spread the cilantro, kimchi, and green onions on top.
8. Serve immediately.

Golden Chicken Burgers

Prep time: 15 minutes | Cook time: 20 minutes | Serves 6 to 8

4 skinless and boneless chicken breasts
1 small head of cauliflowe , sliced into floret
1 jalapeño pepper
3 tablespoons smoked paprika
1 tablespoon thyme
1 tablespoon oregano
1 tablespoon mustard powder
1 teaspoon cayenne pepper
1 egg
Salt and ground black pepper, to taste
2 tomatoes, sliced
2 lettuce leaves, chopped
6 to 8 brioche buns, sliced lengthwise
¾ cup taco sauce
Cooking spray

1. Spritz the air fry basket with cooking spray. Set aside.
2. In a blender, add the cauliflower florets jalapeño pepper, paprika, thyme, oregano, mustard powder and cayenne pepper and blend until the mixture has a texture similar to bread crumbs.
3. Transfer ¾ of the cauliflower mixture to a medium bowl and set aside. Beat the egg in a different bowl and set aside.
4. Add the chicken breasts to the blender with remaining cauliflower mixture. Sprinkle with salt and pepper. Blend until finely chopped and well mi ed.
5. Remove the mixture from the blender and form into 6 to 8 patties. One by one, dredge each patty in the reserved cauliflower mixture, then into the egg. Dip them in the cauliflowe mixture again for additional coating.
6. Place the coated patties into the basket and spritz with cooking spray.
7. Select Air Fry, set temperature to 350°F (180°C) and set time to 20 minutes. Select Start to begin preheating.
8. Once preheated, place the basket into the air fryer. Flip the patties halfway through the cooking time.
9. When cooking is complete, the patties should be golden and crispy.
10. Transfer the patties to a clean work surface and assemble with the buns, tomato slices, chopped lettuce leaves and taco sauce to make burgers. Serve and enjoy.

Golden Chicken Empanadas

Prep time: 25 minutes | Cook time: 12 minutes | Makes 12 empanadas

1 cup boneless, skinless rotisserie chicken breast meat, chopped finel
¼ cup salsa verde
⅔ cup shredded Cheddar cheese
1 teaspoon ground cumin
1 teaspoon ground black pepper
2 purchased refrigerated pie crusts, from a minimum 14.1-ounce (400 g) box
1 large egg
2 tablespoons water
Cooking spray

1. Spritz the air fry basket with cooking spray. Set aside.
2. Combine the chicken meat, salsa verde, Cheddar, cumin, and black pepper in a large bowl. Stir to mix well. Set aside.
3. Unfold the pie crusts on a clean work surface, then use a large cookie cutter to cut out 3½-inch circles as much as possible.
4. Roll the remaining crusts to a ball and flatten into a circle which has the same thickness of the original crust. Cut out more 3½-inch circles until you have 12 circles in total.
5. Make the empanadas: Divide the chicken mixture in the middle of each circle, about 1½ tablespoons each. Dab the edges of the circle with water. Fold the circle in half over the filling to shape li e a half-moon and press to seal, or you can press with a fork.
6. Whisk the egg with water in a small bowl.
7. Arrange the empanadas in the basket and spritz with cooking spray. Brush with whisked egg.
8. Select Air Fry, set temperature to 350°F (180°C) and set time to 12 minutes. Select Start to begin preheating.
9. Once preheated, place the basket into the air fryer. Flip the empanadas halfway through the cooking time.
10. When cooking is complete, the empanadas will be golden and crispy.
11. Serve immediately.

Air Fried Crispy Spring Rolls

Prep time: 10 minutes | Cook time: 18 minutes | Serves 4

4 spring roll wrappers
½ cup cooked vermicelli noodles
1 teaspoon sesame oil
1 tablespoon freshly minced ginger
1 tablespoon soy sauce
1 clove garlic, minced
½ red bell pepper, deseeded and chopped
½ cup chopped carrot
½ cup chopped mushrooms
¼ cup chopped scallions
Cooking spray

1. Spritz the air fry basket with cooking spray and set aside.
2. Heat the sesame oil in a saucepan on medium heat. Sauté the ginger and garlic in the sesame oil for 1 minute, or until fragrant. Add soy sauce, red bell pepper, carrot, mushrooms and scallions. Sauté for 5 minutes or until the vegetables become tender. Mix in vermicelli noodles. Turn off the heat and remove them from the saucepan. Allow to cool for 10 minutes.
3. Lay out one spring roll wrapper with a corner pointed toward you. Scoop the noodle mixture on spring roll wrapper and fold corner up over the mixture. Fold left and right corners toward the center and continue to roll to make firm y sealed rolls.
4. Arrange the spring rolls in the basket and spritz with cooking spray.
5. Select Air Fry, set temperature to 340ºF (171ºC) and set time to 12 minutes. Select Start to begin preheating.
6. Once the air fryer has preheated, place the basket into the air fryer. Flip the spring rolls halfway through the cooking time.
7. When done, the spring rolls will be golden brown and crispy.
8. Serve warm.

Beef Burgers with Korean Mayo

Prep time: 15 minutes | Cook time: 10 minutes | Serves 4

Burgers:
1 pound (454 g) 85% lean ground beef
2 tablespoons gochujang
¼ cup chopped scallions
2 teaspoons minced garlic
2 teaspoons minced fresh ginger
1 tablespoon soy sauce
1 tablespoon toasted sesame oil
2 teaspoons sugar
½ teaspoon kosher salt
4 hamburger buns
Cooking spray

Korean Mayo:
1 tablespoon gochujang
¼ cup mayonnaise
2 teaspoons sesame seeds
¼ cup chopped scallions
1 tablespoon toasted sesame oil

1. Combine the ingredients for the burgers, except for the buns, in a large bowl. Stir to mix well, then wrap the bowl in plastic and refrigerate to marinate for at least an hour.
2. Spritz the air fry basket with cooking spray.
3. Divide the meat mixture into four portions and form into four balls. Bash the balls into patties.
4. Arrange the patties in the basket and spritz with cooking spray.
5. Select Air Fry, set temperature to 350ºF (180ºC) and set time to 10 minutes. Select Start to begin preheating.
6. Once the air fryer has preheated, place the basket into the air fryer. Flip the patties halfway through the cooking time.
7. Meanwhile, combine the ingredients for the Korean mayo in a small bowl. Stir to mix well.
8. When cooking is complete, the patties should be golden brown.
9. Remove the patties from the air fryer and assemble with the buns, then spread the Korean mayo over the patties to make the burgers. Serve immediately.

Golden Tilapia Tacos

Prep time: 20 minutes | Cook time: 5 minutes | Serves 4

2 tablespoons milk
1/3 cup mayonnaise
1/4 teaspoon garlic powder
1 teaspoon chili powder
1½ cups panko bread crumbs
½ teaspoon salt
4 teaspoons canola oil
1 pound (454 g) skinless tilapia fillets, cut into 3-inch-long and 1-inch-wide strips
4 small flour tortilla
Lemon wedges, for topping
Cooking spray

1. Spritz the air fry basket with cooking spray.
2. Combine the milk, mayo, garlic powder, and chili powder in a bowl. Stir to mix well. Combine the panko with salt and canola oil in a separate bowl. Stir to mix well.
3. Dredge the tilapia strips in the milk mixture first, then dunk the strips in the panko mixture to coat well. Shake the excess off.
4. Arrange the tilapia strips in the basket.
5. Select Air Fry, set temperature to 400°F (205°C) and set time to 5 minutes. Select Start to begin preheating.
6. Once the air fryer has preheated, place the basket into the air fryer. Flip the strips halfway through the cooking time.
7. When cooking is complete, the strips will be opaque on all sides and the panko will be golden brown.
8. Unfold the tortillas on a large plate, then divide the tilapia strips over the tortillas. Squeeze the lemon wedges on top before serving.

Shrimp and Zucchini Potstickers

Prep time: 35 minutes | Cook time: 5 minutes | Serves 10

½ pound (227 g) peeled and deveined shrimp, finely chopped
1 medium zucchini, coarsely grated
1 tablespoon fish sauce
1 tablespoon green curry paste
2 scallions, thinly sliced
¼ cup basil, chopped
30 round dumpling wrappers
Cooking spray

1. Combine the chopped shrimp, zucchini, fish sauce, curry paste, scallions, and basil in a large bowl. Stir to mix well.
2. Unfold the dumpling wrappers on a clean work surface, dab a little water around the edges of each wrapper, then scoop up 1 teaspoon of filling in the middle of each wrapper.
3. Make the potstickers: Fold the wrappers in half and press the edges to seal.
4. Spritz the air fry basket with cooking spray.
5. Transfer the potstickers to the basket and spritz with cooking spray.
6. Select Air Fry, set temperature to 350°F (180°C) and set time to 5 minutes. Select Start to begin preheating.
7. Once preheated, place the basket into the air fryer. Flip the potstickers halfway through the cooking time.
8. When cooking is complete, the potstickers should be crunchy and lightly browned.
9. Serve immediately.

Turkey Sliders with Chive Mayo

Prep time: 10 minutes | Cook time: 15 minutes | Serves 6

12 burger buns
Cooking spray

Turkey Sliders:
¾ pound (340 g) turkey, minced
1 tablespoon oyster sauce
¼ cup pickled jalapeno, chopped
2 tablespoons chopped scallions
1 tablespoon chopped fresh cilantro
1 to 2 cloves garlic, minced
Sea salt and ground black pepper, to taste

Chive Mayo:
1 tablespoon chives
1 cup mayonnaise
Zest of 1 lime
1 teaspoon salt

1. Spritz the air fry basket with cooking spray.
2. Combine the ingredients for the turkey sliders in a large bowl. Stir to mix well. Shape the mixture into 6 balls, then bash the balls into patties.
3. Arrange the patties in the basket and spritz with cooking spray.
4. Select Air Fry, set temperature to 365°F (185°C) and set time to 15 minutes. Select Start to begin preheating.
5. Once preheated, place the basket into the air fryer. Flip the patties halfway through the cooking time.
6. Meanwhile, combine the ingredients for the chive mayo in a small bowl. Stir to mix well.
7. When cooked, the patties will be well browned.
8. Smear the patties with chive mayo, then assemble the patties between two buns to make the sliders. Serve immediately.

Air Fried Cream Cheese Wonton

Prep time: 5 minutes | Cook time: 6 minutes | Serves 4

2 ounces (57 g) cream cheese, softened
1 tablespoon sugar
16 square wonton wrappers
Cooking spray

1. Spritz the air fry basket with cooking spray.
2. In a mixing bowl, stir together the cream cheese and sugar until well mixed. Prepare a small bowl of water alongside.
3. On a clean work surface, lay the wonton wrappers. Scoop ¼ teaspoon of cream cheese in the center of each wonton wrapper. Dab the water over the wrapper edges. Fold each wonton wrapper diagonally in half over the filling to form a triangle.
4. Arrange the wontons in the basket. Spritz the wontons with cooking spray.
5. Select Air Fry, set temperature to 350°F (180°C) and set time to 6 minutes. Select Start to begin preheating.
6. Once preheated, place the basket into the air fryer. Flip the wontons halfway through the cooking time.
7. When cooking is complete, the wontons will be golden brown and crispy.
8. Divide the wontons among four plates. Let rest for 5 minutes before serving.

Eggplant Hoagies

Prep time: 15 minutes | Cook time: 12 minutes | Makes 3 hoagies

6 peeled eggplant slices (about ½ inch thick and 3 inches in diameter)
¼ cup jarred pizza sauce
6 tablespoons grated Parmesan cheese
3 Italian sub rolls, split open lengthwise, warmed
Cooking spray

1. Spritz the air fry basket with cooking spray.
2. Arrange the eggplant slices in the basket and spritz with cooking spray.
3. Select Air Fry, set temperature to 350°F (180°C) and set time to 10 minutes. Select Start to begin preheating.
4. Once the air fryer has preheated, place the basket into the air fryer. Flip the slices halfway through the cooking time.
5. When cooked, the eggplant slices should be lightly wilted and tender.
6. Divide and spread the pizza sauce and cheese on top of the eggplant slice
7. Select Air Fry, set temperature to 375°F (190°C) and set time to 2 minutes. Place the basket into the air fryer. When cooked, the cheese will be melted.
8. Assemble each sub roll with two slices of eggplant and serve immediately.

Cabbage and Pork Gyoza

Prep time: 10 minutes | Cook time: 10 minutes | Makes 48 gyozas

1 pound (454 g) ground pork	1 teaspoon minced fresh ginger
1 head Napa cabbage (about 1 pound / 454 g), sliced thinly and minced	1 tablespoon minced garlic
½ cup minced scallions	1 teaspoon granulated sugar
1 teaspoon minced fresh chives	2 teaspoons kosher salt
1 teaspoon soy sauce	48 to 50 wonton or dumpling wrappers
	Cooking spray

1. Spritz the air fry basket with cooking spray. Set aside.
2. Make the filling: Combine all th ingredients, except for the wrappers in a large bowl. Stir to mix well.
3. Unfold a wrapper on a clean work surface, then dab the edges with a little water. Scoop up 2 teaspoons of the fillin mixture in the center.
4. Make the gyoza: Fold the wrapper over to filling and press the edges to seal Pleat the edges if desired. Repeat with remaining wrappers and fillings
5. Arrange the gyozas in the basket and spritz with cooking spray.
6. Select Air Fry, set temperature to 360ºF (182ºC) and set time to 10 minutes. Select Start to begin preheating.
7. Once preheated, place the basket into the air fryer. Flip the gyozas halfway through the cooking time.
8. When cooked, the gyozas will be golden brown.
9. Serve immediately.

Baked Turkey Hamburger

Prep time: 10 minutes | Cook time: 20 minutes | Serves 4

1 cup leftover turkey, cut into bite-sized chunks	2 bell peppers, deveined and chopped
1 leek, sliced	2 tablespoons Tabasco sauce
1 Serrano pepper, deveined and chopped	½ cup sour cream
	1 heaping tablespoon fresh cilantro, chopped
1 teaspoon hot paprika	salt
¾ teaspoon kosher	½ teaspoon ground black pepper
	4 hamburger buns
	Cooking spray

1. Spritz a baking pan with cooking spray.
2. Mix all the ingredients, except for the buns, in a large bowl. Toss to combine well.
3. Pour the mixture in the baking pan.
4. Select Bake, set temperature to 385ºF (196ºC) and set time to 20 minutes. Select Start to begin preheating.
5. Once preheated, place the pan into the air fryer.
6. When done, the turkey will be well browned and the leek will be tender.
7. Assemble the hamburger buns with the turkey mixture and serve immediately.

Cheesy Chicken Taquitos

Prep time: 15 minutes | Cook time: 12 minutes | Serves 4

1 cup cooked chicken, shredded	Mozzarella cheese
¼ cup Greek yogurt	Salt and ground black pepper, to taste
¼ cup salsa	4 flour tortilla
1 cup shredded	Cooking spray

1. Spritz the air fry basket with cooking spray.
2. Combine all the ingredients, except for the tortillas, in a large bowl. Stir to mix well.
3. Make the taquitos: Unfold the tortillas on a clean work surface, then scoop up 2 tablespoons of the chicken mixture in the middle of each tortilla. Roll the tortillas up to wrap the filling
4. Arrange the taquitos in the basket and spritz with cooking spray.
5. Select Air Fry, set temperature to 380ºF (193ºC) and set time to 12 minutes. Select Start to begin preheating.
6. Once preheated, place the basket into the air fryer. Flip the taquitos halfway through the cooking time.
7. When cooked, the taquitos should be golden brown and the cheese should be melted.
8. Serve immediately.

Cheesy Potato Tortilla

Prep time: 5 minutes | Cook time: 6 minutes | Makes 12 taquitos

2 cups mashed potatoes
½ cup shredded Mexican cheese
12 corn tortillas
Cooking spray

1. Line a baking pan with parchment paper.
2. In a bowl, combine the potatoes and cheese until well mixed. Microwave the tortillas on high heat for 30 seconds, or until softened. Add some water to another bowl and set alongside.
3. On a clean work surface, lay the tortillas. Scoop 3 tablespoons of the potato mixture in the center of each tortilla. Roll up tightly and secure with toothpicks if necessary.
4. Arrange the filled tortillas, seam side down, in the prepared baking pan. Spritz the tortillas with cooking spray.
5. Select Air Fry, set temperature to 400ºF (205ºC) and set time to 6 minutes. Select Start to begin preheating.
6. Once preheated, place the pan into the air fryer. Flip the tortillas halfway through the cooking time.
7. When cooked, the tortillas should be crispy and golden brown.
8. Serve hot.

Cheesy Chicken Wraps

Prep time: 30 minutes | Cook time: 5 minutes | Serves 12

2 large-sized chicken breasts, cooked and shredded
2 spring onions, chopped
10 ounces (284 g) Ricotta cheese
1 tablespoon rice vinegar
1 tablespoon molasses
1 teaspoon grated fresh ginger
¼ cup soy sauce
⅓ teaspoon sea salt
¼ teaspoon ground black pepper, or more to taste
48 wonton wrappers
Cooking spray

1. Spritz the air fry basket with cooking spray.
2. Combine all the ingredients, except for the wrappers in a large bowl. Toss to mix well.
3. Unfold the wrappers on a clean work surface, then divide and spoon the mixture in the middle of the wrappers.
4. Dab a little water on the edges of the wrappers, then fold the edge close to you over the filling. uck the edge under the filling and roll up to seal
5. Arrange the wraps in the basket.
6. Select Air Fry, set temperature to 375ºF (190ºC) and set time to 5 minutes. Select Start to begin preheating.
7. Once preheated, place the basket into the air fryer. Flip the wraps halfway through the cooking time.
8. When cooking is complete, the wraps should be lightly browned.
9. Serve immediately.

Avocado and Tomato Egg Rolls

Prep time: 10 minutes | Cook time: 5 minutes | Serves 5

10 egg roll wrappers
3 avocados, peeled and pitted
1 tomato, diced
Salt and ground black pepper, to taste
Cooking spray

1. Spritz the air fry basket with cooking spray.
2. Put the tomato and avocados in a food processor. Sprinkle with salt and ground black pepper. Pulse to mix and coarsely mash until smooth.
3. Unfold the wrappers on a clean work surface, then divide the mixture in the center of each wrapper. Roll the wrapper up and press to seal.
4. Transfer the rolls to the basket and spritz with cooking spray.
5. Select Air Fry, set temperature to 350ºF (180ºC) and set time to 5 minutes. Select Start to begin preheating.
6. Once the air fryer has preheated, place the basket into the air fryer. Flip the rolls halfway through the cooking time.
7. When cooked, the rolls should be golden brown.
8. Serve immediately.

Crispy Chicken Egg Rolls

Prep time: 10 minutes | Cook time: 23 to 24 minutes | Serves 4

1 pound (454 g) ground chicken
2 teaspoons olive oil
2 garlic cloves, minced
1 teaspoon grated fresh ginger
2 cups white cabbage, shredded
1 onion, chopped
¼ cup soy sauce
8 egg roll wrappers
1 egg, beaten
Cooking spray

1. Spritz the air fry basket with cooking spray.
2. Heat olive oil in a saucepan over medium heat. Sauté the garlic and ginger in the olive oil for 1 minute, or until fragrant. Add the ground chicken to the saucepan. Sauté for 5 minutes, or until the chicken is cooked through. Add the cabbage, onion and soy sauce and sauté for 5 to 6 minutes, or until the vegetables become soft. Remove the saucepan from the heat.
3. Unfold the egg roll wrappers on a clean work surface. Divide the chicken mixture among the wrappers and brush the edges of the wrappers with the beaten egg. Tightly roll up the egg rolls, enclosing the filling. Arange the rolls in the basket.
4. Select Air Fry, set temperature to 370°F (188°C) and set time to 12 minutes. Select Start to begin preheating.
5. Once the air fryer has preheated, place the basket into the air fryer. Flip the rolls halfway through the cooking time.
6. When cooked, the rolls will be crispy and golden brown.
7. Transfer to a platter and let cool for 5 minutes before serving.

Beef Burgers with Mayo

Prep time: 15 minutes | Cook time: 10 minutes | Serves 4

1 teaspoon cumin seeds
1 teaspoon mustard seeds
1 teaspoon coriander seeds
1 teaspoon dried minced garlic
1 teaspoon dried red pepper fla es
1 teaspoon kosher salt
2 teaspoons ground black pepper
1 pound (454 g) 85% lean ground beef
2 tablespoons Worcestershire sauce
4 hamburger buns
Mayonnaise, for serving
Cooking spray

1. Spritz the air fry basket with cooking spray.
2. Put the seeds, garlic, red pepper fla es, salt, and ground black pepper in a food processor. Pulse to coarsely ground the mixture.
3. Put the ground beef in a large bowl. Pour in the seed mixture and drizzle with Worcestershire sauce. Stir to mix well.
4. Divide the mixture into four parts and shape each part into a ball, then bash each ball into a patty. Arrange the patties in the basket.
5. Select Air Fry, set temperature to 350°F (180°C) and set time to 10 minutes. Select Start to begin preheating.
6. Once the air fryer has preheated, place the basket into the air fryer. Flip the patties with tongs halfway through the cooking time.
7. When cooked, the patties will be well browned.
8. Assemble the buns with the patties, then drizzle the mayo over the patties to make the burgers. Serve immediately.

Appendix 1: Measurement Conversion Chart

VOLUME EQUIVALENTS(DRY)

US STANDARD	METRIC (APPROXIMATE)
1/8 teaspoon	0.5 mL
1/4 teaspoon	1 mL
1/2 teaspoon	2 mL
3/4 teaspoon	4 mL
1 teaspoon	5 mL
1 tablespoon	15 mL
1/4 cup	59 mL
1/2 cup	118 mL
3/4 cup	177 mL
1 cup	235 mL
2 cups	475 mL
3 cups	700 mL
4 cups	1 L

VOLUME EQUIVALENTS(LIQUID)

US STANDARD	US STANDARD (OUNCES)	METRIC (APPROXIMATE)
2 tablespoons	1 fl.oz.	30 mL
1/4 cup	2 fl.oz.	60 mL
1/2 cup	4 fl.oz.	120 mL
1 cup	8 fl.oz.	240 mL
1 1/2 cup	12 fl.oz.	355 mL
2 cups or 1 pint	16 fl.oz.	475 mL
4 cups or 1 quart	32 fl.oz.	1 L
1 gallon	128 fl.oz.	4 L

TEMPERATURES EQUIVALENTS

FAHRENHEIT(F)	CELSIUS(C) (APPROXIMATE)
225 °F	107 °C
250 °F	120 °C
275 °F	135 °C
300 °F	150 °C
325 °F	160 °C
350 °F	180 °C
375 °F	190 °C
400 °F	205 °C
425 °F	220 °C
450 °F	235 °C
475 °F	245 °C
500 °F	260 °C

WEIGHT EQUIVALENTS

US STANDARD	METRIC (APPROXIMATE)
1 ounce	28 g
2 ounces	57 g
5 ounces	142 g
10 ounces	284 g
15 ounces	425 g
16 ounces (1 pound)	455 g
1.5 pounds	680 g
2 pounds	907 g

Appendix 2: Recipe Index

A

Air Fried Avocado Tacos   165
Air Fried Bacon-Wrapped Scallops   56
Air Fried Beef Kofta   70
Air Fried Beef Satay   63
Air Fried Carne Asada   64
Air Fried Cheesy Steak   167
Air Fried Cream Cheese Wonton   172
Air Fried Crispy Fish Sticks   43
Air Fried Crispy Spring Rolls   170
Air Fried Egg and Avocado Burrito   38
Air Fried Eggs in Pepper Rings   23
Air Fried Ham and Cheese Toast   28
Air Fried Lahmacun (Turkish Pizza)   66
Air Fried Lamb Kofta   65
Air Fried London Broil   70
Air Fried Milky Cod Fillets   45
Air Fried Paprika Shrimp   51
Air Fried Peppered Maple Bacon Knots   25
Air Fried Pineapple Rings   154
Air Fried Pork Rib   75
Air Fried Pork Tenderloin   80
Air Fried Steak and Spinach Rolls   68
Air Fried Veal Loin   67
Air Fried Venison   64
Air Fryer Rotisserie Beef Roast   168
Air-Fried Acorn Squash   121
Air-Fried Breaded Chicken Wings   139
Air-Fried Broccoli with Hot Sauce   118
Air-Fried Cheesy Broccoli Tots   104
Air-Fried Cheesy Cabbage Wedges   113
Air-Fried Cheesy Zucchini Tots   127
Air-Fried Crispy Chicken Skin   97
Air-Fried Crunchy Chickpeas   135
Air-Fried Duck Leg Quarters   96
Air-Fried Edamame   129
Air-Fried Korean Chicken Wings   95
Air-Fried Old Bay Chicken Wings   138
Air-Fried Pecan-Crusted Cat ish   52
Air-Fried Pickle Spears   132
Air-Fried Polenta Fries with Mayo   132
Air-Fried Winter Veggies   104
Apple Wedges with Apricots   152
Apple Wedges with Yogurt   134
Apricot-Glazed Drumsticks   89

Aromatic Air Fried Shrimp   57
Aromatic Air-Fried Scallop   54
Aromatic Baked Cod Fillet   48
Aromatic Beef and Onion Tacos   168
Aromatic Coconut-Crusted Prawns   51
Aromatic French Toast Sticks   35
Aromatic Parmesan Fish Fillets   52
Aromatic Shrimp with Parsley   55
Aromatic Steaks with Cucumber and Snap Pea Salad   69
Arrowroot-Crusted Zucchini   122
Asian Spicy Broccoli   110
Authentic Char Siu   83
Avocado and Tomato Egg Rolls   174

B

Bacon-Wrapped Cheesy Chicken   90
Bacon-Wrapped Filets Mignons   63
Bacon-Wrapped Hot Dogs   73
Bacon-Wrapped Stuffed Dates   140
Baked Apple Fritters   146
Baked Apple-Glazed Pork   61
Baked Apple-Peach Crisp   149
Baked Asparagus and Cheese Strata   27
Baked Beef and Spinach Meatloaves   82
Baked Beef and Tomato Sauce Meatloaf   66
Baked Beef Steak   67
Baked Bourbon Vanilla French Toast   29
Baked Cheesy Marinara Chicken   100
Baked Chocolate Pie   153
Baked Coconut Cake   145
Baked Corn Casserole   157
Baked Egg in a Hole   27
Baked Flounder Fillets   54
Baked Garlicky Whole Chicken   89
Baked Golden Beer-Battered Cod   46
Baked Mini Cinnamon Rolls   33
Baked Pork Chops and Apple   80
Baked Quesadillas with Blueberries   38
Baked Scalloped Potatoes   119

Baked Sweet Apple   151
Baked Tilapia with Garlic Aioli   47

Baked Turkey and Carrot Meatloaves   97
Baked Turkey Hamburger   173
Baked Turnip, Zucchini, Onion   110
Baked Veggies with Basil   106
Baked Walnuts Tart   150
Baked Whole-Wheat Muffins with   lueberries   34
Baked Zucchini Ground Beef   71
Balck Bean Cheese Tacos   106
Balsamic Asparagus   119
Balsamic Asparagus Spears   109
Balsamic Marmalade Duck Breasts   93
Balsamic Sausages and Red Grapes   82
Bangers and Cauliflower Mash   7
Barbecue Chicken Tostadas with Coleslaw   92
Barbecue Herby Sausage Pizza   139
BBQ Sausage, Pineapple and Peppers   79
BBQ-Honey Basted Drumsticks   89
Beef and Chile Cheese Casserole   162
Beef and Mushroom Casserole   157
Beef Burgers with Korean Mayo   170
Beef Burgers with Mayo   175
Beef Meatballs with Marinara Sauce   63
Beer Cod Tacos   165
Bell Peppers with Garlic   108
Berry Crisp with Coconut Chip   148
Blackberry Butter Cake   154
Blueberry and Peach Galette   147
Blueberry Cupcakes   144
Bo Luc Lac   81
Breadcrumb-Crusted Catfish Nuggets   55
Breadcrumb-Crusted Fish Sticks   50

Breaded Banana with Chocolate Sauce   153

Breaded Brussels Sprouts with Sage   121

Breaded Calamari Ring with Lemon   56
Breaded Chicken Nuggets   91
Breaded Eggplant Slices   111
Breaded Golden Wasabi Spam   71
Broccoli Cheese Casserole   161
Broiled Goulash   91
Browned Ricotta Capers   131
Bruschetta with Tomato Sauce   141
Buffalo Chicken Drumettes   91
Butter-Juicy Salmon Steak   48

Buttermilk Cake   149
Buttery Catfish Cakes with Cheese   51
Buttery Chocolate Cheesecake   149
Buttery Chocolate Cookies   146
Buttery New York Strip   64
Buttery Scampi   58
Buttery Shortbread   145
Buttery Shrimp with Cherry Tomato   56

C-D

Cabbage and Pork Gyoza   173
Cajun Chicken Drumsticks   92
Caramelized Cinnamon Peach   135
Caramelized Eggplant with Yogurt   108
Caramelized Fruit Kebabs   152
Caramelized Peach Wedge   142
Caramelized Wax Beans   108
Cauliflower and Chicken Casserole   156
Cheesy Artichoke-Mushroom Frittata   33
Cheesy Avocado with Eggs   38
Cheesy Bacon and Egg Wraps   166
Cheesy Beef and Pork Sausage Meatloaf   73
Cheesy Beef Rolls   62
Cheesy Chicken and Pepperoni Pizza   90
Cheesy Chicken Crouton   156
Cheesy Chicken Ham Casserole   160
Cheesy Chicken Taquitos   173
Cheesy Chicken Wraps   174
Cheesy Corn and Black Bean Salsa   142
Cheesy Corn Casserole   121
Cheesy Corn on the Cob   120
Cheesy Crab Meat Toasts   141
Cheesy Dijon Turkey Burgers   99
Cheesy Egg Florentine with Spinach   31
Cheesy Fried Cheese Grits   31
Cheesy Green Bean Casserole   158
Cheesy Green Chiles Nachos   128
Cheesy Mini Brown Rice Quiches   37
Cheesy Parmesan-Crusted Salmon Patties   43
Cheesy Potato and Black Bean Burritos   167
Cheesy Potato Tortilla   174
Cheesy Rice, Shrimp, and Spinach Frittata   37
Cheesy Salmon with Asparagus   42
Cheesy Sausage and Mushroom Calzones   78

Cheesy Sausage Balls   129
Cheesy Shrimp Salad with Caesar   53
Cheesy Spinach and Bacon Roll-ups   26
Cheesy Spinach and Mushroon Frittata   162
Cheesy Stuffed Beef Tenderloin   69
Cheesy Tuna Patties   40
Cheesy Vegan Quesadilla   113
Cheesy Vegetable Frittata   159
Cherry-Glazed Whole Duck   95

Chessy Asparagus and Prosciutto Tart   81
Chessy Sausage and Broccoli Casserole   158
Chicken Tacos with Peanut Sauce   87
Chicken Thighs on Waffles with Honey   9
Chicken Thighs with Veggies   102
Chicken with Mashed Potato and Corn   101
Chicken, Bell Pepper and Onion Rolls   92
Chocolate Cake   151
Chuck and Sausage Sandwiches   74
Classic Hawaiian Chicken Bites   90
Classic Marinara Sauce   20
Coconut Brown Rice Porridge with Dates   34

Coconut Milky Fish Curry with Tomato   55
Cod Fingers Gratin   141
Coffee Coconut Cake   150
Cornfla es-Crusted Tofu Sticks   111
Cream Glazed Cinnamon Rolls   184

Creamy Bacon and Egg Bread Cups   31
Creamy Raspberry Muffin   14
Crispy Bacon-Wrapped Sausage   72
Crispy Breadcrumb Scallops   49
Crispy Chicken Egg Rolls   175
Crispy Chili Okra   116
Crispy Cinnamon Apple Chips   134

Crispy Crab Cakes with Bell Peppers   59
Crispy Golden Schnitzel   71
Crispy Lechon Kawali   79
Crispy Parmesan Asparagus   122
Crispy Pork Tenderloin   73
Crispy Spiced Apple Chips   134
Crispy Veggies with Mixed Herbs   115
Crunchy Tonkatsu   78
Crusted Beef Steaks   70

Cuban Turkey Sandwiches   142
Deviled Eggs with Paprika   126
Dijon Pork with Squash and Apple   84

E

Easy Fried Salmon Patties   42
Easy Lamb Chops with Asparagus   72
Easy Shawarma Spice Mix   20
Easy Spicy Tortilla Chips   137
Easy Thai Curry Beef Meatballs   66
Eggplant Hoagies   172
Eggy Crustless Broccoli Quiche   30
Eggy Hash Brown Cups   30
Eggy Sausage and Cheese Quiche   23
Eggy Spinach, Leek and Cheese Frittata   24
Eggy Veggie Frittata   25

F

Fast Carrot Chips   134
Fast Cripsy Artichoke Bites   139
Fired Shrimp with Mayonnaise Sauce   59
Fried Chicken and Roma Tomato   93
Fried Potatoes with Peppers and Onions   32
Fudge Pie   154

G

Garlic-Butter Shrimp with Sausage   50
Garlicky Button Mushrooms   130
Garlicky Carrots with Sesame   115
Garlicky Stuffed WhiteMushroom   110
Ginger Flavored Tuna Lettuce Wraps   46
Glazed Strawberry Toast   23
Goat Cheese and Asparagus Frittata   161
Golden Breaded Fish Fillets   41
Golden Butternut Squash Croquettes   123
Golden Chicken Burgers   169
Golden Chicken Empanadas   169
Golden Chicken Schnitzel   94
Golden Cod Tacos with Salsa   164
Golden Hush Puppies   130
Golden Italian Rice Balls   138
Golden Lamb Chops   72
Golden Lemony Pork Chop   74
Golden Mushroom and Spinach Calzones   140
Golden Sweet-Sour Chicken Nuggets   98
Golden Tilapia Tacos   171
Green Tomato with Horseradish   137

Grilled Breakfast Tater Tot Casserole   22
Grits and Asparagus Casserole   162

H-I

Herbed Broccoli with Yellow Cheese   114
Herbed Dijon Turkey Breast   100
Herbed Salmon with Roasted Asparagus   45
Homemade Air-Fried Chicken Wings   88
Homemade Baked Almonds   126
Homemade Maple Pecan Granola   105
Homemade Paprika Potato Chips   131
Homemade Salsa Beef Meatballs   65
Honey Snack Mix   133
Honey-Glazed Chicken Breasts   96
Honeyed Halibut Steaks with Parsley   46
Italian Spiced Tofu   116

J

Juicy Caesar Salad Dressing   19
Juicy Chicken Breakfast Sausages   32
Juicy Salmon Bowl   47
Juicy Swordfish Steaks   4

K

Kung Pao Tofu   105

L

Lemon-Honey Snapper with Fruit   41
Lemon-Pepper Chicken Wings   128
Lemony Cheese Cake   153
Lemony Red Snapper Fillet   49 Lemony Tahini Kale   106

M-N

Maple Brussels Sprouts   118
Maple-Rosemary Turkey Breast   87
Meat and Rice Stuffed Bell Peppers   61
Meaty Breakfast Casserole   32

Meaty Canadian Bacon Muffin Sandwiches   2

Milky Air Fryer Baked Rice   20
Milky air fryer Grits   19
Milky Buttermilk Biscuits   24

Milky Chocolate Banana Bread   22
Milky Hash Brown Casserole   29
Milky Maple Walnut Pancake   34
Milky Mixed Berry Dutch Baby Pancake   35

Milky Cajun and Lemon Pepper Cod 47

Milky Spinach and Bacon English Muffins   2
Milky Western Omelet   30
Mozzarella Pepperoni Rolls   128
Muffuletta Sliders with Olives   136
Mustard-Crusted Sole Fillets   44
Nuts Crusted Pork Rack   76

O

Oily Basil Salmon with Tomatoes   43
Oily Cauliflower Fritters   4
Oily Cinnamon Sweet Potato Chips   28
Oily Corned Beef Hash with Eggs   36
Oily Fish Tacos   45
Olives, Kale, and Pecorino Baked Eggs   37

P

Panko Crab Sticks with Mayo Sauce   57

Panko Crusted Calf's Liver Strips   65
Panko Parmesan Zucchini Chips   116
Panko-Crusted Avocado Chips   136
Panko-Crusted Cauliflower Fritters   19

Panko-Crusted Cheesy Broccoli   120
Panko-Crusted Chicken Cutlets   98
Panko-Crusted Chicken Livers   96
Panko-Crusted Green Beans   114
Panko-Ctusted Chicken Fingers   88
Paprika Chicken Skewers   97
Paprika Pork Chops   84
Parma Prosciutto-Wrapped Pear   132
Parmesan Buttered Broccoli   119
Parmesan Cauliflower Florets   12
Parmesan Chicken Skewers with Corn   102
Parmesan-Crusted Hake with Garlic Sauce   53
Pastrami Cheese Casserole   159
Peach-Blueberry Tart   151
Peach-Glazed Chicken with Cherry   99

Pecans Nuts Cookies   148
Pork and Carrot Momos   166
Pork Cutlets with Aloha Salsa   85
Pork Steak and Squash   77
Potato and Asparagus with Cheese Sauce   112
Prawn and Cabbage Egg Rolls Wraps   164
Pumpkin Pudding with Vanilla Wafers   150

R

Ratatouille   113

Rhubarb Oatmeal Crumble   145
Rice Shrimp Patties   57
Riced Cauliflower Ok a Casserole   160
Ritzy Chicken and Vegetable Casserole   158
Ritzy Turkey Breast Casserole   160
Roasted Cinnamon Celery Roots   109
Roasted Crab with Onion and Tomato   54
Roasted Honey Grapes   130
Roasted Honey-Glazed Carrot   110
Roasted Lamb Chops with Potatoes   76
Roasted Parmesan Snack Mix   138
Roasted Parmesan-Crusted Halibut Fillets   41
Roasted Pork Chop   82
Roasted Ratatouille   112
Roasted Ribeye Steaks   80
Roasted Sausage and Onion Rolls   125
Roasted Scallops with Snow Peas   49
Roasted Spicy Cabbage   119
Roasted Tuna Melts   125
Roasted Veggies and Rice   115
Roasted Veggies Balls   107
Rosemary Butternut Squash   114
Rosemary Red Potatoes   123
Rotisserie Spiced Chicken with Lemon   199
Rump Steak with Broccoli   67
Russet Potatoes with Yogurt and Chives   123

S

Salmon and Carrot Croquettes   191
Salty Crunchy Tortilla Chips   188
Sardines with Tomato Sauce   127
Sauce Flavored Asian Dipping Sauce   20
Savory King Prawn   59
Savory Lamb Loin Chops   62
Savory Pork Butt with Chilled Sauce   77
Savory Roasted Shrimp   52
Savory Steak with Mushroom Gravy   68
Savory Tilapia Fillet   50
Scallops with Broccoli and Bean   48
Shrimp and Zucchini Potstickers   171
Shrimp Paella with Artichoke Heart   58
Shrimp Toasts with Thai Chili Sauce   133
Simple Flavor Packed Teriyaki Sauce   19
Smoked Paprika Cauliflower   10
Smoked Sausage and Mushroom Empanadas   131
Smoked Trout and Crème Fraiche Frittata   159
Spanakopita (Spinach Pie)   186
Spiced Whole Chicken   197
Spicy Chicken Wings   188
Spicy Chicken, Sausage and Pepper   101

Spicy Honey Broccoli   105
Spicy Kale Chips   137
Spicy Pork with Lettuce   83
Spicy-Sweet Walnut   136
Spinach and Cheese Pockets   166
Spinach and Chickpea Casserole   157
Strawberry-Glazed Turkey Breast   93
Stuffed Chicken with Bruschetta   88
Stuffed Jalapeño Poppers with Cheese   127
Stuffed Mushroom with Ham   135
Stuffed Mushrooms with Cheese   126
Sumptuous Breakfast Cheese Sandwiches   25
Sumptuous Spring Roll   168
Super Cheesy Sandwiches   140
Sweet Bacon Pinwheels   193
Sweet Cornmeal Pancake   35
Sweet Milky Monkey Bread   27
Sweet Roasted Mixed Nuts   133
Syrupy Banana and Oat Bread Pudding   29
Syrupy Breakfast Blueberry Cobbler   24
Syrupy Vanilla Granola   26

T

Tangy Balsamic-Glazed Carrots   122
Tangy Cake   144
Tangy Cake   152
Tangy Cilantro Chicken Breast   98
Tangy Shrimp   58
Tangy Sriracha Beef and Broccoli   85
Tangy Sweet Potatoes   120
Tasty Turkey Breakfast Sausage Patties   26
Teriyaki Cauliflower Florets   11
Teriyaki Country Pork Ribs   79
Teriyaki Pork Skewers   75
Thai Spicy Veggies with Nuts   109
Tilapia and Rockfish Casserole   16
Tomato-Corn Frittata with Avocado Dressing   36
Tortellini and Vegetable   107
Turkey Sliders with Chive Mayo   172

V

Vinegary Enchilada Sauce   19
Vinegary Hoisin Tuna   44

W-Y

Walnut Butter Baklava   147
Yummy Oily Teriyaki Salmon   44